CLARK GABLE, CIRCA 1930s

ROBERT MITCHUM IN *OUT OF THE PAST*, 1947

FOREWORD BY ROBERT OSBORNE

INTRODUCTION BY MOLLY HASKELL

TEXT BY FRANK MILLER

Leading
MEN

THE 50 MOST UNFORGETTABLE ACTORS OF THE STUDIO ERA

CHRONICLE BOOKS
SAN FRANCISCO

Except as set forth below, all film images contained in this book are the property of Turner Entertainment Co., a Time Warner Company, or RKO Pictures, Inc. All Rights Reserved.

Artcinema Corporation (*The Son of the Sheik*); Batjac Productions (*Hondo*); Columbia Pictures (*The Bridge on the River Kwai, From Here to Eternity, Guess Who's Coming to Dinner, Lawrence of Arabia, Mr. Smith Goes to Washington, On the Waterfront, Twentieth Century*); Embassy (*The Lion in Winter*); First National (*The Kid*); The Harold Lloyd Trust (*Safety Last, Speedy*); Kino (*The General, The Thief of Bagdad*); KirchMedia (*La Strada*); Paramount (*The Godfather, The Odd Couple, Roman Holiday, Seconds, Shane, The Sheik, Sunset Boulevard, White Christmas*); Rainbow Productions, Inc. (*Lilies of the Field*); Republic Entertainment (*Force of Evil, High Noon, It's a Wonderful Life*); Samuel Goldwyn (*Wuthering Heights*); Seven Arts Productions, Inc. (*The Misfits*); 20th Century Fox (*Butch Cassidy and the Sundance Kid, The Grapes of Wrath, How To Steal a Million, Zorba the Greek*); United Artists (*The Apartment, Elmer Gantry, The Night of the Hunter, Some Like It Hot, Sweet Smell of Success*); Universal (*The Blue Dahlia, Cape Fear, My Man Godfrey, The Palm Beach Story, Road to Utopia, Scarface, Sullivan's Travels, This Gun For Hire, To Kill A Mockingbird*); Warner Bros. (*Bullitt, Cool Hand Luke, Giant, Rebel Without a Cause, A Streetcar Named Desire, The Wild Bunch*).

All of the films in this book, along with countless other classics, can be seen completely commercial-free, on Turner Classic Movies.

A concerted effort has been made to trace the ownership of all material included in this book. Any errors that may have occurred are inadvertent and will be corrected in subsequent editions, provided sufficient notification is sent to the publisher in a timely manner.

Library of Congress Cataloging-in-Publication Data available.

ISBN 10: 0-8118-5467-1
ISBN 13: 978-0-8118-5467-2

Manufactured in China

Designed by Affiche Design

Distributed in Canada by Raincoast Books
9050 Shaughnessy Street
Vancouver, British Columbia V6P 6E5

10 9 8 7 6 5 4 3

Chronicle Books LLC
680 Second Street
San Francisco, California 94107
www.chroniclebooks.com

FRANK SINATRA IN *ANCHORS AWEIGH*, 1945

STEVE MCQUEEN IN *BULLITT*, 1968

ACKNOWLEDGMENTS

As with all great film productions this book reflects the collaborative efforts of many: from the Academy of Motion Picture Arts and Sciences & Margaret Herrick Library, Sue Guldin and Faye Thompson; from The Everett Collection, Glenn Bradie and Ron Harvey; from The Kobal Collection, Jamie Vuignier and Ayzha Wolf; from Photofest, Howard Mandelbaum; from the Warner Bros. Corporate Image Archive, Cynthia Graham and Jeff Stevens; from Turner Image Management, David Diodate, Brandy Ivins, Christopher Grakal, Melissa Jacobson, Cynthia Martinez, Sam Morris, Christian Pierce, Matthew Rond, and Kim Vardeman.

TCM contributors to project development and management and to editorial and research include: Carrie Beers, Kristin Ramsey Clyde, Tanya Coventry-Strader, Katherine Evans, Alexa Foreman, Talia Gerecitano, Randy Gragg, Tom Karsch, Scott McGee, Genevieve McGillicuddy, Chris Merrifield, Dennis Millay, R. Anna Millman, Robert Osborne, John Renaud, Mary Rindlesbach, Charles Tabesh, Lee Tsiantis, Eric Weber, and Michon Wise.

Thanks to our friends and colleagues for their relentless enthusiasm and commitment to TCM: Anne Borchardt, Brooks Branch, Britt Else, Molly Haskell, and Frank Miller.

FOREWORD
ROBERT**OSBORNE**

"Can't act. Slightly bald. Also dances." That's the clinical observation made by a Hollywood studio executive after seeing Fred Astaire's first screen test.

"His ears are too big and he looks like an ape." So said Warner Bros. executive Darryl F. Zanuck about Clark Gable after testing him for the lead in Warner's gangster drama *Little Caesar*.

"The young man who embodies the sprig is what is usually and mercifully described as inadequate." Thus was the first critical notice taken of Humphrey Bogart, written by Alexander Wolcott.

And you thought you've made a wrong judgment or two in your life . . .

It's hard to believe now, but there was once a time before their stardom when the former Frederic Austerliz Jr., of Omaha, Nebraska, William Clark Gable, of Cadiz, Ohio, and Humphrey DeForest Bogart, of New York City, did not yet rule the earth, or at least the silver screen. And we know now how empty our universe known as "the movies" would have been without them. Can you really imagine a world without Astaire gliding across those art deco ballrooms with Ginger Rogers? Or someone other than Gable, frankly, not giving a damn? Or anyone but Bogie running Rick's Café Americain? Unthinkable!

Each of the fifty leading men in this book—Astaire, Gable, and Bogart included—is part of an extremely rare breed. Every one stands out like a water tower in the Sahara from all the millions who've tried, with varying degrees of success, to make their marks in the motion picture industry—the peers, the competitors, the imitators, and the wannabes who have swarmed to Hollywood and to every locale where a camera has been purring since the nickelodeon was in flower. The men you'll be reading about in this book all made the grade, in spades.

As was true in assembling the companion volume to this book, *Leading Ladies: The 50 Most Unforgettable Actresses of the Studio Era*, it was extremely difficult to narrow our list to fifty. In a way, it would have been easier to come up with a list of only twenty since there seem to be about that number who would most likely be on anyone's list of "essentials," namely (and in alphabetical order) Astaire, Bogart, Brando, Cagney, Chaney, Chaplin, Cooper, Fairbanks, Flynn, Fonda, Gable, Grant, Keaton, Peck, Stewart, Tracy, Valentino, Wayne . . . I leave it to you to fill in the other two.

From that point, it gets dizzying and somewhat mystifying to name only thirty more. Limiting ourselves with few exceptions to the studio era meant ruling out actors such as Robert Redford, Sean Connery, and Michael Caine, who rose to fame after the heyday when Hollywood's major studios kept stables of stars under contract. It also meant largely excluding champs from the silent era, such as Ramon Novarro and Wallace Reid. There are other omissions, including any number of Roberts (Montgomery, Donat, Ryan, Walker, Young); Van Johnson isn't here, though nobody was bigger at the box office during World War II; no Walter Pidgeon, Leslie Howard, Orson Welles, Tony Curtis, Fred MacMurray, Melvyn Douglas, Glenn Ford, Wallace Beery, Douglas Fairbanks Jr., Dana Andrews, Richard Widmark, Lew Ayres, Dick Powell, John Payne, Stewart Granger . . . you get the point. If everyone who deserves to be in this book were to be included, you'd need a crane to lift it.

But I'm particularly proud that we've chosen to include Charles Boyer, Ronald Colman, John Garfield, Fredric March, Bing Crosby, and Paul Muni in these pages, all of them shining lights who too often get short shrift because their magic is so little known by most of today's moviegoers. When I was growing up, Alan Ladd was the movie hero I admired most, especially in noir films such as *This Gun for Hire*, *Lucky Jordan*, *Salty O'Rourke*, and *The Blue Dahlia*. I'm pleased he has made the cut, as well as Robert Mitchum— the only actor I've ever met who had no concept of what a great talent he possessed. I'm glad others recognized his worth, even if Mitchum himself never really did.

This book is full of interesting tidbits. Did you know that Montgomery Clift, not William Holden, was originally signed and set for the lead in *Sunset Blvd.*? Or that Fred Astaire was offered *Yankee Doodle Dandy* before it was given to Jimmy Cagney? Or that John Garfield was up for the role of Stanley Kowalski in *A Streetcar Named Desire*, but his demands were so great that the producers gave the role to a new boy named Brando?

You'll also learn that Jimmy Stewart's father was so offended by the sexual content in his son's film *Anatomy of a Murder* that Papa took out an ad in his local Indiana, Pennsylvania, newspaper telling people not to go see the movie. And Cary Grant was actually older than the actress (Jessie Royce Landis) who played his mother in *North by Northwest*. Henry Fonda lost what would have been one of the defining roles of his career when his agent, on Fonda's behalf, turned down the lead in the original production of *Who's Afraid of Virginia Woolf*? later explaining "You don't want to be in a play about four people yelling at each other all the time." (Fonda changed agents, pronto.)

Such facts flourish in the pages ahead, along with personal data on each of the fifty men we're celebrating, a listing of five "must-see" films made by each, behind-the-scenes info, and an explanation of the legacy each has left behind. And, in case you were curious, their height. It turns out the tallest man on the list is John Wayne, measuring 6 feet 4½". (Runners-up: Rock Hudson at 6 feet 4" and Jimmy Stewart at 6 feet 3½".) The shortest: Mickey Rooney at 5 feet 3", with Edward G. Robinson and Charlie Chaplin (both 5 feet 5") not much taller. There's always been the legend that Alan Ladd was the smallest male among major stars; actually, he stood taller than many at 5 feet 6" and was only one inch shorter than several who may surprise you: Gene Kelly, Charles Boyer, and James Cagney, all of whom were 5 feet 7".

This is one of those books I suspect you'll dig into many times and enjoy for many moons to come. We guarantee some fascinating discoveries every time you travel the magical, elite trail from *A* in Astaire to *W* in Wayne.

INTRODUCTION
MOLLY**HASKELL**

The lingo may change, but the principle is the same: the star is the sine qua non, the Must Factor, the beginning and end point in the way a movie is made and received. In current parlance, it's the "bankable" star who "gets on board" and anchors the "package," thereby getting the project "greenlighted." Under the studio system, it was the name above the title, and long hours were spent negotiating the size and shape of those letters, which of two costars' names came first, and where those names were positioned on the screen.

Who can explain how a little squirt like Mickey Rooney or a skinny dancer like Fred Astaire or a guy with jug ears and no moustache named Clark Gable ended up as stars? And stars for all seasons and all audiences, as almost no movie personality is today. Luck, studio grooming, the right agent, a niche waiting to be filled, an electrifying role in which an actor suddenly connects with the audience and establishes a persona: these are some of the elements that separate the wannabes from the successes. There's no single formula, and all our understanding is after the fact. For movie lovers, it's fascinating to watch films while simultaneously examining the ins and outs of stars' careers in a book like this: it affords us a double vision. Knowing their stardom as a fait accompli, we get to marvel at how it might have been otherwise. It's a game anyone can play: observe this or that personal favorite, now enthroned in the memory, in one of those exceedingly minor (or miscast), early roles, one that might as easily have been quick-sand as a stepping stone to stardom, and wonder if you would have picked him for a future star. Watch Humphrey Bogart as the villain in *The Petrified Forest*, grizzled and snarling, or even as the genuinely hard-boiled detective in *The Maltese Falcon*, and can you possibly foresee the man who inspires passion in such forties beauties as Ingrid Bergman (*Casablanca*) and Lauren Bacall (*To Have and Have Not*)?

Whereas women's careers depended on the same mixture of luck and talent and timing, their rise, based more exclusively on looks, is easier to predict on the basis of early films. The greater latitude afforded men is reflected in the number and enormous variety of the male stars under consideration (extremely difficult to whittle down to fifty), the types of roles in which they excelled, and the kinds of films—the genres—devoted to every conceivable masculine pursuit, both fantasized and real. Gangster films, westerns and war films, political fables and adventure epics, science fiction and silent comedy—all were heavily stacked with masculine presence and preeminence. The roles ran the gamut from swashbucklers to senators, from sports figures to criminals, from gangsters and cowboys to lovers and seducers, from comedians to cops and kings. Heroic as these roles often were, male stars could also play seedy or shiftless or sinister, nasty or brutish; they could be unsavory and downright ugly, not to mention small or fat and slapstick funny. Unlike the women, for whom stardom was and is virtually synonymous with glamour, male stars didn't even have to be beautiful.

Lon Chaney, the man of a thousand mostly grotesque faces; Edward G. Robinson, the plug-ugly yet charismatic guy—a woman who looked like either of them wouldn't get to first base in the romantic sweepstakes and would be consigned (if she were very lucky) to character parts. The male star didn't have to be a hunk, or even good-looking, to get the girl; witness comedians like Buster Keaton's heroic nebbish or Charlie Chaplin's impecunious tramp who courted and won (if just barely) princesses above their stations, or the clownish but romantically resilient Bob Hope. Needless to say, any woman not alluring enough to nail down her leading man was out of the running for stardom.

This may be the place to note that the term *leading man* has a different and more limited meaning than star. Leading man refers to a relationship—a partnership with a woman, inevitably of an amorous kind (as in *romantic lead*). Not all leading men were stand-alone stars, and not all stars played leading men. It might be a starting point, as it was for Laurence Olivier, or an end point (Cary Grant and Rock Hudson), or never even a possibility, as was the case with Robinson.

The leading man can be a consort to a female diva, stuck in torchbearer mode, as were many of Garbo's and Dietrich's screen lovers. Or they could graduate to or from leading man roles. *Leading man* could be used as a diminutive in another way: the world of love and the emotions was considered a lesser plane of human activity compared to the more virile (and American!) adventures of war, crime, and business. It was one of the reasons Charles Boyer, French, velvet voiced, and the quintessential screen lover, wasn't taken seriously as an actor. It was one of the reasons Laurence Olivier, prince of the stage, didn't take his lover roles (*Wuthering Heights*, *The Prince and the Showgirl*) seriously.

Socially conscious critics dismissed the "woman's film" (domestic melodramas and stories of impossible love and sacrifice) as somehow trivial, less important, than the "serious" matters of the day. Love was nothing but a "hill of beans" as Bogey has it, in *Casablanca*, in the Nazi-threatened world of the forties. Some of the impatience with love came legitimately, when women were shoehorned into all-male preserves as an obligatory love interest, to bolster appeal to female moviegoers (quaint consideration, that!); and that gave love itself a bad name. Great lovers and great leading men (Boyer, Grant, Hudson) didn't get Oscars. But from a later, more indulgent perspective, and with a revisionist view, we now realize how great those "mere" lovers could be, not just Cary Grant, but an actor like Joel McCrea, who wins deserved star status in this book for a body of work that ranges from enchanting westerns to drama and comedy, where his relaxed charm and absence of narcissism allowed him to be a great listener in sexy duets with swans like Claudette Colbert and Veronica Lake.

The same prejudice operated to keep any discussion of male beauty off the table; reviewers could go into raptures over Garbo's face, pant in print over Marilyn Monroe (although even that awaited a more permissive age), but men were not supposed to have that sort of vanity or surface sex appeal; their attraction was in what they did and were, not how they looked. Studios furnished the fan magazines with endless details about a female star's "look," how it was created and maintained, but were mum about men. Models were brought in to help unworldly women walk, talk, and dress, but Henry Willson's similar service to male stars was kept discreetly under wraps. Willson was the gay agent with an eye for studs who discovered and christened a whole stable of one-syllable hunks, most famously Rock Hudson but also Guy Madison, Tab Hunter, and Troy Donahue. These bland cover boys and muscle-beach guys were the era's equivalent of starlets, interchangeable pretty faces until one or another (Hudson, for example) emerged from the pack with real talent. New, demystifying biographies tell how strenuously an icon like Cary Grant worked to fashion his glistening image, as vigilant as any glamour girl in his efforts to stay young and beautiful. But who knew then?

The stories of these fifty men's ascent to stardom are as varied and individual as the men themselves, as full of serendipity as the women's stories but with a greater chance to broaden and deepen, to age "gracefully" when they reached the top. Sometimes retaining the vestiges of lower-class background and struggle, sometimes smoothing the rough edges, they brought who and what they were to screen, but the end result was a persona less fixed and immutable. Garfield and Cagney, for instance, came from rough urban backgrounds and brought a street-smart panache to a wide variety of characters. Others were men who'd had to fight their way up, a pugnacity that shows in every move and expression of Kirk Douglas, son of an immigrant junk dealer—and distinguishes him from the more pampered angst of Hollywood son Michael. Cary Grant transformed himself from a cockney tumbler to a tuxedo-wearing dandy, while William Powell, that other "nob," was the son of an accountant. Loners, cynics, wiseguys (think Robert Mitchum), they were to the manner born, while others, born with the proverbial silver spoon—Humphrey Bogart, Henry Fonda—managed to erase most signs of privilege except a steely confidence.

Men were more likely than women to take career in hand when they were dissatisfied with studio projects, saddled with one mediocre script after another. John Garfield was one of the first to start his own production company; Grant went freelance; Montgomery Clift and others refused to sign long-term studio contracts; and some became directors. Edward G. Robinson preempted any attempts to consign him to character parts by insisting, through his agent, that his name be above the title. Men were expected to exert power, and they did, and that, coupled with longevity and versatility, meant they were more able to shift gears and often continue as stars well beyond middle age. As the decades wore on, Fred Astaire and Cary Grant romanced younger and younger partners, while the women they'd started out with graduated to mother and grandmother roles. The possibilities weren't limitless, and star charisma carried its own risks: once he'd become every woman's fantasy playmate-lover, Cary Grant couldn't play a wife killer as he was meant to in Hitchcock's original script for *Suspicion*. But for the most part, bad-boy behavior, both on and off the screen, added to a man's sex appeal, a moral latitude that didn't extend to women.

On the other hand, many fought and were destroyed, or nearly destroyed, by demons. One of the most corrosive was the suspicion that acting was not a "manly" career—all that pretending, dressing up, like women. Perhaps infected by the old adage that "an actress is something more than a woman; an actor is something less than a man," a self-loathing crept into the behavior, the drinking, the acting up, the eccentricities of Holden, Brando, Olivier. Others repressed awkwardnesses, like being gay, or tried to keep drug habits or jail terms from the eyes of the press (a task in which they were assisted by the ever-vigilant and scandal-fearing studio heads and their minions). And whatever the greater opportunities for men, fairly rigid notions of masculinity still prevailed, which is why, in the fifties, a trio of hypersensitive rebels—Marlon Brando, Montgomery Clift, and James Dean— had a revolutionary impact on Hollywood and changed America's bedrock notions of masculinity, a license that extends to the more coolly and unself-consciously androgynous stars—and "metrosexuals"—of today.

James Dean, the smoldering "rebel without a cause," is a watershed figure, in that he virtually ushered in the whole concept of the teenager as a breed apart. Where once adolescents were adults-in-waiting, they were now alienated from the grown-up world, which would come to be seen, in Salingeresque fashion, as hypocritical, out of touch, beyond the pale. For better or worse, we're living with the consequences of that upheaval: the obsession with youth and the dethroning of the old WASP hierarchy that was enshrined in the studio system have changed the very nature of stardom. Term limits for superstars in the relentless search for new flesh, multiethnic casting, and the fragmentation of the film audience mean the absence of the kind of collective enthusiasms and universal admiration lavished on stars of the past.

Even when they were, or clearly had to be, narcissistic, these men didn't want to be seen as vain or effeminate, and, without wanting to gainsay all the various sexual freedoms of our time, there is something appealing in that appearance of modesty and virility, of men pursuing something more important than the ecstasies and transformations of the self. Who, with any sense of history, can resist peering into this window on the past? Movies, their stories and the stories about them, offer glittering clues to the way people thought and felt and looked, as embodied by these all-purpose heroes and heroines who claimed so much more of our attention and awe than the more transient celebrities of today.

The epitome of grace and charm, he transformed the movie musical, creating a new level of sophistication and style, especially in his legendary team-ups with Ginger Rogers.

FRED
ASTAIRE

The dance duets in Fred Astaire's ten films with Ginger Rogers are like a courtship set to music. He lures, she resists, but within a few beats she's swept into the romance of it all as they glide across the floor in perfect step. Their partnership made both careers but was really an accident. After a successful career on Broadway teamed with his sister, Adele, the newly married Astaire decided to see whether the movies would deliver a more stable life. But he wasn't exactly the stuff leading men were made of. When one studio executive saw an early screen test, he issued the famous judgment: "Can't act. Slightly bald. Also dances." After playing himself in Joan Crawford's *Dancing Lady* (1933), he landed a supporting role in RKO's *Flying Down to Rio* (1933). The film was a vehicle for Dolores Del Rio and Gene Raymond, with Astaire contributing a few numbers, one teamed with Dorothy Jordan. When Jordan got married and left for her honeymoon, however, the studio rushed Ginger Rogers into the role. Their first meeting on the dance floor, dancing "The Carioca," stole the show. Their partnership led to nine more starring films—including *The Gay Divorcee* (1934), *Top Hat* (1935), and *Swing Time* (1936)—that marked a revolution in movie musicals. Astaire and choreographer Hermes Pan developed a more fluid approach to shooting dance numbers, showing the performers' entire bodies, cutting on movement, and doing away with audience-reaction shots. When the team broke up in 1939, Astaire moved on to other dancing partners, including Rita Hayworth and Paulette Goddard. Concerned that he was getting older as his leading ladies got younger, he announced his retirement from the screen in 1946, but MGM lured him back to costar with Judy Garland in *Easter Parade* (1948), and the project revitalized him. Astaire found another memorable dancing partner in Cyd Charisse, most notably in *The Band Wagon* (1953). With the decline in film musicals, he brought his artistry to television for a series of acclaimed specials, this time with dancer Barrie Chase. He also moved into character roles, starting with the nuclear war drama *On the Beach* (1959). He made his final film musical, *Finian's Rainbow*, in 1968, and then won his only Oscar nomination for the all-star disaster film *The Towering Inferno* (1974). Astaire made his last film appearance with fellow veterans Melvyn Douglas, Douglas Fairbanks Jr., and John Houseman in 1981's *Ghost Story*.

Born
Frederic Austerlitz Jr.
May 10, 1899,
Omaha, Nebraska

Died
June 22, 1987,
Los Angeles, California,
of pneumonia

Star Sign
Taurus

Height
5'9"

Wives and Children
Socialite Phyllis Livingstone Potter
(1933–1954, her death)
son, Fred Jr.
daughter, Ava

Jockey Robyn Smith
(1980–1987, his death)

Essential
FREDASTAIREFilms

TOP HAT

(1935) RKO
Fred Astaire introduces his trademark song—Irving Berlin's "Top Hat, White Tie, and Tails"—before romping off to Venice to dance "Cheek to Cheek" with Ginger Rogers in their second costarring vehicle.

YOU WERE NEVER LOVELIER

(1942) Columbia
In the second of two films with his favorite dancing partner, Rita Hayworth, Astaire plays a dancer stranded in Rio who agrees to court a wealthy club owner's romantic daughter.

EASTER PARADE

(1948) MGM
The chance to work with two new dancing partners—Judy Garland and Ann Miller—and another great Irving Berlin score brought Astaire out of retirement to play a vaudeville star in search of a new partner.

ROYAL WEDDING

(1951) MGM
In a plot inspired by Astaire's early teamings with his sister, Adele, he and sister Jane Powell travel to England to entertain during Princess Elizabeth's wedding, with each finding love along the way.

FUNNY FACE

(1957) Paramount
Even as he was nearing sixty, Astaire proved that he could adapt to a new partner—this time the ballet-trained Audrey Hepburn—in this romance set in the world of high fashion.

EASTER PARADE, 1948

SWING TIME, 1936

BEHIND THE SCENES

ASTAIRE'S DANCE DUETS WITH ROGERS HAVE BEEN HAILED AS SOME OF THE MOST ROMANTIC MOMENTS IN SCREEN HISTORY, BUT HE ACTUALLY DEVELOPED THE NUMBERS WITH CHOREOGRAPHER HERMES PAN, WHO FILLED IN FOR ROGERS DURING CHOREOGRAPHY, THEN TAUGHT HER THE STEPS.

ORIGINALLY, ASTAIRE DIDN'T WANT TO KISS ROGERS ON SCREEN, BECAUSE HE WANTED THE DANCES TO BE THEIR LOVE SCENES. WHEN RUMORS BLAMED THEIR NOT KISSING ON HIS WIFE'S JEALOUSY OR THE STARS' DISLIKE OF EACH OTHER, HE PUT A KISS INTO *CAREFREE* (1938).

ASTAIRE'S DANCE CLOTHES HAD A MAJOR INFLUENCE ON MEN'S FASHIONS. HIS ENGLISH-STYLE TAILCOAT, BLACK PATENT LEATHER SHOES, AND TOP HATS BECAME THE NORM FOR THIRTIES EVENING WEAR, AND HIS USE OF THE PRINCE OF WALES DOUBLE-BREASTED SUIT POPULARIZED THAT STYLE FOR BUSINESS USE. FADS HE INTRODUCED INCLUDED WEARING A NECKTIE AS A BELT, AN IDEA HE GOT FROM FRIEND DOUGLAS FAIRBANKS JR.

ALTHOUGH ASTAIRE'S USE OF BLACKFACE FOR THE "BOJANGLES OF HARLEM" NUMBER IN *SWING TIME* (1936) IS NOW CONSIDERED CONTROVERSIAL, HE INTENDED THE PIECE AS A TRIBUTE TO HIS FRIEND, BILL "BOJANGLES" ROBINSON. HE AND HERMES PAN GOT THE IDEA FOR THE DANCING SHADOWS DURING REHEARSALS WHEN THEY NOTICED HOW THE LIGHTS GAVE ASTAIRE MULTIPLE SHADOWS.

IN ORDER TO SHOW ASTAIRE DANCING ON THE WALLS AND CEILINGS FOR A NUMBER IN *ROYAL WEDDING* (1951), DIRECTOR STANLEY DONEN HAD THE SET CONSTRUCTED SO IT WOULD ROTATE WITH THE CAMERA. ALTHOUGH IT APPEARED FRED WAS CLIMBING THE WALLS AND DANCING UPSIDE DOWN, IT WAS REALLY THE SET AND CAMERA THAT MOVED.

ALTHOUGH NOT PRIMARILY KNOWN FOR HIS SINGING, ASTAIRE WAS A FAVORITE OF SOME OF THE SCREEN'S GREATEST SONGWRITERS, INCLUDING GEORGE AND IRA GERSHWIN AND COLE PORTER. AMONG THE HITS THEY WROTE FOR HIM WERE "NIGHT AND DAY," "LET'S FACE THE MUSIC AND DANCE," "THE WAY YOU LOOK TONIGHT," "THEY CAN'T TAKE THAT AWAY FROM ME," AND MANY OTHERS.

"The Great Profile" brought his pedigree as the most acclaimed member of a great theater dynasty to both straightforward romantic leads and offbeat character parts.

JOHN
BARRYMORE

Born
John Sidney Blyth
February 14, 1882
Philadelphia, Pennsylvania

Died
May 29, 1942
Los Angeles, California
of pneumonia and
cirrhosis of the liver

Star Sign
Aquarius

Height
5'10"

Wives and Children
Socialite Katherine Corri Harris
(1910–1917, divorced)

Poet Blanche Oelrichs Thomas/
Michael Strange
(1920–1928, divorced)
daughter, Diana

Actress Dolores Costello
(1928–1934, divorced)
daughter,
Dolores Ethel Mae ("Dede")
son, John Blythe Jr.

Actress Elaine Jacobs/Elaine Barrie
(1936–1940, divorced)

Few stars blazed as brightly or fell as precipitously as John Barrymore. He, sister Ethel, and brother Lionel constituted "the Royal Family of Broadway," with John clearly the king. The three were born into the theater, the third generation of an acting clan presided over by Mrs. John Drew, the grandmother who raised them. Middle child Ethel was the first to reach stardom and stayed with the stage the longest before moving to Hollywood in her later years. Always afraid of audiences, the eldest, Lionel, hid himself in character roles from an early age and was the first to move into films, eventually starring in *A Free Soul* (1931) and *It's a Wonderful Life* (1946). It was the baby, John, who would be acclaimed as one of the greatest actors of his generation. After starting out as a romantic comedian, capitalizing on good looks to become one of the stage's biggest matinee idols, he moved into more serious work, scoring spectacular successes as Shakespeare's Richard III and Hamlet in the twenties. In 1914, he had started making films in New York, often shooting a picture by day while performing on Broadway at night. Most notably, he starred in a 1920 adaptation of *Dr. Jekyll and Mr. Hyde*, winning praise for playing the transformation scene without makeup or trick photography. After playing Hamlet to acclaim in New York and London, he gave up the stage for the chance to make big bucks in Hollywood. Into the early thirties, he commanded the box office with romantic roles in films like *Don Juan* (1926) and *Grand Hotel* (1932), and character parts like *Svengali* (1931) and the recovering lunatic in *A Bill of Divorcement* (1932), in which he played Katharine Hepburn's father in her film debut. He even teamed with Lionel and Ethel for the only time for 1932's *Rasputin and the Empress*. As famous as his acting, however, was his reputation as a drinker and womanizer. When he played the alcoholic actor in MGM's *Dinner at Eight* (1933), Hollywood insiders quipped that he was simply playing himself. As he lost his looks, he took more and more to low-budget projects. To pay his bills, he even played a buffoonish version of himself on singer Rudy Vallee's radio program. During a rehearsal in May 1942, he collapsed. All he could say was, "This is one time I miss my cue." Ten days later, he passed away.

Essential
JOHN**BARRYMORE**Films

DR. JEKYLL AND MR. HYDE
(1920) Famous Players–Lasky
John Barrymore threw himself
wholeheartedly into his
performance as a dedicated
scientist who transforms himself
into a hideous monster.

DON JUAN
(1926) Warner Bros.
Drawing on Barrymore's reputation
as a womanizer, Warner Bros. cast
him as the greatest lover of them
all for their first experiment with
synchronized sound.

GRAND HOTEL
(1932) MGM
Cast as a romantic jewel thief who
connects the all-star production's
various plots, Barrymore flirted with
the young Joan Crawford, tried to
steal scenes from his brother, Lionel,
and became the man Greta Garbo
wanted to be alone with.

DINNER AT EIGHT
(1933) MGM
Barrymore was at the height of his
film career when he played a faded,
alcoholic actor invited to an all-star
dinner party whose participants
included Marie Dressler, Billie Burke,
Jean Harlow, Wallace Beery, and
brother Lionel.

TWENTIETH CENTURY
(1934) Columbia
As egomaniacal Broadway
producer Oscar Jaffe, Barrymore
moves heaven and earth to win
back leading lady Carole Lombard,
in the screwball comedy that made
her a star.

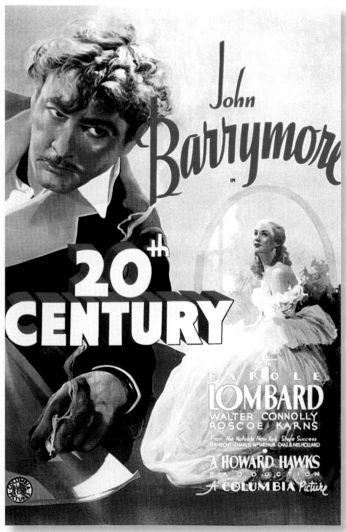

TWENTIETH CENTURY, 1934

WITH LIONEL AND ETHEL BARRYMORE, 1932

GRAND HOTEL, 1932

BEHINDTHESCENES

JOHN BARRYMORE'S HARD LIVING STARTED EARLY IN LIFE. A PSYCHIATRIST LATER SUGGESTED THE SOURCE OF HIS ALCOHOLISM WAS HIS SEDUCTION BY HIS STEPMOTHER WHEN HE WAS 15.

ALTHOUGH SHE HAD ORIGINALLY WANTED ONETIME COSTAR AND EX-LOVER JOHN GILBERT AS HER LEADING MAN IN *GRAND HOTEL* (1932), GRETA GARBO WAS THRILLED TO WORK WITH BARRYMORE. KNOWING HE LIKED TO FAVOR HIS LEFT PROFILE, SHE SPENT ONE LUNCH BREAK REARRANGING THE SET PIECES TO FAVOR THAT SIDE.

WHEN WARNER BROS. BOUGHT THE SCREEN RIGHTS TO *THE MAN WHO CAME TO DINNER* (1941), BETTE DAVIS AGREED TO STAR IN HOPES SHE COULD WIN HIM THE ROLE OF ACERBIC COLUMNIST SHERIDAN WHITESIDE. BARRYMORE SHOT A TEST THAT ALL INVOLVED THOUGHT HE GAVE A BRILLIANT PERFORMANCE. UNFORTUNATELY, STUDIO HEAD JACK WARNER DECIDED NOT TO GAMBLE ON BARRYMORE'S BEHAVIOR AND CAST THE PLAY'S BROADWAY STAR, MONTY WOOLLEY.

ONE OF BARRYMORE'S CLOSEST FRIENDS AND DRINKING BUDDIES WAS SWASHBUCKLING STAR ERROL FLYNN. YEARS AFTER BARRYMORE'S DEATH, FLYNN PLAYED HIM IN *TOO MUCH, TOO SOON* (1958), THE FILM BIOGRAPHY OF BARRYMORE'S ALCOHOLIC DAUGHTER, ACTRESS DIANA BARRYMORE.

BARRYMORE HAD TWO CHILDREN WHO WENT INTO THE THEATER: DIANA AND JOHN JR. NEITHER HAD A GREAT CAREER, AND FOR A WHILE IT SEEMED THE BARRYMORE DYNASTY HAD FADED OUT. THEN, IN 1982, JOHN JR.'S DAUGHTER, DREW BARRYMORE, LAUNCHED HER CAREER WITH *E.T., THE EXTRA-TERRESTRIAL.*

An antihero for the ages, this unlikely leading man built a career playing street-smart gangsters and cynical tough-guys, but is best remembered for his most romantic role, as Rick in *Casablanca.*

HUMPHREY
BOGART

When the Brattle Theatre, near Harvard, started its annual revivals of *Casablanca* (1942) in the sixties, students showed up for screenings dressed as Rick Blaine, their trench coats and snap-brim hats mirroring Humphrey Bogart's screen image just as his tough-guy pose mirrored their own youthful rebellions. Had Bogie been alive, he probably would have been amused and even touched, though he never would have shown it. Cynicism was a hard-won prize for the star. Born into New York society, the son of a prominent doctor and a popular portrait artist, he turned to acting after flunking out of school. Initially cast as callow young sophisticates, his failed attempt to break into films in the early thirties brought him back to Broadway, where he played a psychopathic gangster in *The Petrified Forest.* When the play became a movie in 1936, stage costar and close friend Leslie Howard refused to do the film without him, and Warner Bros. signed Bogie to a long-term contract. They kept him mainly in supporting roles—turning scripts down helped toughen him up, too—until John Huston wrote *High Sierra* (1941) for him and then used his directorial debut with *The Maltese Falcon* (1941) to make Bogart a star. That was enough to win over producer Hal Wallis, who had the script for *Casablanca* written to showcase Bogart's world-weary cynicism. Bogie had already proved himself a surprisingly effective leading man opposite stars like Ingrid Bergman and Ida Lupino, but it was a feisty newcomer who would really bring out the lover in him. Although almost two decades his junior, Lauren Bacall was his match in cynicism and sass when director Howard Hawks paired them in *To Have and Have Not* (1944). The onscreen chemistry continued in three more films together. Offscreen, she provided a stability that had eluded him in three failed marriages. She also gave him two children who brought out a softer side that would have surprised people who only knew him from his film roles. Bacall even put her own career on hold to accompany him during location shooting for *The Treasure of the Sierra Madre* (1948) and *The African Queen* (1951). Their relationship, whether trading barbs in *The Big Sleep* (1946) or simply posing for family photos, was the stuff dreams are made of.

Born
Humphrey DeForest Bogart
December 25, 1899
New York City

Died
January 14, 1957
Holmby Hills, California,
of throat cancer

Star Sign
Capricorn

Height
5'8"

Wives and Children
Actress Helen Menken
(1926–1927, divorced)

Actress Mary Phillips
(1928–1937, divorced)

Actress Mayo Methot
(1938–1945, divorced)

Actress Lauren Bacall
(1945–1957, his death)
son, Stephen Humphrey
daughter, Leslie Howard

Essential
HUMPHREY**BOGART**Films

ACADEMY AWARDS
Won for Best Actor
The African Queen

Nominated for Best Actor
Casablanca
The Caine Mutiny

THE MALTESE FALCON

(1941) Warner Bros.
Humphrey Bogart started his association with film noir when John Huston cast him as detective Sam Spade, a man whose personal code of honor carries him through a tangled web of deceit during the search for a stolen art treasure.

CASABLANCA

(1942) Warner Bros.
The role of Rick Blaine, the cynical nightclub owner trying to remain neutral during the Nazi occupation of Morocco, made Bogart an international star, and his love scenes with Ingrid Bergman made him a sex symbol.

TO HAVE AND HAVE NOT

(1944) Warner Bros.
Bogie met his match on screen when the insolent young Lauren Bacall taught him how to whistle in Howard Hawks's tale of a charter boat captain caught up in the fight against the Nazis.

THE TREASURE OF THE SIERRA MADRE

(1948) Warner Bros.
Director John Huston revealed new depths in Bogart's acting when he showed the paranoid side of toughness in this cynical western about three prospectors in the Mexican mountains who strike it rich, only to find their good fortune undone by their own greed.

THE AFRICAN QUEEN

(1951) United Artists
Bogart endured the rigors of location shooting in Africa and got an Oscar for his performance as a crusty riverboat captain who joins forces with prim missionary Katharine Hepburn while trying to survive World War I.

CASABLANCA, 1942

DARK PASSAGE, 1947

BEHIND THE SCENES

GEORGE RAFT GAVE BOGART A CAREER BOOST BY REFUSING TO MAKE *HIGH SIERRA* (1941), BECAUSE HE DIDN'T WANT HIS CHARACTER TO DIE AT THE FILM'S END, AND THEN TURNING DOWN *THE MALTESE FALCON* (1941) BECAUSE IT WAS A REMAKE, AND HE DIDN'T WANT TO WORK WITH A FIRST-TIME DIRECTOR (JOHN HUSTON). CONTRARY TO RUMOR, RAFT DID NOT TURN DOWN *CASABLANCA* (1942). THAT PICTURE HAD ALREADY BEEN WRITTEN WITH BOGART IN MIND WHEN RAFT MADE AN UNSUCCESSFUL BID FOR THE LEADING ROLE.

BOGART AND HIS THIRD WIFE, ACTRESS MAYO METHOT, WERE NICKNAMED "THE BATTLING BOGARTS" BECAUSE OF THEIR LEGENDARY BRAWLS, PARTICULARLY WHEN ONE OR BOTH HAD BEEN DRINKING. THEIR FIGHTING EVEN GOT THEM KICKED OFF AN OVERSEAS USO TOUR DURING WORLD WAR II FOR FEAR THEY WOULD INTERFERE WITH THE WAR EFFORT.

IN CONTRAST TO HIS TOUGH-GUY IMAGE, BOGART REALLY WANTED A WIFE WHO COULD CONTROL HIM, AND LAUREN BACALL FILLED THE BILL PERFECTLY. SHE COULD EVEN GET HIM TO STOP DRINKING BEFORE HE HAD ONE TOO MANY. WHEN SHE PUSHED HIM TOO FAR WHILE THEY WERE WORKING, HOWEVER, HE COULD GET HER TO BACK DOWN BY SIMPLY CALLING HER "MISS BACALL."

BOGART NAMED HIS SON, STEPHEN, FOR HIS CHARACTER IN *TO HAVE AND HAVE NOT* (1944), THE FILM ON WHICH HE MET THE BOY'S MOTHER, LAUREN BACALL. THEIR DAUGHTER, LESLIE, WAS NAMED FOR THE LATE LESLIE HOWARD, A CLOSE FRIEND.

WRITER-DIRECTOR JOHN HUSTON FORGED A CLOSE FRIENDSHIP WITH BOGART OVER THE COURSE OF SIX FILMS THEY MADE TOGETHER. IT WAS HUSTON WHO MADE HIM A STAR WITH *THE MALTESE FALCON* (1941) AND HELPED HIM WIN AN OSCAR FOR *THE AFRICAN QUEEN* (1951). BUT THE FRIENDSHIP COOLED WITH THE BOX OFFICE FAILURE OF THEIR LAST FILM TOGETHER, *BEAT THE DEVIL* (1953).

BOGIE WAS THE FATHER OF THE RAT PACK, A GROUP OF DRINKING BUDDIES WHO GOT TOGETHER REGULARLY AT MIKE ROMANOFF'S HOLLYWOOD RESTAURANT. FRANK SINATRA WAS ORIGINALLY JUST A RAT PACK MEMBER, BUT HE TOOK OVER LEADERSHIP AFTER BOGIE PASSED AWAY.

WRITER-DIRECTOR-ACTOR WOODY ALLEN CAPTURED THE YOUTHFUL ADULATION OF BOGART THAT HAD GROWN UP AROUND REVIVALS OF HIS FILMS IN HIS PLAY AND FILM *PLAY IT AGAIN, SAM* (1972), IN WHICH THE LOVELORN ALLEN LEARNS FROM BOGART'S SPIRIT, PLAYED BY ACTOR JERRY LACY, HOW TO HANDLE WOMEN.

His hooded gaze, suave manner, and Gallic sophistication made him the quintessential continental lover and a perfect romantic match for the screen's most glamorous leading ladies.

CHARLES
BOYER

The ultimate French ladies' man—suave and sophisticated beyond any woman's wildest dreams—was just a shy small-town boy who discovered the movies and theater at the age of eleven. Working as a hospital orderly during World War I, Charles Boyer started to come out of himself performing comic sketches for the soldiers there. He went to Paris to finish his education but spent most of his time pursuing a theatrical career. In 1920, his quick memory won him a shot at replacing the leading man in a stage production, and he scored an immediate hit. At first Boyer did film roles only for the money, but with the coming of sound, his deep voice made him the perfect romantic star. MGM signed him to a contract, and though he loved life in the United States, nothing much came of his Hollywood stay until fellow French expatriate Claudette Colbert requested him as her leading man in the psychiatric drama *Private Worlds* (1935). During this period, Boyer had continued making European films, and *Mayerling* (1936) made him an international star. The offscreen Boyer was bookish and private, far removed from the Hollywood high life. But on screen he made women swoon as he romanced Marlene Dietrich in *The Garden of Allah* (1936), Greta Garbo in *Conquest* (1937), and Irene Dunne in *Love Affair* (1939). In 1938, he landed his most famous role, as Pepe Le Moko, the thief on the run, in *Algiers*. Although he never invited costar Hedy Lamarr to "Come with me to the Casbah," the line would stick with him, thanks to generations of impressionists. In the forties, Boyer sought more varied assignments, including the role of Ingrid Bergman's villainous husband in *Gaslight* (1944). When another film with Bergman, *Arch of Triumph* (1948), failed at the box office, he started looking for character parts. He also moved into television as one of the pioneering producers and stars of *Four Star Theatre;* Four Star Productions would make him and partners David Niven and Dick Powell rich. Onscreen, he continued to shine with older roles in *Fanny* (1961), *Barefoot in the Park* (1967), and the French film *Stavisky* (1974), the latter winning him the New York Film Critics Circle Award. But his later years were also marked by personal loss. His only child, Michael, committed suicide at twenty-one. Then his wife of more than forty years, former actress Pat Paterson, died after a long bout with cancer. Heartbroken, Boyer took his life two days later.

Born
Charles Boyer
August 28, 1899
Figeac, Lot, Midi-Pyrénées,
France

Died
August 26, 1978
Phoenix, Arizona, of suicide,
sleeping pill overdose

Star Sign
Virgo

Height
5'7"

Wife and Child
British actress Pat Paterson
(1934–1978, her death)
son, Michael

Essential
CHARLESBOYERFilms

MAYERLING
(1936) Nero
Charles Boyer's U.S. career was just picking up when he shot to international stardom in this fictionalized, supremely romantic account of Archduke Ferdinand of Austria's doomed love for the beautiful Marie Vetsera (Danielle Darrieux).

ALGIERS
(1938) United Artists
Doomed love became Boyer's forte when he risked his life for Hedy Lamarr as Pepe Le Moko, a jewel thief hiding out in northern Africa.

LOVE AFFAIR
(1939) RKO
Boyer got to show his lighter side and indulge in some memorable improvisations when Leo McCarey cast him opposite Irene Dunne in this tale of a shipboard romance, later remade by McCarey as *An Affair to Remember* (1957), with Cary Grant and Deborah Kerr.

GASLIGHT
(1944) MGM
Seeking to expand his image, Boyer went after the role of Ingrid Bergman's murderous, manipulative husband in this classic melodrama.

THE EARRINGS OF MADAME DE . . .
(1953) Arlan
Boyer returned to French filmmaking for the first time in almost two decades to reunite with Darrieux (as the wife driven to infidelity by his inattention) in this tale of love and betrayal directed by the legendary Max Ophuls.

LOVE AFFAIR, 1939

GASLIGHT, 1944

TOVARICH, 1937

BEHIND THE SCENES

BOYER'S ROLE AS PEPE LE MOKO WAS ALREADY WORLD FAMOUS WHEN ANIMATOR CHUCK JONES BASED THE CHARACTER OF PEPE LE PEW, THE ROMANTIC SKUNK INTRODUCED IN 1945'S "ODOR-ABLE KITTY," ON BOYER AND HIS MOST WELL-KNOWN PERFORMANCE.

BOYER'S MARRIAGE TO PAT PATERSON WAS AS ROMANTIC AS HIS MOVIES. IT WAS LOVE AT FIRST SIGHT WHEN THEY MET AT A DINNER PARTY IN 1934. TWO WEEKS LATER, THEY WERE ENGAGED. THREE MONTHS LATER, THEY WERE MARRIED.

IN CONTRAST TO HIS GLAMOROUS IMAGE, BOYER BEGAN LOSING HIS HAIR EARLY, HAD A PRONOUNCED PAUNCH, AND WAS NOTICEABLY SHORTER THAN LEADING LADIES LIKE INGRID BERGMAN. WHEN BETTE DAVIS FIRST SAW HIM ON THE SET OF *ALL THIS, AND HEAVEN TOO* (1940), SHE DIDN'T RECOGNIZE HIM AND TRIED TO HAVE HIM REMOVED FROM THE SET.

Credited with introducing Method acting to the screen, his naturalistic performances combined raw sexuality and barely masked sensitivity.

MARLON
BRANDO

Born
Marlon Brando Jr.
April 3, 1924
Omaha, Nebraska

Died
July 1, 2004
Los Angeles, California,
of pulmonary fibrosis

Star Sign
Aries

Height
5'10"

Wives and Children
Actress Anna Kashfi
(1957-1959, divorced)
son, Christian Devi
(acted briefly as Gary Brown)

Actress Movita Castenada
(1960–1962, divorced;
1967, annulled)
son, Miko
daughter, Rebecca
(born after their divorce)

daughter, Liliane, born
out of wedlock to unnamed
Tahitian woman

son, Bobby, born out of wedlock
to unnamed Asian woman,
acknowledged only by Christian

Actress Tarita Tariipaia
(1962–1972, divorced)
son, Simon Tehotu
daughter, Tarita Cheyenne
adopted daughter, Petra Barrett

daughter, Ninna Priscilla and two
other children born out of wedlock
to former maid Christina Ruiz

Biographers have suggested
various other children born out
of wedlock but never openly
acknowledged by Brando

Brando was one of the key figures to introduce a new, more personal approach to acting in the fifties. Although he never considered himself a Method actor, he had studied with New York teacher Stella Adler, who taught him to create impressively realistic performances by dredging up evocative past memories. As the child of alcoholic parents, he had a lot of them. He started acting at an early age to pull his mother out of frequent drunken stupors. Following his actress sister, Jocelyn, to New York in 1943, he did impressive stage work in *I Remember Mama* and *A Streetcar Named Desire* before signing to make his film debut as a paraplegic veteran in *The Men* (1950). He won raves for his performance, but the film that clearly carved his niche on screen was *A Streetcar Named Desire* (1951), in which his animalistic Stanley Kowalski menaced Vivien Leigh's faded Southern belle Blanche DuBois. Although his naturalistic delivery was often derided as mere mumbling and his casual dress led to jokes about the "torn T-shirt" school of acting, he demonstrated his versatility as Marc Antony in MGM's all-star version of Shakespeare's *Julius Caesar* (1953). The fifties were Brando's golden years, capped by an Oscar win for *On the Waterfront* (1954). By the sixties, however, indulgent on-set behavior (particularly during the filming of 1962's *Mutiny on the Bounty*) and offscreen excesses led to complaints that he was squandering his talent. He bounced back when young director Francis Ford Coppola fought to cast him as mafioso Vito Coreleone in *The Godfather* (1972). Although the studio made him test for the role, Brando went after the character with his old enthusiasm, delivering an acclaimed performance that brought him his second Oscar. He alienated the Hollywood establishment by sending a representative to decline the award as a protest against Hollywood's stereotyping of Native Americans, but the notoriety kept him at the top of box office polls. At the same time, Brando was rapidly losing interest in acting. After a highly autobiographical performance in *Last Tango in Paris* (1972) and a record-setting paycheck for a glorified cameo in *Superman* (1978), he gradually withdrew from performing. His few returns to the screen were news, but equally newsworthy were his battles with weight and family problems. At the time of his death, he had recorded the voice of Mrs. Sour, a candy-factory owner, for the animated feature *Big Bug Man* (2006).

Essential
MARLON BRANDO Films

A STREETCAR NAMED DESIRE

(1951) Warner Bros.
The role of Stanley Kowalski had made Marlon Brando a national phenomenon when he played it on Broadway; in the film version, his naturalistic, graceful, and surprisingly funny performance as a lout who destroys his sister-in-law (Vivien Leigh) revolutionized acting and made him an icon.

ON THE WATERFRONT

(1954) Columbia
In another legendary performance, Brando captures all the frustration underlying the moral awakening of a boxer turned longshoreman who risks his life to give evidence against the mob.

THE GODFATHER

(1972) Paramount
After years of box office drought, Brando shot back to the top with his acclaimed performance as Don Vito Coreleone, fathering young costars Al Pacino, James Caan, and Robert Duvall as surely as he had influenced their offscreen development as actors.

LAST TANGO IN PARIS

(1972) United Artists
In this intense battle of the sexes, Brando drew so heavily on his own life experiences, particularly in an improvised speech about his character's mother, that he would later call his performance "embarrassing," but critics called it brilliant.

APOCALYPSE NOW

(1979) Zoetrope/United Artists
Director Francis Ford Coppola, who courted Brando for the role of renegade Green Beret Willard Kurtz in his Vietnam War epic, was shocked when he arrived on set weighing more than 250 pounds, then let him improvise his final scene in a performance that, for all its good qualities, points to the excesses of Brando's later years.

THE GODFATHER, 1972

BEHIND THE SCENES

MARLON BRANDO'S EARLY SCREEN SUCCESSES SET A NEW STANDARD OF ACTING FOR FUTURE GENERATIONS. AMONG THE MANY ACTORS WHO FOLLOWED IN HIS FOOTSTEPS AS A SENSITIVE REBEL WERE PAUL NEWMAN, JAMES DEAN (WHO EVEN COPIED ASPECTS OF BRANDO'S PERSONAL LIFE), STEVE MCQUEEN, AND WARREN BEATTY. YEARS LATER, JACK NICHOLSON WOULD SAY, "WE ARE ALL BRANDO'S CHILDREN."

CONTRARY TO HIS LATER CLAIMS, BRANDO DID NOT IMPROVISE PARTS OF THE TAXI SCENE WITH ROD STEIGER IN *ON THE WATERFRONT* (1954). WHEN HE TRIED TO AD LIB DURING THE SHOOTING, DIRECTOR ELIA KAZAN STOPPED HIM.

BRANDO MARRIED BOTH ACTRESSES WHO PLAYED FLETCHER CHRISTIAN'S LOVE INTERESTS IN DIFFERENT VERSIONS OF *MUTINY ON THE BOUNTY*. HE FIRST MET MOVITA CASTENADA, WHO HAD ACTED OPPOSITE CLARK GABLE IN 1935, WHILE DOING RESEARCH IN MEXICO FOR *VIVA ZAPATA!* (1952), STARTING AN OFF-AND-ON RELATIONSHIP THAT WOULD LAST FOR YEARS. HE MET TARITA TERIIPAIA, HIS COSTAR IN THE 1962 REMAKE, DURING CASTING FOR THAT FILM. THEIRS WAS AN EQUALLY LENGTHY AND TORTUOUS RELATIONSHIP.

BRANDO SENT A WOMAN IDENTIFIED AS SACHEEN LITTLEFEATHER TO REFUSE HIS OSCAR FOR *THE GODFATHER* (1972). ALTHOUGH REPORTERS CLAIMED SHE WAS A MEXICAN ACTRESS NAMED MARIA CRUZ, SHE ACTUALLY WAS PART APACHE AND HAD ADOPTED THE NAME LITTLEFEATHER WHILE WORKING IN THE NATIVE AMERICAN RIGHTS MOVEMENT. SHE AND BRANDO WERE NOT, AS SOME SUGGESTED, LOVERS. SHE WAS MOBBED IN THE PARKING LOT AFTERWARD, INVESTIGATED BY THE FBI, AND EVENTUALLY NEEDED THERAPY TO GET OVER THE CONTROVERSY.

IN MANY OF HIS LATER APPEARANCES, BRANDO REFUSED TO LEARN LINES, DEPENDING ON CUE CARDS AND A SPECIAL HEARING AID THAT FED HIM LINES. HE CLAIMED THIS KEPT HIS PERFORMANCES FRESH, BECAUSE REAL PEOPLE RARELY MEMORIZE WHAT THEY'RE GOING TO SAY FROM MOMENT TO MOMENT.

LONG BEFORE HE BALLOONED TO 300 POUNDS IN LATER YEARS, BRANDO WAS NOTORIOUS FOR HIS EXCESSIVE EATING HABITS, OFTEN REQUIRING THAT HIS COSTUMES BE LET OUT DURING FILMING. FOR A LATE-NIGHT SNACK, HE OFTEN DROVE TO L.A.'S PINK'S HOT DOG STAND AND ATE SIX OF THEM. WHEN HIS WIFE MOVITA SUSPECTED THE HOUSEHOLD STAFF OF RAIDING THE REFRIGERATOR AT NIGHT, SHE HAD A PADLOCK PUT ON IT. WHEN SHE FOUND THE PADLOCK BROKEN AND MORE FOOD MISSING, ONE OF THE SERVANTS EXPLAINED THAT BRANDO WAS RESPONSIBLE.

ON THE WATERFRONT, 1954

Starting out as a song-and-dance man on Broadway, he ultimately found success as one of the screen's most famous gangsters, electrifying audiences with his machine-gun line delivery and aggressive stance.

JAMES
CAGNEY

By the early thirties, America was fed up with crime. With headlines about gang violence appearing almost daily, organized crime was increasingly viewed as a social ill. This new perspective made the gangster genre more prominent than ever. The studios needed leading men who weren't afraid to portray these very human monsters, making James Cagney the right man in the right place. He knew these characters all too well, having grown up in one of New York's poorest neighborhoods, where he learned to fight at an early age. While some of his playmates turned to crime, however, he was too busy helping support his family to get into trouble. Acting at the local settlement house as a way to let off steam led to his first professional job, as part of the ladies' chorus of an all-male musical. His ticket to Hollywood came when Warner Bros. bought the screen rights to his 1929 Broadway flop *Penny Arcade* and signed him and leading lady Joan Blondell for the film version, *Sinner's Holiday* (1930). Originally, Cagney was cast as the second lead in *The Public Enemy* (1931), but director William Wellman moved him into the lead, and his venomous portrayal of gangster Tom Powers made him a star. Typecasting as a tough guy kept Cagney busy on both sides of the law, but he always described himself as "just a song-and-dance man" and got to show off those talents in his Oscar-winning performance as musical star George M. Cohan in *Yankee Doodle Dandy* (1942). At the height of his fame, Cagney left Warner Bros. to produce his own films with brother William at United Artists. When his projects there failed to catch fire at the box office, however, he returned to Warner Bros., starting his new contract with a psychological look at the gangster genre, *White Heat* (1949). Cagney continued to headline through the fifties, but, after finishing director Billy Wilder's Cold War comedy *One, Two, Three* (1961), he retired from the screen. For twenty years, the very private actor contented himself with painting and family life, but he returned for one last feature, *Ragtime* (1981), at the urging of director Milos Forman, who lived near his New York farm. The actor was so ill he could only be photographed sitting down, with a double used for long shots, but the old magic was still there.

Born
James Francis Cagney
July 17, 1899
Yonkers, New York

Died
March 30, 1986
Stanfordville, New York
of a heart attack following a
prolonged bout with diabetes

Star Sign
Cancer

Height
5'7"

Wife and Children
Actress-dancer
Frances Willard ("Bill") Vernon
(1922–1986, his death)
adopted son, James Jr.
adopted daughter,
Cathleen ("Casey")

Essential
JAMESCAGNEYFilms

ACADEMY AWARDS
Won for Best Actor
Yankee Doodle Dandy

Nominated for Best Actor
Angels with Dirty Faces
Love Me or Leave Me

THE PUBLIC ENEMY

(1931) Warner Bros.
In his first starring role as a gangster, James Cagney played a ruthless child of the slums who kills everyone in his way—and shoves a grapefruit in Mae Clark's face but turns into a puppy dog over Jean Harlow.

ANGELS WITH DIRTY FACES

(1938) Warner Bros.
Teamed with offscreen friend and frequent costar Pat O'Brien, Cagney took on the law as a gangster on the run who befriends the juvenile-delinquent Dead End Kids and meets up with a childhood friend who has become a priest (O'Brien).

YANKEE DOODLE DANDY

(1942) Warner Bros.
In a break from gangster roles, Cagney took his tough-guy persona to vaudeville and the Broadway stage, drawing on his song-and-dance roots and studying archival footage of George M. Cohan to capture the stage star's unique dancing style.

WHITE HEAT

(1949) Warner Bros.
The gangster film took a turn into more psychological territory after World War II, with Cagney leading the way as the psychotic Cody Jarrett, a cold-blooded killer with a mother fixation and psychosomatic headaches.

RAGTIME

(1981) Paramount
After twenty years off screen, Cagney returned for his final film, costarring as a New York police chief trying to quash a social revolution in director Milos Forman's adaptation of the critically acclaimed E. L. Doctorow novel.

YANKEE DOODLE DANDY, 1942

ANGELS WITH DIRTY FACES, 1938

THE ROARING TWENTIES, 1939

BEHINDTHESCENES

BECAUSE HE GREW UP IN A JEWISH NEIGHBORHOOD IN NEW YORK'S HELL'S KITCHEN, THE IRISH-NORWEGIAN JAMES CAGNEY WAS FLUENT IN YIDDISH FROM AN EARLY AGE. HE EVEN SPOKE IN THAT LANGUAGE WITH JEWISH COSTARS LIKE SYLVIA SIDNEY.

THE FAMOUS GRAPEFRUIT SCENE IN *THE PUBLIC ENEMY* (1931) WAS A PRACTICAL JOKE CAGNEY AND COSTAR MAE CLARKE DECIDED TO PLAY ON THE CREW WHILE THE CAMERAS WERE ROLLING. DIRECTOR WILLIAM WELLMAN LIKED IT SO MUCH HE PUT IT IN THE PICTURE. THE SCENE MADE CLARKE'S EX-HUSBAND, LEW BRICE, VERY HAPPY. HE SAW THE FILM REPEATEDLY JUST TO SEE THAT SCENE AND OFTEN WAS SHUSHED BY ANGRY PATRONS WHEN HIS DELIGHTED LAUGHTER GOT TOO LOUD.

CAGNEY MODELED HIS PERFORMANCE IN *ANGELS WITH DIRTY FACES* (1938) ON A HUNGARIAN PIMP AND DRUG ADDICT HE HAD SEEN GROWING UP IN NEW YORK. FROM HIM, CAGNEY GOT THE HABITUAL TROUSER HITCH AND NECK MOVEMENT, ALONG WITH THE GREETING, "WHADDA YA HEAR? WHADDA YA SAY?"

CAGNEY WENT AFTER THE ROLE OF GEORGE M. COHAN IN *YANKEE DOODLE DANDY* (1942) AFTER FRED ASTAIRE TURNED IT DOWN. AT THE TIME, HE NEEDED THE FLAG-WAVING FILM BECAUSE OF ACCUSATIONS OF RADICAL ACTIVITIES FOLLOWING HIS WORK TO ESTABLISH THE SCREEN ACTORS' GUILD AND HIS SUPPORT OF PRESIDENT FRANKLIN D. ROOSEVELT.

ALTHOUGH CAGNEY'S OFFSCREEN LIFE WAS SQUEAKY CLEAN, HE HAD ONE RUN-IN WITH THE MOB WHEN ORGANIZED CRIME TRIED TO TAKE OVER THE SCREEN ACTORS' GUILD DURING HIS PRESIDENCY IN THE EARLY FORTIES. THEY PLOTTED TO RUB HIM OUT BY HAVING A HEAVY KLIEG LIGHT DROPPED ON HIS HEAD AT A MOVIE STUDIO, BUT GEORGE RAFT, ANOTHER SCREEN GANGSTER, USED HIS REAL-LIFE MOB CONTACTS TO CALL OFF THE HIT.

The screen's first great horror star, he was dubbed "the Man of a Thousand Faces" for bringing a gallery of grotesque yet sympathetic characters to life.

LON
CHANEY

What amazes audiences discovering Lon Chaney's work for the first time, along with his impressive ability to transform his face and body, is the humanity shining through even the thickest makeup. Chaney was one of the screen's greatest pantomime artists, a skill he developed as a child in order to communicate with his parents, both of whom were deaf. As a young teen, he got a job at the local opera house, where he first learned to use stage makeup and developed a love of acting. During his early theatrical career, he met and married sixteen-year-old singer Cleva Creighton, the mother of his only child, future actor Lon Chaney Jr. When they settled in San Francisco, the marriage fell apart, leading his distraught wife to burst backstage while Lon was working and drink poison in the wings. Although it didn't kill her, it destroyed her voice, the marriage, and Chaney's theatrical career. Chaney won custody of their son but had to put him into foster care until he could support him. To do that, he used his makeup skills to land a wide variety of extra roles and bit parts in silent films. Chaney shot to stardom in 1919 when he used his physical contortions to play the fake cripple in *The Miracle Man* and dazzled audiences. His ability to capture the humanity in the most grotesque characters struck a chord in post—World War I audiences. The use of modern medicine during that war had kept many soldiers alive despite disfiguring injuries; some even wore masks in public like the one Chaney would wear in his biggest success, *The Phantom of the Opera* (1925). That film and *The Hunchback of Notre Dame* (1923) made him one of the era's biggest stars. Initially, Chaney resisted the transition to talking films, afraid that sound would undercut his pantomime skills. When he finally made his first sound film, a new version of *The Unholy Three* (1930), he proved he could shape his voice as much as he had shaped his face and body, using five voices for his role as a con artist. Sadly, it would be his only talking film. Chaney died of lung cancer at the relatively young age of forty-seven, though his genius would remain alive through continuing revivals of his work just as his son, part of a new generation of horror stars, would keep the family name alive.

Born
Leonidas Frank Chaney
April 1, 1883
Colorado Springs, Colorado

Died
August 26, 1930
Hollywood, California,
of lung cancer

Star Sign
Aries

Height
5'8"

Wives and Child
Singer Cleva Creighton
(1905–1914, divorced)
son, Creighton (Lon Chaney Jr.)

Hazel Hastings Bennett
(1914–1930, his death)

Essential
LONCHANEYFilms

THE MIRACLE MAN
(1919) Paramount
Audiences were so impressed with Lon Chaney's star-making performance as a fake cripple who hooks up with a faith healer that in 1921 they voted this the greatest film ever made over such acknowledged classics as Charles Chaplin's *The Kid* (1921) and D. W. Griffith's *Broken Blossoms* (1919).

THE HUNCHBACK OF NOTRE DAME
(1923) Universal
This sumptuous adaptation of Victor Hugo's novel, about the deformed bell ringer Quasimodo and his doomed love for the gypsy Esmeralda (Patsy Ruth Miller), was Chaney's dream project, and one of the most expensive films made to that time.

HE WHO GETS SLAPPED
(1924) MGM
Headlining the infant MGM's first release, Chaney stars opposite Norma Shearer and John Gilbert as a tortured scientist hiding out as a circus clown.

THE PHANTOM OF THE OPERA
(1925) Universal
Audiences fainted when Chaney revealed the skull-like face of Erik, the murderous recluse haunting the Paris Opera, then sobbed as they realized the inner pain behind the character's love for a young singer.

THE UNKNOWN
(1927) MGM
Director Tod Browning built this circus romance around Chaney's suggestion that he play an armless sideshow performer in love with a beautiful circus performer (Joan Crawford).

HE WHO GETS SLAPPED, 1924

WITH MAKEUP CASE, CIRCA 1922

LONDON AFTER MIDNIGHT, 1927

BEHIND THE SCENES

LON CHANEY SPARED HIMSELF NO PAIN TO CREATE HIS CHARACTERS PHYSICALLY. TO PLAY AN AMPUTEE IN *THE PENALTY* (1920), HE HAD HIS LOWER LEGS STRAPPED SO TIGHTLY BEHIND HIS THIGHS IT CAUSED PERMANENT MUSCULAR DAMAGE. FOR *THE HUNCHBACK OF NOTRE DAME* (1923), HE WORE A LEATHER HARNESS AND A FIFTEEN-POUND PLASTER HUMP THAT MADE IT IMPOSSIBLE FOR HIM TO STAND UP STRAIGHT.

CHANEY OFTEN WENT OUT OF HIS WAY TO HELP OTHERS. FILM STARS JOAN CRAWFORD AND LORETTA YOUNG SPOKE KINDLY OF HIS HELPFULNESS WHEN THEY WORKED WITH HIM EARLY IN THEIR CAREERS. CHANEY ALSO HELPED FUTURE HORROR STAR BORIS KARLOFF GET STARTED IN FILMS, A DEBT KARLOFF WOULD ACKNOWLEDGE THE REST OF HIS LIFE.

CHANEY'S REPUTATION FOR CHANGING HIS APPEARANCE WITH EACH ROLE WAS SO WELL KNOWN THAT DURING THE TWENTIES IT INSPIRED THE CATCHPHRASE "DON'T STEP ON THAT SPIDER; IT MIGHT BE LON CHANEY!"

ONCE CHANEY WAS SPOTTED REPLACING SOME BABY BIRDS THAT HAD FALLEN OUT OF THEIR NEST. HE SWORE THE WITNESS TO SILENCE, SAYING, "I WILL NEVER HEAR THE END OF IT. EVERYONE THINKS I AM SO HARD-BOILED."

MANY OF CHANEY'S MOST POPULAR FILMS ARE CONSIDERED LOST. HIS VAMPIRE THRILLER *LONDON AFTER MIDNIGHT* (1927) WAS UNAVAILABLE FOR YEARS UNTIL FILMMAKER RICK SCHMIDLIN SPEARHEADED A RECONSTRUCTION THAT CREATED A VERSION CONSISTING OF PRODUCTION STILLS AND TITLES.

As the Little Tramp—the prankster with the heart of gold, as prone to heartache as mischief—"Charlie" was one of the world's most recognized figures, one of the first truly international stars.

CHARLES
CHAPLIN

The shot of the Little Tramp walking down a deserted road has become one of the screen's most memorable images, an icon of human resilience, thanks to the genius of Charles Chaplin. As actor, writer, director, producer, and composer, he played a key role in establishing the movies as a legitimate art form by combining humor and sentiment in a series of timeless classics. The sentiment was influenced by his youth as the son of a music-hall-singer mother whose mental problems often left Chaplin and his half-brother, Syd, alone and penniless. His comic skills were honed by a lifetime of performing, starting when he was five and would go onstage to save his mother's act whenever she faltered. At seventeen, he joined Fred Karno's vaudeville troupe, which brought him to the United States, where he landed a contract with film-comedy director Mack Sennett. For his second film, *Kid Auto Races at Venice* (1914), he threw together various costume pieces and invented the Little Tramp. After a year with Sennett, Chaplin moved through a series of studios until he joined Douglas Fairbanks, Mary Pickford, and D. W. Griffith in 1919 to create United Artists. This new freedom allowed him to lavish time and attention on films like *The Gold Rush* (1925) and *The Circus* (1928). Chaplin was Hollywood's biggest holdout against the coming of sound, using only synchronized scores for *City Lights* (1931) and *Modern Times* (1936). His first talkie, *The Great Dictator* (1940), ignited controversy because he dared to poke fun at Hitler and the rise of Fascism, but it still scored at the box office. Political controversy became a dominant factor in his life, as the liberal politics expressed in his films, which often criticized the government, law enforcement, and big business, increasingly came under fire in the conservative times following World War II. The pacifist message of his next picture, the black comedy *Monsieur Verdoux* (1947), inspired protest demonstrations that curtailed its distribution in the United States. When he traveled to England for the premiere of *Limelight* in 1952, he was denied reentry into the United States and retired to Switzerland with his fourth wife, Oona O'Neill. Even as late as 1972, a decision to honor him with a special Academy Award was considered controversial, though it marked the start of a series of late-life honors for the man who helped invent motion pictures.

Born
Charles Spencer Chaplin
April 16, 1889
Walworth, London, England

Died
December 25, 1977
Vevey, Switzerland,
of natural causes

Star Sign
Aries

Height
5'5"

Wives and Children
Actress Mildred Harris
(1918–1920, divorced)
son, Norman Spencer

Actress Lita Grey
(1924–1927, divorced)
sons, Charles Spencer Jr.
and Sydney Earle

Actress Paulette Goddard
(1936–1942, never legally proven)

Actress Oona O'Neill
(1943–1977, his death)
daughters, Geraldine,
Josephine Hannah, Victoria,
Jane Cecil, and Annette Emily
sons, Michael John,
Eugene Anthony,
and Christopher James

Essential
CHARLESCHAPLINFilms

THE KID
(1921) First National
With his first feature, Charles Chaplin scored laughs and tears as an unemployed man who finds new hope when he adopts a foundling, played by Jackie Coogan in the role that made him the screen's first major child star.

THE GOLD RUSH
(1925) United Artists
Some of Chaplin's most famous comic routines—including eating one of his shoes to fend off starvation and an improvised dance with a pair of dinner rolls—highlight this tale of the Little Tramp's efforts to strike it rich in the Klondike gold rush.

CITY LIGHTS
(1931) United Artists
While the rest of Hollywood was rushing to make talking films, Chaplin proved silence still could be golden when his Little Tramp devised a series of schemes to restore a blind flower seller's sight.

THE GREAT DICTATOR
(1940) United Artists
Playing off his resemblance to Adolf Hitler, Chaplin used his first talking film to poke fun at him, playing both dictator Adenoid Hynkel and a look-alike Jewish barber.

MONSIEUR VERDOUX
(1947) United Artists
Chaplin dropped all vestiges of the Little Tramp to play a serial killer who bumps off rich widows to support his invalid wife, justifying his crimes as insignificant in comparison to what the world's nations had done in World War II.

ON-SET DIRECTING *THE GOLD RUSH*, 1925

THE KID, 1921

BEHINDTHE**SCENES**

TO CREATE THE LITTLE TRAMP, CHARLES CHAPLIN BORROWED COSTUME PIECES FROM OTHER MEMBERS OF THE MACK SENNETT COMPANY, INCLUDING BAGGY PANTS THAT HAD ONCE BEEN A PERFECT FIT FOR ROSCOE "FATTY" ARBUCKLE, SIZE 14 SHOES FROM FORD STERLING, AND MACK SWAIN'S CREPE MOUSTACHE. THE BAMBOO WALKING STICK ACTUALLY BELONGED TO CHAPLIN.

ALL OF CHARLES CHAPLIN'S WIVES WERE ACTRESSES, AND ALL WERE STILL IN THEIR TEENS WHEN THEY FIRST BECAME INVOLVED WITH HIM. HIS FIRST TWO WEDDINGS, TO HARRIS AND EQUALLY YOUTHFUL LITA GREY, WERE NATIONAL SCANDALS, AND HIS LOVE LIFE WAS REPUTEDLY THE INSPIRATION BEHIND VLADIMIR NABOKOV'S CONTROVERSIAL NOVEL *LOLITA*.

ONE OF THE SCREEN'S GREATEST PERFECTIONISTS, CHAPLIN WOULD PRINT AS MANY AS ONE HUNDRED VERSIONS OF A SCENE, THEN GO BACK AND SHOOT IT AGAIN BASED ON WHAT HE HAD SEEN IN THE EDITING ROOM. IT TOOK 342 TAKES—STILL A RECORD—BEFORE HE WAS SATISFIED WITH THE SCENE IN *CITY LIGHTS* (1931) IN WHICH THE BLIND LEADING LADY SELLS A FLOWER TO THE LITTLE TRAMP.

CHAPLIN'S MUSICAL SKILLS TURNED ONE OF HIS RARE BOX OFFICE DISAPPOINTMENTS INTO A MONEYMAKER. HIS SONG "THIS IS MY SONG," WRITTEN FOR HIS LAST FILM, *THE COUNTESS FROM HONG KONG* (1967), BECAME AN INTERNATIONAL HIT FOR PETULA CLARK. HIS OTHER BIG SONG HIT WAS "SMILE," WRITTEN AS THE THEME FOR *MODERN TIMES* (1936) AND A HIT ALMOST TWENTY YEARS LATER WHEN NAT "KING" COLE RECORDED IT.

OONA O'NEILL, CHAPLIN'S FOURTH WIFE, WAS THE DAUGHTER OF PLAYWRIGHT EUGENE O'NEILL, WHO TRIED TO STOP HIS SEVENTEEN-YEAR-OLD DAUGHTER FROM MARRYING THE CONTROVERSIAL COMIC AND REFUSED TO SPEAK TO HER AFTER THE WEDDING.

IN A BIZARRE POSTSCRIPT TO THE CHAPLIN LEGEND, HIS COFFIN WAS STOLEN AND HELD FOR RANSOM IN MARCH 1978, ALMOST THREE MONTHS AFTER HIS DEATH. POLICE TRACED THE RANSOM CALLS TO A PAIR OF EASTERN EUROPEAN POLITICAL DISSIDENTS WHO HAD BURIED THE BODY TEN MILES AWAY FROM ITS PLACE OF INTERMENT. THE BODY WAS RETURNED TO CHAPLIN'S FAMILY THREE MONTHS LATER AND NOW RESTS IN A VAULT ENCASED IN CEMENT.

Fans and critics alike swooned over the riveting combination of physical beauty, psychological nuance, and vulnerability that he brought to his introspective, alienated characters.

MONTGOMERY
CLIFT

The life of Montgomery Clift is one of Hollywood's most tragic stories. In many ways the sensitivity and emotional openness that made him a star in films like *A Place in the Sun* (1951) and *From Here to Eternity* (1953) contributed to his fall from stardom. Clift's family background—domineering mother and emotionally absent father—seemed to have come out of a psychiatry text. For all his problems with his mother, however, he made his Broadway debut at fourteen thanks largely to her dogged pursuit of acting jobs for him. The first key influence on his career was the acting couple Alfred Lunt and Lynne Fontanne, with whom he costarred in *There Shall Be No Night* (1940). From them he learned a simple, emotionally honest approach to acting that made him one of the stage's top young leading men. Family problems, the stress of hiding his homosexuality, and recurrent bouts of dysentery and colitis contributed to a drinking problem that would grow worse through the years. Clift turned down all Hollywood offers that came with a studio contract attached, but when director Howard Hawks offered him a one-shot deal to costar with John Wayne in *Red River* (1948), he accepted. When postproduction work delayed that film's release, he made his screen debut in the realistic post—World War II drama *The Search* (1948). Stardom created more emotional strain for Clift. During location shooting for *From Here to Eternity* (1953), he spent most of his nights out drinking with costar Frank Sinatra, and a four-year hiatus from the screen heightened the problem. While shooting his comeback picture, *Raintree County* (1957), he suffered a near-fatal automobile accident that damaged his good looks and left him in constant pain, prompting him to add prescription drugs to his alcohol consumption. Despite strong performances as a victim of Nazi persecution in *Judgment at Nuremberg* (1961) and a worn-out rodeo rider in *The Misfits* (1961), he was virtually unemployable. Longtime friend Elizabeth Taylor tried to salvage his career by demanding he be cast as her husband in *Reflections in a Golden Eye* (1967). To get back into shape, he signed up for a low-budget spy thriller, *The Defector* (1966). But the strain of filmmaking was too much for somebody who had already seriously compromised his health. A few months after completing the film, he was found dead in his New York home.

Born
Edward Montgomery Clift
October 17, 1920
Omaha, Nebraska

Died
July 23, 1966
New York, New York,
of occlusive coronary
artery disease

Star Sign
Libra

Height
5'10"

Essential
MONTGOMERYCLIFTFilms

ACADEMY AWARDS
Nominated for Best Actor
The Search
A Place in the Sun
From Here to Eternity

Nominated for
Best Supporting Actor
Judgment at Nuremberg

THE SEARCH
(1948) MGM
For his screen debut, as a soldier trying to help an abandoned child (Ivan Jandl) find his mother in the aftermath of World War II, Montgomery Clift lived among GIs to master their physical habits and forged a close mentoring relationship with his young costar, who had never acted before.

RED RIVER
(1948) United Artists
Clift proved a cowboy could be sensitive and introspective without losing any of his manly swagger when he played John Wayne's adopted son and the leader of a cattle-trail uprising against the Duke.

A PLACE IN THE SUN
(1951) Paramount
As a boy from the wrong side of the tracks who falls in love with a beautiful heiress, Clift shared some legendary love scenes with good friend Elizabeth Taylor that reflected their offscreen rapport.

FROM HERE TO ETERNITY
(1953) Columbia
Clift cornered the market on vulnerability in the role of an alienated army boxer, turning in the performance most critics hail as the definitive embodiment of his star persona.

THE MISFITS
(1961) United Artists
This modern-day western has taken on a special patina because it was the last for its two stars—Marilyn Monroe and Clark Gable—and for the eerie similarities between Clift's personal life and his role as a mother-fixated rodeo rider suffering the physical effects of an injury in the ring.

THE MISFITS, 1961

BEHIND THE SCENES

IT TOOK THREE DAYS TO TEACH CLIFT TO THROW A BELIEVABLE PUNCH FOR HIS CLIMACTIC FIGHT WITH JOHN WAYNE IN *RED RIVER* (1948). ACCORDING TO LEGEND, THE FIRST TIME HE TRIED, WAYNE BURST OUT LAUGHING. CLIFT'S HUMILIATION MAY HAVE MADE HIM LOOK EVEN MORE DETERMINED THAN REQUIRED IN THE SCENE.

SHORTLY AFTER DEPARTING A SUPPER PARTY AT ELIZABETH TAYLOR'S HOUSE, CLIFT FOLLOWED FELLOW GUEST KEVIN MCCARTHY IN HIS OWN CAR, WHEN SUDDENLY THE ACTOR CRASHED INTO A TREE. TAYLOR WAS ON THE SCENE BEFORE THE AMBULANCE AND SAVED HIS LIFE BY REMOVING TWO LOOSENED TEETH THAT WERE LODGED IN HIS THROAT. WHEN THE PRESS ARRIVED, SHE KEPT THEM FROM TAKING PICTURES OF CLIFT'S BATTERED FACE, THREATENING TO HAVE ANY REPORTER WHO PHOTOGRAPHED HIM BARRED FROM WORKING WITH HER.

MARLON BRANDO DISCOVERED CLIFT'S ADDICTION TO ALCOHOL AND PAINKILLERS BY ACCIDENT. WHEN THEY WERE COSTARRING IN *THE YOUNG LIONS* (1958), BRANDO TOOK A BAD FALL AND DISLOCATED HIS SHOULDER. TO EASE THE PAIN, CLIFT OFFERED HIM A DRINK FROM THE THERMOS HE BROUGHT TO THE SET EVERY DAY. WHEN HE TOOK THE DRINK, BRANDO WAS SURPRISED TO DISCOVER THE CONTAINER HELD A COMBINATION OF VODKA AND THE SEDATIVE CHLORAL HYDRATE.

WITH ELIZABETH TAYLOR, 1949

RED RIVER, 1948

With his mellifluous voice and debonair wit, he was the rare silent-era star whose career soared with talkies.

RONALD
COLMAN

Although born to middle-class parents, young Ronald Colman was taught from an early age to play the gentleman, training that would serve him well as an actor. Unable to pursue a college education after his father's death, he sank into an office job, the tedium only relieved when he started performing in amateur theatrical productions. Injured after only two months' service in World War I, he returned to England to seek work on stage and in silent films. When a postwar economic slump made stage work harder to find, he gave New York a try, sleeping on park benches until he could find a decent job. It took two years, but he finally landed a Broadway lead that brought him to the attention of Lillian Gish, who gave him the lead in her first independent film production, *The White Sister* (1923). The film's popularity brought him a contract with producer Samuel Goldwyn, who starred him in a series of historical romances, usually opposite Hungarian beauty Vilma Banky. When talking films arrived, Colman's British accent perfectly suited his romantic image while also allowing him to insert a little much-needed wit into even the most turgid script. With his talkie debut, as the titular British secret agent in *Bulldog Drummond* (1929), he became the first silent star to become even bigger in sound films. After leaving Goldwyn, Colman resisted signing any more long-term contracts, but he flourished as a freelance actor in MGM's sumptuous *A Tale of Two Cities* (1935), director Frank Capra's *Lost Horizon* (1937), independent producer David O. Selznick's swashbuckling *The Prisoner of Zenda* (1937), and the historical romance *If I Were King* (1938). Colman's involvement in the war effort took time from screen acting, but he made one of his most personal films playing a wounded veteran (the character even came from the same part of England as he did) in *Random Harvest* (1942), with Greer Garson. After the war, he chose to slow down his career but pulled out all the stops for one of his most dramatic roles, the classical actor who goes mad in *A Double Life* (1947). The performance brought him an Oscar that served as a fitting tribute to his body of work. In the fifties, he focused mainly on radio and television work, costarring in both media with wife Benita Hume in the comedy series *The Halls of Ivy*.

Born
Ronald Charles Colman
February 9, 1891
Richmond, Surrey, England

Died
May 19, 1958
Santa Barbara, California,
of a lung infection

Star Sign
Aquarius

Height
5'10"

Wives and Child
Actress Thelma Victoria Raye
(1920–1935, divorced)

Actress Benita Hume
(1938–1958, his death)
daughter, Juliet

Essential
RONALDCOLMANFilms

BEAU GESTE

(1926) Paramount
In his first swashbuckler, Ronald Colman stars as the eldest of three brothers who defend the family name by joining the Foreign Legion in the first adaptation of a classic tale that would be filmed two more times.

A TALE OF TWO CITIES

(1935) MGM
Neither the MGM version of the French Revolution nor such memorable scene stealers as Basil Rathbone, Edna May Oliver, and Blanche Yurka could outshine Colman's performance as the alcoholic Sydney Carton, who faces the guillotine to save the woman he loves.

LOST HORIZON

(1937) Columbia
Only an actor as cultured and sincere as Colman could have brought credibility to novelist James Hilton's tale of a philosophical diplomat who flees an Asian revolution, only to stumble upon the mythical paradise of Shangri-La.

RANDOM HARVEST

(1942) MGM
In his second Hilton adaptation, amnesiac Colman marries music hall performer Greer Garson only to regain his memory of everything but his one true love.

A DOUBLE LIFE

(1947) Universal-International
Colman delivers an Oscar-winning performance as a stage star whose performance as the murderously jealous Othello bleeds over into his relationships with his ex-wife (Signe Hasso) and a sluttish waitress (Shelley Winters, in her first major screen role).

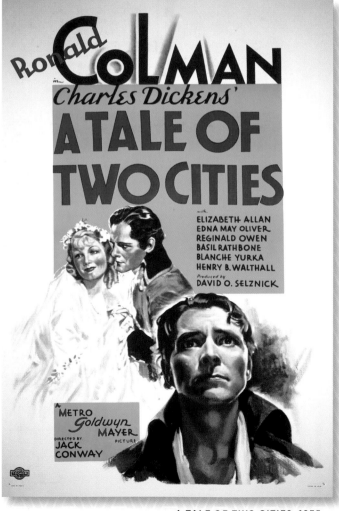

A TALE OF TWO CITIES, 1935

BEHIND THE SCENES

IN THE EARLY THIRTIES, A POLL OF HOLLYWOOD ACTRESSES TO NAME THE SCREEN'S HANDSOMEST ACTOR SELECTED RONALD COLMAN BY A WIDE MARGIN, OVER RUNNERS-UP CLARK GABLE AND FREDRIC MARCH.

DIRECTOR FRANK CAPRA CONSIDERED COLMAN SUCH A PERFECT FIT WITH THE LEADING ROLE IN *LOST HORIZON* (1937) THAT HE POSTPONED PRODUCTION A YEAR UNTIL THE ACTOR WAS AVAILABLE TO DO THE FILM.

AFTER A DISASTROUS FIRST MARRIAGE, COLMAN WAS RELUCTANT TO GET INVOLVED AGAIN. THEN HE MET BRITISH ACTRESS BENITA HUME ON THE SET OF *A TALE OF TWO CITIES* (1935). BUT AFTER THREE YEARS OF DATING, SHE TOOK OFF FOR NEW YORK, CONVINCED HE WOULD NEVER MARRY AGAIN. BY THE TIME HER TRAIN REACHED ALBUQUERQUE, NEW MEXICO, COLMAN HAD TELEGRAPHED HER TO PROPOSE MARRIAGE.

ONE OF COLMAN'S HAPPIEST WORKING EXPERIENCES WAS ON *RANDOM HARVEST* (1942). HE APPRECIATED THE FACT THAT DIRECTOR MERVYN LEROY AND PRODUCER SIDNEY FRANKLIN ALLOWED HIM AND COSTAR GREER GARSON TO SUGGEST SCRIPT REVISIONS. WHEN THE FILM WRAPPED, HE SAID, "THIS IS ONE PICTURE I HATE TO FINISH!" SHORTLY AFTERWARD, HE FINISHED REMODELING HIS HOLLYWOOD HOME AND DUBBED THE PLACE RANDOM HOUSE.

RANDOM HARVEST, 1942

THE PRISONER OF ZENDA, 1937

With his lanky good looks, bashful smile, and no-nonsense masculinity, he commanded the screen in low-key performances that turned stoic men into American movie icons.

GARY
COOPER

Gary Cooper's upbringing—born on a Montana ranch but sent to England for his education—provides a key to the man's character. Although he achieved his greatest stardom as a simple man of few words, the offscreen Cooper was a sophisticated man of the world, respected for his taste in literature and modern art and notorious for his amorous exploits. That sophistication fed his screen image, giving his all-American characters an edge and putting some extra heat into his love scenes. "Coop's" western upbringing helped him get into movies, where he started out as a stunt rider. Before long, he was landing small roles, leading to a scene-stealing second lead in the western *The Winning of Barbara Worth* (1926) that won him a contract at Paramount. A small part in *Wings* (1927), the first Oscar winner for Best Picture, inspired impressive amounts of fan mail, so the studio started putting him into bigger roles. Although he had already started making westerns, Coop was equally popular in sophisticated fare like Marlene Dietrich's American debut film, *Morocco* (1930), and the Noel Coward comedy *Design for Living* (1933), both of which capitalized on his youthful sex appeal. His image as the ideal American was established when director Frank Capra went after him to play small-town poet Longfellow Deeds in *Mr. Deeds Goes to Town* (1936), a huge hit that made him one of Hollywood's top stars. Parts like the World War I hero in *Sergeant York* (1941) and champion slugger Lou Gehrig in *The Pride of the Yankees* (1942), along with well-chosen forays into comedy for *Meet John Doe* and *Ball of Fire* (both 1941), kept his star on the rise. By the late forties, however, Cooper was going through personal crises. Not only was he dissatisfied with his films, but also he left his wife for a five-year affair with the much younger Patricia Neal, his costar in *The Fountainhead* (1949). In the midst of this period, he rejuvenated his career with the role of U.S. Marshal Will Kane in *High Noon* (1952), one of the most acclaimed westerns ever made. Cooper was hoping to film either *The Sundowners* (1960) or *Ride the High Country* (1962) when recurring health problems were traced to lung cancer. He died a few months after receiving a special Oscar "for his many memorable screen performances and the international recognition he, as an individual, has gained for the motion picture industry."

Born
Frank James Cooper
May 7, 1901
Helena, Montana

Died
May 13, 1961
Beverly Hills, California,
of lung cancer

Star Sign
Taurus

Height
6'3"

Wife and Child
Socialite-actress
Veronica "Rocky" Balfe
(1933–1961, his death)
daughter, Maria

Essential
GARY COOPER Films

ACADEMY AWARDS
Won for Best Actor
Sergeant York
High Noon

Nominated for Best Actor
Mr. Deeds Goes to Town
The Pride of the Yankees
For Whom the Bell Tolls

Special Oscar in 1961

MOROCCO

(1930) Paramount
In the film that brought
Marlene Dietrich to Hollywood,
Gary Cooper more than matched
her sophistication and sizzling
sexuality as the legionnaire who
wins her love.

MR. DEEDS GOES TO TOWN

(1936) Columbia
Frank Capra's comedy about
a small-town poet who faces
off against corrupt big-city
businessmen catapulted Cooper
to stardom and set his image as a
simple man representing the best
of the American spirit.

MEET JOHN DOE

(1941) Warner Bros.
Almost the flip side of *Mr. Deeds*,
this dark political comedy-drama
stars Cooper as a nobody turned
into a national hero by reporter
Barbara Stanwyck and a corrupt
political machine.

SERGEANT YORK

(1941) Warner Bros.
Coop's performance as the
backwoods pacifist who fights after
reconciling his religious beliefs
with duty to country captured the
imagination of a United States on
the brink of war.

HIGH NOON

(1952) United Artists
Cooper wasn't the first choice to
play lawman Will Kane (director
Fred Zinnemann had proposed
Marlon Brando and Montgomery
Clift), but he made the role his own
in a film that brought the western to
new levels of artistic achievement
while also mirroring the state of
America during the anti-Communist
hysteria of the fifties.

MOROCCO, 1930

HIGH NOON, 1952

BEHIND THE SCENES

OFTEN DURING FILMING, ONLOOKERS WOULD THINK GARY COOPER WASN'T DOING ANYTHING. BUT WHEN PEOPLE LOOKED AT THE DAY'S RUSHES, THEY REALIZED THAT ALL THE ACTING WAS ON THE SCREEN. ONLY THE CAMERA CAUGHT HIS SUBTLE UNDERACTING, BUT THEN, IN THE MOVIES, THAT'S ALL IT TAKES TO MAKE A GREAT ACTOR. AS COSTAR CHARLES LAUGHTON ONCE SAID, "WE ACT; HE IS."

COOP'S REPUTATION AS A MAN OF FEW WORDS WAS WELL ESTABLISHED BY 1938, WHEN HE APPEARED ON VENTRILOQUIST EDGAR BERGEN'S RADIO SHOW AND DID A SKETCH IN WHICH HE RESPONDED "YUP" TO EVERY QUESTION UNTIL HE WAS ASKED WHETHER THAT WAS ALL HE COULD SAY. TO THAT, HE SAID, "NOPE."

COOPER'S IMAGE AS AN ALL-AMERICAN COWBOY WAS BELIED BY THE SOPHISTICATION BRED FROM HIS EDUCATION AND LATER WORLD TRAVELS. OFFSCREEN, THE COWBOY STAR COLLECTED MODERN ART AND COUNTED WRITERS ERNEST HEMINGWAY AND JOHN O'HARA AND PAINTER PABLO PICASSO AMONG HIS CIRCLE OF FRIENDS.

TO PLAY BASEBALL GREAT LOU GEHRIG IN *THE PRIDE OF THE YANKEES* (1942), COOPER SPENT WEEKS IN BASEBALL CAMP. SINCE GEHRIG WAS FAMOUS FOR BATTING LEFT-HANDED, AND COOPER WAS RIGHT-HANDED, DIRECTOR SAM WOOD HAD THE BASEBALL SCENES FLIPPED IN THE EDITING ROOM. DOING THIS MEANT THE ENTIRE SCENE HAD TO BE DESIGNED IN REVERSE, INCLUDING THE NUMBERS AND LETTERING ON THE PLAYERS' UNIFORMS.

A NOTORIOUS WOMANIZER BEFORE HIS MARRIAGE, PARAMOUNT'S PUBLICISTS DUBBED COOPER "PARAMOUNT'S PARAMOUNT SKIRT-CHASER." AMONG HIS EARLY LOVES WERE CLARA BOW, WHO WAS INSTRUMENTAL IN HELPING HIM LAND BETTER ROLES AT THE STUDIO, LUPE VELEZ, MARLENE DIETRICH, AND THE COUNTESS DOROTHY DI FRASSO.

HIS DAUGHTER MARIA WAS NAMED AFTER INGRID BERGMAN'S CHARACTER IN *FOR WHOM THE BELL TOLLS* (1943).

ALTHOUGH COOPER HAD BEEN ONE OF THE FRIENDLY WITNESSES TESTIFYING BEFORE THE HOUSE UN-AMERICAN ACTIVITIES COMMITTEE'S INVESTIGATIONS OF ALLEGED COMMUNIST INFILTRATION OF HOLLYWOOD, HE TRIED TO SUPPORT BLACKLISTED WRITER CARL FOREMAN, WHO HAD WRITTEN THE SCREENPLAY FOR *HIGH NOON* (1952). HE EVEN OFFERED TO JOIN A PRODUCTION COMPANY THE WRITER WAS TRYING TO START. AS PRESSURE IN HOLLYWOOD AND THE PRESS MOUNTED, FOREMAN RELEASED COOPER FROM THEIR VERBAL AGREEMENT BUT LATER WOULD REFER TO HIM GRATEFULLY AS THE ONLY MAJOR HOLLYWOOD FIGURE TO STAND UP FOR HIM.

An influential, chart-topping pop crooner and the world's first multimedia star, he brought his laid-back musical style to the big screen, infusing roles both comic and serious with an endearing warmth and intimacy.

BING
CROSBY

Casual was Bing Crosby's stock in trade. He was the first crooner, possessed of an intimate singing style that was perfect for the movies. That laid-back intimacy carried into his acting, giving American audiences worn out by the Depression and later World War II a comfort zone where they knew everything would work out fine. A set of mail-order drums started his career while he was still in college. Before long, he had dropped out of school and was singing with the era's most popular big band, the Paul Whiteman Orchestra, and he made his screen debut when the band headlined the early musical *The King of Jazz* (1930). New, more sensitive microphones showcased Crosby's easygoing singing style on early recordings that caught the attention of CBS Radio head William S. Paley. He put Crosby on the air, which led to a role as himself in Paramount's *The Big Broadcast* (1932). He stuck to that persona for the rest of his career. Crosby's casual air provided a perfect complement for Bob Hope's comic antics when they teamed for *Road to Singapore* (1940), the first of seven *Road* films in which they vied for Dorothy Lamour's affections while kidding more serious adventure films, the movie business, and even their own images. Recordings and radio appearances kept audiences turning out for his films, particularly when he introduced "White Christmas" in *Holiday Inn* (1942). With more than thirty million copies sold, the song would set an industry record. Crosby hit number one at the box office when he took on the role of Father O'Malley, the singing priest in *Going My Way* (1944), which brought him the Oscar for Best Actor. He earned a second nomination when he reprised the role in *The Bells of St. Mary's* (1945), costarring Ingrid Bergman. Playing against type as an embittered alcoholic in *The Country Girl* (1954), he won still another Oscar nomination. The same year, he scored his biggest box office hit with *White Christmas*. After costarring with Grace Kelly and Frank Sinatra in *High Society* (1956), Crosby started cutting back on screen work. By this point, he was a very rich man thanks to astute investments in land and oil wells and a profitable production company. He continued to record and sing in concerts, but he was happy to make more time for golf. He had just finished a game in Spain when he suffered a fatal heart attack in 1977.

Born
Harry Lillis Crosby
May 2, 1903
Tacoma, Washington

Died
October 14, 1977
Madrid, Spain,
of a heart attack

Star Sign
Taurus

Height
5'8"

Wives and Children
Singer Dixie Lee
(1930–1952, her death)
sons, Gary, Dennis,
Eddie, and Lindsay

Actress Kathryn Grant
(1957–1977, his death)
son, Harry Jr.
daughter, Mary Frances
son, Nathaniel

Essential
BINGCROSBYFilms

ACADEMY AWARDS
Won for Best Actor
Going My Way

Nominated for Best Actor
The Bells of St. Mary's
The Country Girl

ROAD TO MOROCCO
(1942) Paramount
Crosby sells Bob Hope into slavery, then enlists Arab princess Dorothy Lamour to help free him in one of the more outrageous *Road* movies, complete with sarcastic commentary from a talking camel.

GOING MY WAY
(1944) Paramount
Father O'Malley (Crosby) is assigned to save a failing parish over the protests of its aging priest (Barry Fitzgerald) in a film wartime audiences took to their hearts, making it the year's top box office picture.

WHITE CHRISTMAS
(1954) Paramount
Crosby and show business partner Danny Kaye travel to Vermont to woo a beautiful sister act (Rosemary Clooney and Vera-Ellen) and help an old army buddy.

THE COUNTRY GIRL
(1954) Paramount
Hot-shot director William Holden tries to revive the career of washed-out alcoholic Crosby despite the protests of the man's bitter wife (Oscar winner Grace Kelly) in this adaptation of the hit play.

HIGH SOCIETY
(1956) MGM
In this musical adaptation of *The Philadelphia Story* with a score by Cole Porter, Crosby takes on Cary Grant's role as a carefree playboy trying to woo ex-wife Kelly from her fiancé and tough-talking reporter Frank Sinatra.

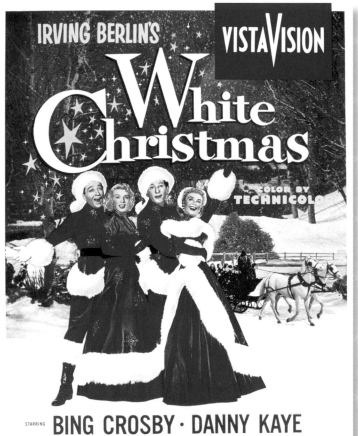

WHITE CHRISTMAS, 1954

WITH BOB HOPE ON THE SET OF *ROAD TO SINGAPORE*, 1940

HIGH SOCIETY, 1956

BEHINDTHESCENES

CROSBY INTRODUCED MORE BEST SONG OSCAR WINNERS THAN ANY OTHER SINGER: "SWEET LEILANI," FROM *WAIKIKI WEDDING* (1937); "WHITE CHRISTMAS," FROM *HOLIDAY INN* (1942); "SWINGIN' ON A STAR," FROM *GOING MY WAY* (1944); AND "IN THE COOL COOL COOL OF THE EVENING," FROM *HERE COMES THE GROOM* (1951).

CROSBY AND BOB HOPE KNEW EACH OTHER ONLY CASUALLY WHEN THEY PERFORMED SOME OLD VAUDEVILLE ROUTINES AT THE OPENING OF CROSBY'S DEL MAR RACETRACK. INTRIGUED BY THEIR BYPLAY, A PARAMOUNT EXECUTIVE DUG OUT AN UNPRODUCED SCRIPT TITLED *ROAD TO MANDALAY* THAT HAD ORIGINALLY BEEN WRITTEN FOR GEORGE BURNS AND GRACIE ALLEN AND THEN REWRITTEN FOR FRED MACMURRAY AND JACK OAKIE. THE RESULT WAS *ROAD TO SINGAPORE* (1940).

AS A RECORDING ARTIST, CROSBY HAD 41 SINGLES AND ONE ALBUM REACH THE TOP OF THE CHARTS, A RECORD THAT STILL STANDS. IN ALL, HE RECORDED MORE THAN 1,700 SONGS, RANKING AS THE MOST SUCCESSFUL RECORDING ARTIST OF ALL TIME.

CROSBY'S CROONING INFLUENCED THE NEXT GENERATION OF SINGING STARS—INCLUDING PERRY COMO AND DEAN MARTIN—BUT THE ONLY ONE TO RIVAL HIM IN POPULARITY WAS FRANK SINATRA, WHOSE BOYISH, VULNERABLE PERSONA ATTRACTED A HORDE OF FEMALE FANS. THE TWO PLAYED OUT THEIR RIVALRY ON RADIO IN THE NAME OF RATINGS BUT COOLED IT OFF WHEN AN ANGRY CROSBY FAN STABBED A SINATRA FAN WITH AN ICE PICK.

IMPRESSED WITH A DEMONSTRATION OF HIGH-FIDELITY AUDIOTAPE, WHICH HAD BEEN DISCOVERED IN NAZI RECORDING LABS AFTER WORLD WAR II, CROSBY BECAME A MAJOR INVESTOR IN THE TECHNOLOGY AND WAS THE FIRST RADIO STAR TO PRERECORD HIS RADIO SHOW. WITH THE ARRIVAL OF TELEVISION, HE ALSO INVESTED IN THE DEVELOPMENT OF VIDEOTAPE.

Despite having only three starring roles before he died at twenty-four, he captured the soul of a generation and has become one of the screen's most iconic figures.

JAMES
DEAN

Sensitive and masculine in equal measures, James Dean made his mark playing sincere, searching youths hungry for emotional honesty. His pained cry to his parents—"You're tearing me apart!"—in *Rebel Without a Cause* (1955) was emblematic of an entire misunderstood generation. Dean's intensely personal acting added to his mystique, blurring the dividing line between actor and character so much that his legions of fans, even half a century after his death, still envision him as the mixed-up kid he played on screen. Pain came early to his life—his mother died when he was just nine—but so did the arts. As a child he studied the violin, tap dancing, and drawing. As a teen, he developed a love of racing—first motorcycles, then cars—that would shape his destiny. But it was as an actor that he made his mark, starting in high school productions and eventually moving to Los Angeles, where he played unbilled walk-ons in four films. After moving to New York, he won a place at the prestigious Actors Studio. In 1954, a flashy supporting role as an Arab hustler in the play *The Immoralist* brought him to the attention of Warner Bros. talent scouts. He made an acclaimed starring debut as Raymond Massey's tormented son in *East of Eden* (1955), a John Steinbeck adaptation directed by Elia Kazan. When his next film, *Giant* (1956), was temporarily postponed because of leading lady Elizabeth Taylor's pregnancy, Warner's shifted him into the juvenile delinquency drama *Rebel Without a Cause*. Dean shone in all three films, but the latter two were released after his sudden death. Driving to compete in an auto race in Salinas, California, he was killed in a collision with another vehicle. The youthful angst he captured in his three starring films brought him a devoted fan following who continue to clamor for images of their idol and flock to his grave in Fairmount, Indiana, where an annual tribute honors his memory. Among those keeping the legend alive, *Giant* costar and good friend Dennis Hopper mourned what he called "my sense of destiny destroyed—the great films he would have directed, the great performances he would have given, the great humanitarian he would have become, and, yet, he's the greatest actor and star I have ever known."

Born
James Byron Dean
February 8, 1931
Marion, Indiana

Died
September 30, 1955
Cholame, California,
in an automobile accident

Star Sign
Aquarius

Height
5'8"

Essential
JAMESDEANFilms

EAST OF EDEN

(1955) Warner Bros.
James Dean could draw on his own family history to play the small-town bad boy who vies with his good-boy brother (Richard Davalos) for the approval of their father (Raymond Massey) in this adaptation of John Steinbeck's classic tale.

REBEL WITHOUT A CAUSE

(1955) Warner Bros.
As a troubled teen, Dean summed up the torment of a generation with his love for Natalie Wood's Judy, his attempts to bond with the even more sensitive Plato (Sal Mineo), and his failed efforts to stay out of trouble.

GIANT

(1956) Warner Bros.
In his last film, Dean stars as a shy, withdrawn ranch hand who strikes it rich and sets out to destroy business and romantic rival Rock Hudson.

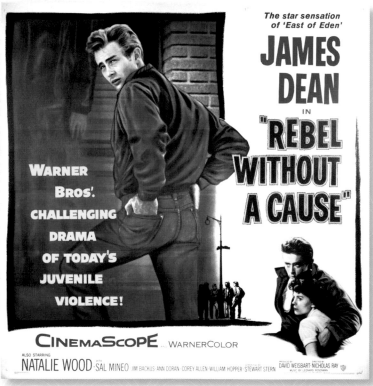

REBEL WITHOUT A CAUSE, 1955

GIANT, 1956

BEHINDTHESCENES

JAMES DEAN'S FIRST PROFESSIONAL JOB WAS A 1950 PEPSI COMMERCIAL. DURING HIS EARLY YEARS IN NEW YORK, HE WORKED A VARIETY OF ODD JOBS, INCLUDING TESTING STUNTS FOR THE POPULAR GAME SHOW *BEAT THE CLOCK*.

DURING FILMING OF *REBEL WITHOUT A CAUSE* (1955), DEAN ASKED ONSCREEN FATHER JIM BACKUS TO TEACH HIM THE VOICE HE USED IN THE "MR. MAGOO" CARTOONS. DEAN THEN USED IT FOR THE LINE, "DROWN THEM LIKE PUPPIES."

DEAN FILMED A HIGHWAY-SAFETY COMMERCIAL WITH ACTOR GIG YOUNG ON THE SET OF *GIANT* (1956). THE SPOT WAS INCLUDED IN THE 1984 COMPILATION FILM *HOLLYWOOD OUTTAKES*.

FAILURE ANALYSIS ASSOCIATES OF MENLO PARK, CALIFORNIA, RECONSTRUCTED DEAN'S FATAL CRASH TO PROVE THAT, CONTRARY TO LEGEND, HE WAS NOT SPEEDING AT THE TIME OF THE ACCIDENT. THEY PLACED HIS SPEED AT 55 OR 56 MPH. NONETHELESS, HE HAD BEEN ISSUED A SPEEDING TICKET ABOUT TWO HOURS BEFORE THE ACCIDENT.

BEFORE *GIANT* WAS RELEASED, DIRECTOR GEORGE STEVENS RECEIVED LETTERS FROM GRIEVING FANS THREATENING TO KILL HIM IF HE CUT ANY OF DEAN'S FOOTAGE FROM THE FILM.

WHEN THE ACADEMY AWARD NOMINATIONS WERE ANNOUNCED IN EARLY 1956, DEAN'S PERFORMANCE IN *EAST OF EDEN* (1955) MADE HIM THE FIRST ACTOR TO RECEIVE A POSTHUMOUS NOMINATION. HE WON ANOTHER NOD FOR *GIANT,* MAKING HIM THE ONLY ACTOR EVER TO RECEIVE TWO POSTHUMOUS NOMINATIONS.

AT THE TIME OF HIS DEATH, DEAN WAS PLANNING FOR THREE ROLES: BOXING CHAMPION ROCKY GRAZIANO IN *SOMEBODY UP THERE LIKES ME* (1956), BRICK IN *CAT ON A HOT TIN ROOF* (1958), AND THE SINGING BASEBALL PLAYER IN *DAMN YANKEES* (1958). THE FIRST TWO HELPED MAKE PAUL NEWMAN A STAR, WHILE THE LAST WENT TO TAB HUNTER.

WHEN WARNER BROS. ANNOUNCED PLANS TO MAKE *THE JAMES DEAN STORY* (1957), ELVIS PRESLEY LOBBIED TO WIN THE TITLE ROLE, ONLY TO DISCOVER THE FILM WAS GOING TO BE A DOCUMENTARY.

His straight-from-the-guts acting style simmered with restrained intensity in portraying men who refused to submit to authority.

KIRK
DOUGLAS

Kirk Douglas gave some of his best performances as men bucking the system, taking on everything from the artistic establishment as Vincent van Gogh in *Lust for Life* (1956) to conventional morality as the unscrupulous hero of *Champion* (1949) and *The Bad and the Beautiful* (1952). His searing intensity and husky physique made him seem a born battler, and he had just the right voice for characters that often spoke through clenched teeth. He actually beat the system in real life, rising from his beginnings as the son of an immigrant junk dealer (he titled his 1988 memoir *The Ragman's Son*) to become an international superstar. He developed his love of acting in high school, leading him to enroll in the American Academy of Dramatic Art, where one of his best friends was Betty Joan Persky. Moving to Hollywood as Lauren Bacall, she pushed producer Hal Wallis to test him, leading to Douglas's screen debut as Barbara Stanwyck's husband in *The Strange Love of Martha Ivers* (1946). Initially cast as neurotics and weaklings, Douglas broke out as a star when he took a salary cut to play the brutal boxer in *Champion*. He demonstrated his range with roles like the romantic English professor in *A Letter to Three Wives* (1949) and sailor Ned Land in *20,000 Leagues Under the Sea* (1954). He was most identified with intense, driven characters like those in *Detective Story, Ace in the Hole* (both 1951), *The Bad and the Beautiful,* and *Lust for Life;* the latter performance was often hailed as his best. In the late fifties, Douglas moved into independent production, working with director Stanley Kubrick on two of his best films, *Paths of Glory* (1957) and *Spartacus* (1960). Douglas took a chance on a tragic modern western with *Lonely Are the Brave* (1962), a box office failure that became a cult classic. More commercial were his sixties westerns and war films, including two with John Wayne, *In Harm's Way* (1965) and *The War Wagon* (1967). In the seventies, Douglas moved into character roles, as the driven father in *The Fury* (1978), an egocentric film star in *Home Movies* (1979), and the Wile E. Coyote—like gunman in *The Villain* (1979). A 1995 stroke slowed him considerably, though he has still been able to make selected screen appearances, most notably in the comedy *It Runs in the Family* (2003), with his son Michael Douglas, grandson Cameron Douglas, and ex-wife Diana Dill.

Born
Issur Danielovich Demsky
December 9, 1916
Amsterdam, New York

Star Sign
Sagittarius

Height
5'9"

Wives and Children
Actress Diana Dill
(1943–1951, divorced)
sons, Michael and Joel

Actress Anne Buydens
(1954–)
sons, Peter and Eric

Essential
KIRKDOUGLASFilms

ACADEMY AWARDS
Nominated for Best Actor
Champion
The Bad and the Beautiful
Lust for Life

Honorary Oscar in 1996
"as a creative and moral force"

ACE IN THE HOLE
(A.K.A. THE BIG CARNIVAL)
(1951) Paramount
In his most hard-boiled role,
Douglas plays a disgraced reporter
who finds his ticket back to the
big time when a local story about a
man trapped in a mine becomes
a national sensation.

THE BAD AND
THE BEAUTIFUL
(1952) MGM
In one of the most popular films
ever made about Hollywood,
film star Lana Turner, writer Dick
Powell, and director Barry Sullivan
reveal why they'll never again work
with the producer (Douglas) who
launched their careers.

LUST FOR LIFE
(1956) MGM
Working with director Vincente
Minnelli, Douglas created one
of the screen's most acclaimed
portraits of artistic creation, giving
himself completely to Vincent van
Gogh's madness, his vision, and his
tortured relationships with friends
like Paul Gauguin (Anthony Quinn).

PATHS OF GLORY
(1957) United Artists
Douglas produced this trenchant
antiwar drama, starring under
Stanley Kubrick's direction as a
French officer fighting to save
three soldiers selected at random
to stand trial for cowardice after
a futile suicide mission during the
final days of World War I.

SPARTACUS
(1960) Universal
As the rebellious slave Spartacus,
Douglas toplined one of
Hollywood's most intelligent
epics, taking on a Roman empire
represented by Laurence Olivier
and Charles Laughton.

LUST FOR LIFE, 1956

WITH SON, MICHAEL DOUGLAS, CIRCA 1949

BEHINDTHE**SCENES**

ONE OF DOUGLAS'S FAVORITE COSTARS WAS LONGTIME FRIEND BURT LANCASTER. THEIR ATHLETIC PHYSIQUES AND INTENSELY PHYSICAL PERFORMING STYLES MADE THEM A PERFECT MATCH EITHER AS ADVERSARIES OR ALLIES. THEY FIRST TEAMED IN THE CRIME FILM *I WALK ALONE* (1948), FOLLOWED BY MEMORABLE PAIRINGS FOR *GUNFIGHT AT THE O.K. CORRAL* (1957), *SEVEN DAYS IN MAY* (1964), AND THEIR FINAL FILM TOGETHER, *TOUGH GUYS* (1986).

DOUGLAS ORIGINALLY HAD TO PASS ON THE LEADING ROLE IN *PATHS OF GLORY* (1957) BECAUSE HE WAS COMMITTED TO STAR IN A BROADWAY PLAY. BY THE TIME RICHARD BURTON, JAMES MASON, AND GREGORY PECK HAD PASSED ON THE PRODUCTION AS WELL, DOUGLAS'S PLAY HAD BEEN POSTPONED, MAKING HIM AVAILABLE FOR ONE OF HIS GREATEST FILMS.

DOUGLAS HELPED BREAK THE COLD WAR—ERA HOLLYWOOD BLACKLIST WHEN HE INSISTED THAT "HOLLYWOOD TEN" MEMBER DALTON TRUMBO BE GIVEN SCREEN CREDIT FOR WRITING *SPARTACUS* (1960). DESPITE THREATS OF BOYCOTTS, THE FILM WAS A BOX OFFICE SUCCESS.

TO ASSEMBLE THE ALL-STAR CAST FOR *SPARTACUS*, DOUGLAS HAD DIFFERENT SCRIPTS PREPARED, EACH EMPHASIZING THE ROLE HE WAS TRYING TO CAST.

BECAUSE OF RESTRICTIONS AGAINST FILMING AT THE PENTAGON, JOHN FRANKENHEIMER, DIRECTOR OF *SEVEN DAYS IN MAY* (1964), SIMPLY PUT DOUGLAS IN UNIFORM AND HAD HIM WALK UP THE STEPS, WITH THE CAMERA HIDDEN IN A NEARBY STATION WAGON. THE GUARDS SALUTING HIM IN THAT SCENE ARE THE REAL THING.

AFTER STARRING IN THE STAGE ADAPTATION OF KEN KESEY'S *ONE FLEW OVER THE CUCKOO'S NEST* ON BROADWAY, DOUGLAS STRUGGLED FOR YEARS TO GET A FILM VERSION MADE. BY THE TIME HIS SON, MICHAEL DOUGLAS, GOT IT PRODUCED, HE WAS TOO OLD FOR THE LEAD, WHICH BROUGHT JACK NICHOLSON HIS FIRST OSCAR AND HIS SON A BEST PICTURE OSCAR.

The first great action star, introducing both Robin Hood and Zorro to the screen, his high energy and charisma carried over into his real life trailblazing as a founding father of Hollywood's movie industry.

DOUGLAS
FAIRBANKS

Born
Douglas Elton Thomas Ulman
May 23, 1883,
Denver, Colorado

Died
December 12, 1939
Santa Monica, California,
of a heart attack

Star Sign
Gemini

Height
5'9"

Wives and Child
Socialite Anna Beth Sully
(1907–1919, divorced)
son, Douglas Jr.

Actress Mary Pickford
(1920–1936, divorced)

Lady Sylvia Ashley
(1936–1939, his death)

Douglas Fairbanks did it all. In addition to starring in a fourteen-year string of box office hits, he cowrote most of his screenplays, produced all of his pictures from 1917 on, and directed two of them—and in his spare time he wrote self-help books and campaigned tirelessly for the advancement of motion pictures. He and wife Mary Pickford were the world's most famous and beloved married couple in the twenties. They were the first stars to preserve their footprints in cement in front of Graumann's Chinese Theatre and were among the founders of the Motion Picture Academy. Their home, Pickfair, was the Graceland of its day, and the couple was mobbed in public by fans eager for a glimpse of their idols. Originally, Fairbanks had come to Hollywood in 1915 to star in comedies after some middling successes on Broadway. In *His Picture in the Papers* (1916), he started adding athletic stunts to his films, and they became his trademark. When his characters were happy, they jumped across rooftops or bounded over walls. By 1917, he was so popular, he started his own production company. In 1919, he joined with Mary Pickford (whom he would marry in 1920), Charles Chaplin, and director D. W. Griffith to form United Artists, the prototype for the modern film studio. A year later, he switched to historical adventures. *The Mark of Zorro* (1920) made him a bigger star than ever and led to a series of popular swashbucklers, including *Robin Hood* (1922) and *The Thief of Bagdad* (1924). One factor distinguishing his adventures was their historical accuracy: Fairbanks hired teams of experts for each film to guarantee their authenticity in every department. He tackled talkies and teamed with Pickford for the only time for *The Taming of the Shrew* (1929), but his age was beginning to show. When his later talking films did poorly at the box office, he announced his retirement in 1933. Underlying his problems with advancing age was the arrival of Douglas Fairbanks Jr., his son from an earlier marriage. Fairbanks Sr. resented the young man's decision to pursue an acting career in Hollywood, and they only became close when each suffered marital problems. Fairbanks and Pickford divorced in 1936, while his son was involved in a tempestuous marriage to Joan Crawford. At the time of his death from a heart attack, Fairbanks was working on a screenplay to star his son, who would carry on the family name in his own adventure films.

Essential
DOUGLAS**FAIRBANKS**Films

THE MARK OF ZORRO

(1920) United Artists
In his first swashbuckling role,
Douglas Fairbanks starred as
Don Diego, who dons the mask
of Zorro when the Spaniards
kidnap his true love (Margaret De
La Motte), leading to one of the
screen's great chase scenes.

THE THREE MUSKETEERS

(1921) United Artists
In the fourth of twenty big-screen
versions of Alexandre Dumas's
adventure classic, Fairbanks is
the young D'Artagnan, fighting to
retrieve the queen's stolen necklace
and win the love of her beautiful
lady-in-waiting (De La Motte).

ROBIN HOOD

(1922) United Artists
The first screen depiction of the
exploits of the man who stole
from the rich to give to the poor
focuses on how he became
Robin Hood (Fairbanks) while
also supplying enough pageantry
(including the largest set built to
that time) to make it the year's top
box office attraction.

THE THIEF OF BAGDAD

(1924) United Artists
Fairbanks topped himself, using
larger sets than ever (designed
by William Cameron Menzies in
his first major assignment) and
incorporating special effects that
still impress for this *Arabian Nights*
story of a thief who sets out to
win the love of a princess.

THE BLACK PIRATE

(1926) United Artists
Adding color to the mix,
Fairbanks starred as a nobleman
who disguises himself as a pirate
to rescue a beautiful princess
(Billie Dove) and exact vengeance
on the cutthroats who murdered
his father.

THE THIEF OF BAGDAD, 1924

BEHIND THE SCENES

WHEN DOUGLAS FAIRBANKS FIRST HIT HOLLYWOOD, HE FILMED SOME TESTS FOR DIRECTING LEGEND D. W. GRIFFITH. GRIFFITH'S ASSESSMENT, "HE HAS A HEAD LIKE A CANTALOUPE, AND HE CAN'T ACT," WOULD HAVE STOPPED A LESS COURAGEOUS ACTOR IN HIS TRACKS, BUT FAIRBANKS'S CAREER TOOK OFF ANYWAY. YEARS LATER, HE EVEN INVITED GRIFFITH TO JOIN IN THE CREATION OF UNITED ARTISTS.

IN RESPONSE TO FAN MAIL ASKING THE SOURCE OF HIS ENERGY, FAIRBANKS WROTE A SERIES OF SELF-HELP BOOKS IN THE LATE TEENS. WITH TITLES LIKE *LAUGH AND LIVE* AND *MAKING LIFE WORTHWHILE,* THEY PREACHED A PHILOSOPHY OF SELF-AWARENESS, SELF-RELIANCE, AND SELF-CONFIDENCE.

FAIRBANKS WAS THE FIRST PRESIDENT OF THE ACADEMY OF MOTION PICTURE ARTS AND SCIENCES.

FAIRBANKS'S FIRST TALKING FILM, *THE TAMING OF THE SHREW* (1929), ALLEGEDLY INCLUDED ONE OF THE MOST FAMOUS CREDIT LINES IN FILM HISTORY: "BY WILLIAM SHAKESPEARE, WITH ADDITIONAL DIALOGUE BY SAM TAYLOR."

FAIRBANKS WAS ONE OF THE INSPIRATIONS FOR BATMAN. CREATOR BOB KANE WAS A FAN AND WOULD LATER SAY HE HAD CREATED THE CAPED CRUSADER AS A MODERN-DAY WINGED ZORRO.

WITH SON, DOUGLAS FAIRBANKS JR., CIRCA 1920s

MARY PICKFORD, D. W. GRIFFITH, CHARLIE CHAPLIN, AND DOUGLAS FAIRBANKS, 1919

Devil-may-care swagger and exceptional good looks were fitting for the valiant heroes he portrayed, the roles seemingly inspired by his real-life adventures and exploits.

ERROL
FLYNN

Adventure was in Errol Flynn's blood. He was a descendant of two key HMS *Bounty* mutineers who settled in the South Pacific. From childhood, his one true love was the ocean, thanks to his father, a marine biologist. As a young adult, he jaunted around the Pacific in a variety of jobs, including police officer, gold prospector, and even sheep castrator. He accepted his first film role out of curiosity, playing his ancestor Fletcher Christian in the semi-documentary *In the Wake of the Bounty* (1933). Inspired by the experience, Flynn took off for London to pursue an acting career. Stage work brought him a Warner Bros. contract, but at first he had only minor roles. Then established star Robert Donat bowed out of Warner's first historical adventure, *Captain Blood* (1935), due to illness, and executives decided to take a chance on the young Australian. Cast opposite Olivia de Havilland, his costar in eight films, Flynn became an overnight sensation. With his roguish smile and the hint of an Australian accent, he triumphed in a series of swashbucklers, including *The Adventures of Robin Hood* (1938) and *The Sea Hawk* (1940). Offscreen, he indulged in his own brand of swashbuckling: Hard drinking and womanizing were part of his daily routine. His 1942 trial for statutory rape (he was acquitted when the accusers' testimony failed to stand up in court) would have sunk many other actors, but it made Flynn more popular. Eventually, however, hard living started to affect his work. He was persistently late and unprepared on the set, and it became harder and harder to disguise the ravages of drink in his appearance. After leaving Warner Bros., Flynn had trouble finding suitable roles and seemed to prefer writing on his yacht. To pay the bills, he moved into character roles, often as alcoholics, surprising fans and critics with the depth of his acting in such films as *The Sun Also Rises* (1957) and *Too Much, Too Soon* (1958). While separated from his third wife, Flynn began a relationship with fifteen-year-old Beverly Aadland, promoting her career and casting her in his last film, *Cuban Rebel Girls* (1959). The same year, he passed away, the victim of a heart attack at fifty. Yet for him, it was probably just one more great adventure. According to legend, his last words were, "I've had a hell of a lot of fun, and I've enjoyed every minute of it!"

Born
Errol Leslie Thomson Flynn
June 20, 1909
Hobart, Tasmania, Australia

Died
October 14, 1959
Vancouver,
British Columbia, Canada,
of a heart attack

Star Sign
Gemini

Height
6'2"

Wives and Children
Actress Lili Damita
(1931–1942, divorced)
son, Sean

Salesgirl Nora Eddington
(1943–1949, divorced)
daughters, Deirdre and Rory

Actress Patrice Wymore
(1950–1959, his death)
daughter, Arnella Roma

Essential
ERROLFLYNN**Films

CAPTAIN BLOOD
(1935) Warner Bros.
Errol Flynn shot to stardom as an escaped slave who takes up a life of piracy for revenge against his British tormentors and the chance to win Olivia de Havilland's heart.

THE DAWN PATROL
(1938) Warner Bros.
In a remake of the 1930 hit, Flynn starred as an air squadron commander forced to send his men (including offscreen friend David Niven) on near-suicidal raids over enemy territory during World War I.

THE ADVENTURES OF ROBIN HOOD
(1938) Warner Bros.
A distant descendant of the man many historians consider the historical Robin Hood, Flynn stole from the rich and gave to the poor in his rebellion against the corrupt Prince John, winning the loyalty of his Merrie Men and the heart of Maid Marian (de Havilland).

GENTLEMAN JIM
(1942) Warner Bros.
In his favorite role, Flynn starred as the famed boxer who rose from lower-class roots to invade San Francisco society and win the heart of a judge's daughter (Alexis Smith).

THE SUN ALSO RISES
(1957) 20th Century–Fox
Flynn moved into character roles to play a hard-drinking expatriate engaged to Lady Brett Ashley (Ava Gardner) but unable to prevent her unrequited love for journalist Jake Barnes (Tyrone Power) in this popular adaptation of the Ernest Hemingway novel.

THE DAWN PATROL, 1938

THE ADVENTURES OF ROBIN HOOD, 1938

BEHIND THE SCENES

TIMING IS EVERYTHING. WHEN ERROL FLYNN AND OLIVIA DE HAVILLAND FIRST WORKED TOGETHER ON *CAPTAIN BLOOD* (1935), SHE HAD A CRUSH ON HIM, BUT HE WAS STILL HAPPILY MARRIED TO FRENCH ACTRESS LILI DAMITA. BY THE TIME THEY MADE *THE ADVENTURES OF ROBIN HOOD* (1938), HIS MARRIAGE WAS FALTERING, AND HE TRIED TO SEDUCE HIS COSTAR, BUT DE HAVILLAND WAS PUT OFF BY HIS RECKLESS LIFESTYLE. AT ONE POINT DURING LOCATION SHOOTING IN NORTHERN CALIFORNIA, HE STORMED HER HOTEL ROOM IN FULL COSTUME, AND GUESTS IN THE NEIGHBORING ROOMS HAD TO CARRY THE DRUNKEN BUT AMOROUS ACTOR AWAY.

FLYNN HAD WRITTEN ARTICLES FOR A SYDNEY NEWSPAPER IN HIS YOUTH AND CONTINUED WRITING THROUGHOUT HIS LIFE. ALONG WITH NUMEROUS MAGAZINE ARTICLES AND SHORT STORIES, HE WROTE A FICTIONALIZED ACCOUNT OF HIS YOUTHFUL TRAVELS, *BEAM ENDS* (1937), AND ANOTHER NOVEL, *SHOWDOWN*, IN 1946. THE LATTER FEATURES A PARROT NAMED HEDDA, A STAB AT GOSSIP COLUMNIST HEDDA HOPPER.

"ERROL FLYNN KILLED IN SPAIN?" THAT'S WHAT HEADLINES ANNOUNCED IN 1938, WHEN THE ACTOR WAS OFF ON A REAL-LIFE ADVENTURE TO COVER THE SPANISH CIVIL WAR AS A JOURNALIST. HE WAS ONLY INJURED WHEN HE GOT TOO CLOSE TO A FALLING BALCONY. FLYNN RECOVERED FROM HIS INJURY BUT WOULD LONG BE HAUNTED BY RUMORS THAT HE HAD FOUGHT FOR GENERAL FRANCO'S LOYALISTS AND WAS A NAZI SYMPATHIZER.

FLYNN'S TRIAL FOR STATUTORY RAPE IN 1942 MADE HIM A PART OF THE ENGLISH LANGUAGE WHEN THE PHRASE "IN LIKE FLYNN," MEANING "ASSURED OF SUCCESS," WAS APPLIED TO HIS SEDUCTIVE EFFECT ON WOMEN. WHEN HE PUBLISHED HIS MEMOIR, *MY WICKED, WICKED WAYS,* IN 1959, HE QUIPPED THAT HE HAD WANTED TO CALL IT *IN LIKE ME.*

WHILE SEVERAL MAJOR STARS DECLINED THE ROLE OF HUMBERT HUMBERT, THE COLLEGE PROFESSOR IN LOVE WITH A PREPUBESCENT GIRL IN *LOLITA*, ERROL FLYNN ACTUALLY PUT IN A BID FOR THE ROLE, HOPING THE FILM COULD BE ANOTHER VEHICLE FOR HIMSELF AND HIS MUCH YOUNGER PROTÉGÉ, BEVERLY AADLAND. DIRECTOR STANLEY KUBRICK REJECTED THE IDEA.

An American Everyman of Midwestern strength and integrity, his natural delivery revealed the tender side of characters struggling against injustice.

HENRY
FONDA

Whether loping down the streets of Tombstone in *My Darling Clementine* (1946), standing up against injustice in *The Grapes of Wrath* (1940), arguing a seemingly lost cause in *12 Angry Men* (1957), or facing old age head-on with Katharine Hepburn in *On Golden Pond* (1981), Henry Fonda personified the frontier spirit. It's no surprise that Fonda was a child of the Midwest, born in Nebraska, where he got his start acting in community theater productions with Marlon Brando's mother. Stock work put him into contact with his lifelong friend James Stewart and eventually brought him to Broadway. His early stage hit *The Farmer Takes a Wife* sent him to Hollywood to reprise his role in 1935. Fonda quickly established himself as a reliable leading player, particularly as the man on the run in *You Only Live Once* (1937) and Bette Davis's suitor in *Jezebel* (1938), but the role that established him as a major screen presence was Tom Joad in *The Grapes of Wrath*. To obtain the part, he had to sign a long-term contract with 20th Century–Fox, where later assignments rarely lived up to his talents. World War II service gave Fonda a harder edge that served him well in *My Darling Clementine*. Shortly after finishing his Fox contract, he left Hollywood for seven years, starring in a series of Broadway hits, most notably the World War II comedy-drama *Mister Roberts*. When he brought the role to the screen in 1955, it was as though he had never left. He tried producing with the jury room drama *12 Angry Men* and played both a presidential candidate in *The Best Man* and the real thing in *Fail-Safe* (both 1964). When his children, Jane and Peter, emerged as actors in their own right, their tales of a cold, often absent father tarnished his image slightly but dovetailed with his appearance in a rare villainous role in the Sergio Leone spaghetti Western *Once upon a Time in the West* (1968). Over time, Fonda reconciled with his children, finally joining Jane on screen for *On Golden Pond*. During production, the Motion Picture Academy voted him a Honorary Oscar. A year later, he won Best Actor for what would be his last theatrical feature; he died a few months afterward.

Born
Henry Jaynes Fonda
May 16, 1905
Grand Island, Nebraska

Died
August 12, 1982
Los Angeles, California,
of cardiorespiratory arrest

Star Sign
Taurus

Height
6'1½"

Wives and Children
Actress Margaret Sullavan
(1931–1933, divorced)

Socialite Frances Seymour Brokaw
(1936–1950, her death)
daughter, Jane
son, Peter

Susan Blanchard
(1950–1956, divorced)
adopted daughter, Amy

Baronessa Afdera Franchetti
(1957–1961, divorced)

Stewardess/model
Shirlee Mae Adams
(1965–1982, his death)

Essential
HENRY FONDA Films

THE GRAPES OF WRATH
(1940) 20th Century–Fox
Henry Fonda won his first Oscar nomination as Tom Joad, who gets out of prison in time to help his dispossessed Oklahoma family travel cross-country in search of a new life.

THE LADY EVE
(1941) Paramount
Preston Sturges cast the usually dramatic Fonda against type in this romantic comedy as a wealthy snake expert driven to distraction by con artist Barbara Stanwyck, the woman Fonda always cited as his favorite costar.

12 ANGRY MEN
(1957) United Artists
In his only stint as a film producer, Fonda wisely hired first-time director Sidney Lumet to helm this tense account of a jury deadlocked over a murder case, with Fonda as the holdout battling to turn the verdict around.

ONCE UPON A TIME IN THE WEST
(1968) Paramount
Fonda played the villain for the first time as a ruthless gang leader trying to make a killing off a new rail line despite opposition from mystery man Charles Bronson.

ON GOLDEN POND
(1981) Universal
In a tantalizing reflection of his offscreen life, Fonda played a retired college professor struggling with the inevitability of old age while trying to repair his shattered relationship with his daughter (Jane Fonda).

THE LADY EVE, 1941

WITH PETER AND JANE FONDA, 1957

BEHIND THE SCENES

EVEN AT 6'1½", FONDA WAS TOO SHORT TO PLAY ABRAHAM LINCOLN IN *YOUNG MR. LINCOLN* (1939), SO HE HAD TO WEAR SPECIAL BOOTS WITH LIFTS IN THEM. SPECIAL MAKEUP AND COSTUME WAS NOT REQUIRED FOR HIS FIRST VILLAINOUS ROLE IN *ONCE UPON A TIME IN THE WEST* (1968), SERGIO LEONE MADE HIM SHAVE A MUSTACHE AND DISCARD THE DARK CONTACT LENSES FONDA HAD ORDERED FOR THE ROLE. THE DIRECTOR WANTED HIS ALL-AMERICAN STAR TO RESEMBLE HIS EARLIER HEROIC CHARACTERS.

THE BEST ROLE THAT GOT AWAY FROM FONDA WAS GEORGE IN THE ORIGINAL BROADWAY PRODUCTION OF *WHO'S AFRAID OF VIRGINIA WOOLF?* HIS AGENT TURNED DOWN THE PLAY WITHOUT TELLING HIM, LATER CLAIMING, "YOU DON'T WANT TO BE IN A PLAY ABOUT FOUR PEOPLE YELLING AT EACH OTHER ALL THE TIME." THE ARGUMENT DIDN'T STOP FONDA FROM CHANGING AGENTS.

THE INVITATION TO THE WEDDING OF FONDA AND LUCILLE BALL'S CHARACTERS IN *YOURS, MINE, AND OURS* (1968) WAS THE ONE USED WHEN THE REAL-LIFE COUPLE MARRIED (THE TRUE LIFE STORY ALSO INSPIRED *THE BRADY BUNCH.*) ACCORDING TO JANE FONDA, HER FATHER MIGHT HAVE WELCOMED THE CHANCE TO MARRY BALL IN REAL LIFE, TOO, AS HE FELL IN LOVE WITH HER DURING PRODUCTION.

ON THE FIRST DAY OF SHOOTING FOR *ON GOLDEN POND* (1981), COSTAR KATHARINE HEPBURN GAVE FONDA A FISHING HAT THAT HAD BELONGED TO HER LONGTIME COMPANION SPENCER TRACY. HE WORE IT THROUGHOUT THE FILM.

THE GRAPES OF WRATH, 1940

To millions of film fans, he *was* Rhett Butler, the cynical rogue whose romantic heart, killer smile, and macho presence were the irresistible stuff of earthy virility.

CLARK
GABLE

Born
William Clark Gable
February 1, 1901
Cadiz, Ohio

Died
November 16, 1960
Los Angeles, California,
of a heart attack

Star Sign
Aquarius

Height
6'1"

Wives and Children
Drama teacher Josephine Dillon
(1924–1930, divorced)

Houston socialite Maria (Ria)
Franklin Prentiss Lucas Langham
(1931–1939, divorced)

daughter, Judy Lewis
born to Loretta Young
out of wedlock

Actress Carole Lombard
(1939–1942, her death)

Lady Sylvia Ashley
(1949–1952, divorced)

Kay Williams Spreckles
(1955–1960, his death)
son, John Clark

Clark Gable was a star tailor-made for the thirties. Stage training gave him a perfect voice for talking pictures, while his size and rough features made him both heroic and down-to-earth—a fitting idol for Depression-weary Americans who wished they could stand up to adversity so well. Gable always joked that he turned to acting in search of an easy job. In truth, as a motherless child, he fell in love with the stage, eventually dropping out of school to join a touring company. His first important film assignment was as the gangster who roughs up Norma Shearer in *A Free Soul* (1931). MGM production head Irving G. Thalberg had suggested the violence to make Gable's character less sympathetic, but fans found his presence so exciting they didn't care. When the studio capitalized on that by teaming him with Jean Harlow in *Red Dust* (1932), his career took off. For a while, Gable was so typecast in roughhouse roles he started refusing scripts in that vein. Studio head Louis B. Mayer decided to punish him with a loan-out to Columbia, a much less successful studio, for a film that seemed to be just another programmer. Instead, *It Happened One Night* (1934) was a huge hit that put director Frank Capra on the map, won Gable an Oscar, and made him a bigger star by adding a touch of roguish humor to his image. When the book *Gone with the Wind* became a runaway best seller, fans clamored for him to play Rhett Butler. Gable resisted (he hated period films after the failure of 1937's *Parnell*) but gave in when MGM agreed to pay a divorce settlement to his second wife so he could marry Carole Lombard. Three years later, Lombard's death in a plane crash sent him into a tailspin. Over the studio's objections, he enlisted in the U.S. Army Air Corps, distinguishing himself with wartime service. Returning home, he had trouble regaining his career momentum, and MGM ultimately decided to let him go. Then his last two films at the studio—*Mogambo* (1953), with Grace Kelly and Ava Gardner, and *Betrayed* (1954), with Lana Turner—were surprise hits, putting him in a position to launch his own production company. He got the best role of his later years when director John Huston cast him opposite Marilyn Monroe in *The Misfits* (1961). During production, he also was thrilled when he learned his fifth wife was pregnant. Sadly, he died before his only son was born.

Essential
CLARKGABLEFilms

ACADEMY AWARDS
Won Best Actor
It Happened One Night

Nominated for Best Actor
Mutiny on the Bounty
Gone with the Wind

RED DUST
(1932) MGM
Whether trading barbs with streetwalker Jean Harlow or sharing a clinch with married woman Mary Astor, Gable was pure sex in his role as a plantation overseer in Indochina torn between the two very different ladies.

IT HAPPENED ONE NIGHT
(1934) Columbia
Gable cemented his image as the screen's most lovable and masculine rogue when he played the newspaper reporter who helps runaway heiress Claudette Colbert survive life on the road.

MUTINY ON THE BOUNTY
(1935) MGM
At first Gable didn't want to make this Oscar-winning historical adventure, but audiences loved watching him stand up to the tyrannical Charles Laughton as Captain Bligh and romancing the Tahitian beauties in the cast.

GONE WITH THE WIND
(1939) MGM
Gable's performance as the Charleston blockade runner who finally won the tempestuous Scarlett O'Hara's (Vivien Leigh) heart only when it was too late for him to care was the stuff legends are made of.

THE MISFITS
(1961) United Artists
In his last film, Gable stars as an aging modern-day cowboy mixed up with a fragile divorcee (Marilyn Monroe, in her last film as well) during an emotional hunt for wild horses.

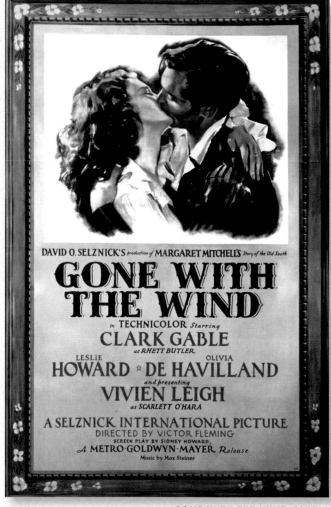

GONE WITH THE WIND, 1939

NO MAN OF HER OWN, 1932

BEHINDTHE**SCENES**

ONE OF CLARK GABLE'S EARLIEST SCREEN TESTS WAS FOR THE TITLE ROLE IN *LITTLE CAESAR* (1931). WARNER BROS. PRODUCTION CHIEF DARRYL F. ZANUCK TOOK ONE LOOK AT HIM AND SAID, "HIS EARS ARE TOO BIG; HE LOOKS LIKE AN APE," AND EVENTUALLY GAVE THE PART TO EDWARD G. ROBINSON.

GABLE TRIGGERED A CRISIS FOR UNDERWEAR MANUFACTURERS SIMPLY BY REMOVING HIS SHIRT IN *IT HAPPENED ONE NIGHT* (1934). WHEN HE REVEALED HE WASN'T WEARING ANYTHING UNDERNEATH, UNDERSHIRT SALES PLUMMETED.

SUPERMAN CREATORS JERRY SIEGEL AND JOEL SCHUSTER CHOSE THE NAME OF THE SUPERHERO'S SECRET IDENTITY, CLARK KENT, IN HONOR OF GABLE AND ACTOR KENT TAYLOR.

WHILE SHOOTING *GONE WITH THE WIND*, LEIGH BEGGED SELZNICK TO CUT BACK ON HER KISSING SCENES WITH GABLE BECAUSE HIS DENTURES SMELLED SO BAD. NOTORIOUSLY CHEAP, GABLE WOULDN'T SPEND THE MONEY TO GET A DECENT SET OF FALSE TEETH.

GABLE WAS SO INSECURE ABOUT PLAYING RHETT BUTLER IN *GONE WITH THE WIND* (1939) THAT WHEN HE REALIZED DIRECTOR GEORGE CUKOR WAS FOCUSING MOST OF HIS ATTENTIONS ON LEADING LADIES VIVIEN LEIGH AND OLIVIA DE HAVILLAND, HE DEMANDED A MORE CONGENIAL DIRECTOR. TO KEEP HIS STAR HAPPY, PRODUCER DAVID O. SELZNICK BROUGHT IN GABLE'S FRIEND VICTOR FLEMING AS A REPLACEMENT.

WHEN WORLD WAR II STARTED, CAROLE LOMBARD ENCOURAGED GABLE TO JOIN THE ARMED FORCES. JUST BEFORE HER FATAL PLANE CRASH, SHE WIRED HIM FROM HER INDIANA WAR-BOND TOUR, "HEY, PAPPY. YOU BETTER GET INTO THIS MAN'S ARMY." AFTER HER DEATH, THAT'S EXACTLY WHAT GABLE DID, AS A TRIBUTE TO HIS LATE WIFE.

Breaking the polished studio mold with a dynamic mix of angst, toughness, and sensitivity, he created defiant urban outsiders in performances so naturalistic they feel contemporary.

JOHN GARFIELD

John Garfield was a fighter all his life, taking on the Hollywood establishment, the House Un-American Activities Committee, and even his colleagues in the legendary Group Theatre. As a motherless child in the New York slums, he had to fight to survive. He fell naturally into clowning, performing for fellow gang members to win their support and protection. A teacher rescued him from a life of crime by channeling his energy into acting, which eventually led to his involvement with the Group Theatre. With the pioneering company, he studied the teachings of Konstantin Stanislavsky and the use of theater as a political tool. When the leading role in *Golden Boy,* which Clifford Odets had promised him, went to another actor, Garfield decided to accept an offer from Warner Bros. As a tryout, the studio cast him as a struggling composer in the family drama *Four Daughters* (1938), and he stole the show with his natural acting and sarcastic delivery, becoming an overnight sensation. When the studio typecast him in similar roles, he rebelled by refusing pictures until he couldn't afford not to work. With his popularity growing thanks to a loan-out to MGM for the classic film noir *The Postman Always Rings Twice* and then back home for Warner Bros.' romantic drama *Humoresque* (both 1946), he decided not to renew his contract. Garfield became one of the first Hollywood stars to form his own production company, named Enterprises, scoring a hit with the boxing drama *Body and Soul* (1946). His next production, the crime exposé *Force of Evil* (1948), was less successful on its initial release but is now regarded as a cult classic. But disaster struck when Garfield refused to name names for the House Un-American Activities Committee during its investigations of alleged communist infiltration of the motion picture industry. Although he had devoted much of his free time during World War II to working with the USO and was a cofounder of the Hollywood Canteen, he was blacklisted as a dangerous subversive. He cleared his name to the extent that he could find sporadic work, but the situation left him estranged from his family, and he drank heavily and slept little. In 1952, he was found dead of a heart attack at the age of thirty-nine. Ten thousand fans mobbed his funeral in New York, the biggest such event since the death of silent screen star Rudolph Valentino.

Born
Jacob Julius Garfinkle
March 4, 1913
New York, New York

Died
May 21, 1952
New York, New York,
of coronary thrombosis

Star Sign
Pisces

Height
5'7"

Wife and Children
Actress Roberta Siedman
(1935–1952, his death)
daughters, Katharine
and Julie
son, David

Essential
JOHNGARFIELDFilms

FOUR DAUGHTERS
(1938) Warner Bros.
John Garfield starred as a cynical composer whose troubled genius brings the cold winds of reality into the idyllic lives of a family of female musicians headed by Claude Rains.

PRIDE OF THE MARINES
(1945) Warner Bros.
As a blinded World War II veteran, Garfield struggled to find a reason to live while haunted by nightmares that made the film ahead of its time in its depiction of the subconscious.

THE POSTMAN ALWAYS RINGS TWICE
(1946) MGM
In one of the all-time classic films noirs, Garfield starred as a cynical drifter seduced into murdering Lana Turner's husband, only to end up paying for a crime he doesn't commit.

BODY AND SOUL
(1947) United Artists
As a boxer mixed up with the mob, Garfield turned in one of his most popular performances, facing off against his criminal tormentors with the line, "What are you gonna do? Kill me? Everybody dies."

FORCE OF EVIL
(1948) MGM
As an ambitious, crooked lawyer, Garfield gets mixed up with the numbers racket in a film that suggests crooked business dealings in America go far beyond organized crime.

THE POSTMAN ALWAYS RINGS TWICE, 1946

FORCE OF EVIL, 1948

BEHIND THE SCENES

AFTER HE COMPLETED HIS SUPPORTING ROLE IN *FOUR DAUGHTERS* (1938), GARFIELD WAS RUSHED INTO THE LOW-BUDGET PRISON PICTURE *BLACKWELL'S ISLAND* (1939). WHEN *FOUR DAUGHTERS* PUT HIM ON THE MAP, HOWEVER, STUDIO EXECUTIVES DIDN'T WANT TO HINDER HIS RISE TO STARDOM BY FOLLOWING IT WITH A B-PICTURE. *BLACKWELL'S ISLAND* WAS PUT BACK IN PRODUCTION JUST AS IT WAS ABOUT TO GO INTO THEATERS, WITH DIRECTOR MICHAEL CURTIZ ASSIGNED TO ADD NEW SCENES TO BEEF IT UP TO THE BIG-BUDGET LEVEL.

WHEN JOAN CRAWFORD MET GARFIELD AT THE START OF WORK ON *HUMORESQUE* (1946), SHE OFFERED HIM HER HAND, BUT HE PINCHED HER BREAST INSTEAD. SHE WAS SHOCKED FOR A MOMENT AND THEN QUIPPED, "YOU KNOW, I THINK WE'RE GOING TO GET ON JUST FINE." THEY ENDED UP CLOSE FRIENDS AND, ACCORDING TO HOLLYWOOD GOSSIP, LOVERS.

GARFIELD WAS UP FOR THE ROLE OF STANLEY KOWALSKI IN THE ORIGINAL BROADWAY PRODUCTION OF *A STREETCAR NAMED DESIRE,* BUT HE WOULD ONLY GUARANTEE A FOUR-MONTH RUN AND WANTED A CLAIM ON THE ROLE IF THE PLAY WERE FILMED. THESE DEMANDS COST HIM THE PART.

THE HOLLYWOOD BLACKLIST COST GARFIELD HIS PRODUCTION COMPANY AND LED UNITED ARTISTS TO BACK OUT OF ITS DEAL TO DISTRIBUTE THE STAR'S LAST PRODUCTION, *FORCE OF EVIL* (1948). MGM PICKED UP THE FILM AND DUMPED IT IN THEATERS DURING CHRISTMAS WEEK, HARDLY THE BEST TIME TO RELEASE A VIOLENT FILM NOIR. THROUGH TELEVISION SHOWINGS AND THE VIDEO MARKET, THE PICTURE HAS BECOME A CULT CLASSIC CREDITED BY DIRECTOR MARTIN SCORSESE AS AN INFLUENCE ON HIS FILMS ABOUT ORGANIZED CRIME.

ALTHOUGH HE WAS A MAJOR STAR AT THE TIME *GENTLEMAN'S AGREEMENT* (1947) WAS MADE, GARFIELD GLADLY ACCEPTED A SUPPORTING ROLE IN IT (THOUGH AT HIS FULL SALARY) BECAUSE OF ITS DEPICTION OF ANTI-SEMITISM. HIS ONLY CONDITION WAS THAT THE STUDIO NOT BLUNT THE EFFECTIVENESS OF MOSS HART'S ORIGINAL SCREENPLAY.

He was a superstar of the silents, his passion and energy hitting romantic heights in celebrated pairings with offscreen love Greta Garbo, their chemistry igniting the screen.

JOHN
GILBERT

In 1928, John Gilbert was the screen's top and highest-paid male star. Three years later, he couldn't crack the top one hundred. His was one of the biggest falls from grace triggered by the arrival of talking pictures. Gilbert's road to heartache was paved early by actress mother Ida Adair, who farmed him out to anybody willing to care for him, including a New York seamstress whose prostitute daughter entertained clients in front of the six-year-old child. His mother's marriage to comic William Gilbert, from whom the star took his surname, allowed the boy to go to boarding school, but her death after an extended illness left him homeless at the age of fourteen. After a series of odd jobs, Gilbert ended up in Hollywood, where between 1915 and 1917 he rose from extra work to leading roles. From 1919 to 1924, he worked at Fox, where he played adventurous roles in films like director John Ford's *Cameo Kirby* (1923). But it was his move to MGM that made him a major star. In 1925, back-to-back hits in director Erich von Stroheim's *The Merry Widow* and King Vidor's *The Big Parade,* the first major film to depict the horrors of World War I, did the trick. Paired with Greta Garbo for the first time, in *Flesh and the Devil* (1926), he became the screen's biggest star. MGM reteamed the two for *Love* (1927) and *A Woman of Affairs* (1928) while exploiting their offscreen love affair. When Garbo left him at the altar in 1927, it led to a fistfight with MGM production chief Louis B. Mayer, who swore to destroy his career. That's exactly what happened with Gilbert's first sound film, *His Glorious Night* (1929). The light voice audiences heard along with too flowery dialogue was out of synch with his image as a great lover; they laughed the film off the screen. This was not a problem with his later films (some have speculated that Mayer ordered the soundtrack altered), but the damage was done. Although he was the highest-paid actor at MGM, Mayer saw to it that Gilbert didn't get good scripts or directors. He got a last chance at success in *Queen Christina* (1933) because Garbo refused to make the film without him. With widespread stories about his drinking, though, his career was finished, and he died of a heart attack at the age of thirty-eight.

Born
John Cecil Pringle
July 10, 1897
Logan, Utah

Died
January 9, 1936
Los Angeles, California,
of heart failure

Star Sign
Cancer

Height
5'11"

Wives and Children
Olivia Burwell
(1918–1921, divorced)

Actress Leatrice Joy
(1921–1925, divorced)
daughter,
Leatrice Gilbert Fountain

Actress Ina Claire
(1929–1931, divorced)

Actress Virginia Bruce
(1932–1934, divorced)
daughter, Susan Ann

Essential
JOHNGILBERTFilms

THE MERRY WIDOW
(1925) MGM
Director Erich von Stroheim turned the thrice-filmed operetta into a study of the decadence underlying the European aristocracy, with Gilbert as the one man who truly loves wealthy widow Mae Murray for herself, rather than her money— or her feet.

THE BIG PARADE
(1925) MGM
With Gilbert as an innocent doughboy whose eyes are opened by the horrors of war and Renee Adoree as the French girl he loves, director King Vidor made this the biggest hit of the silent era.

FLESH AND THE DEVIL
(1926) MGM
Gilbert and Greta Garbo teamed for the first time for this steamy tale of a femme fatale who comes between childhood friends.

A WOMAN OF AFFAIRS
(1928) MGM
Family animosity and scandal tear apart childhood sweethearts Gilbert and Garbo in their third film together.

QUEEN CHRISTINA
(1933) MGM
In his last romantic role, Gilbert is the Spanish ambassador who wins the love of Sweden's greatest export, Garbo, as Sweden's greatest queen.

A WOMAN OF AFFAIRS, 1928

LOVE, 1927

BEHIND THE SCENES

WHEN GRETA GARBO MET GILBERT ON THE SET OF *FLESH AND THE DEVIL* (1926), IT WAS LOVE—OR AT LEAST LUST—AT FIRST SIGHT. THEY HAD TO KISS IN THEIR FIRST SCENE, AND WHEN DIRECTOR CLARENCE BROWN CALLED CUT, THE STARS DIDN'T STOP.

WHEN GILBERT AND GARBO FILMED *LOVE* (1927), AN ADAPTATION OF LEO TOLSTOY'S CLASSIC *ANNA KARENINA,* MGM SHOT ONE ENDING AS IN THE BOOK, WITH GARBO THROWING HERSELF IN FRONT OF A TRAIN, AND ANOTHER WITH THEM REUNITED, AND ALLOWED EXHIBITORS TO CHOOSE. IN THE UNITED STATES, MOST THEATERS SHOWED THE HAPPY ENDING, WHILE EUROPEAN THEATERS LARGELY SHOWED THE TRAGIC ONE.

THERE WERE SO MANY HEAVY DRINKERS WORKING ON GILBERT'S LAST FILM, *THE CAPTAIN HATES THE SEA* (1934), THAT WHEN COLUMBIA PICTURES HEAD HARRY COHN CABLED DIRECTOR LEWIS MILESTONE, URGING HIM ON WITH THE MESSAGE "HURRY UP. THE COSTS ARE STAGGERING," HE WIRED BACK, "SO IS THE CAST."

SHORTLY AFTER HER ARRIVAL IN HOLLYWOOD, MARLENE DIETRICH HEARD OF GILBERT'S FALL FROM GRACE AND SET OUT TO SAVE HIM. SHE GOT HIM TO STOP DRINKING UNTIL SHE LEFT HIS BED FOR GARY COOPER'S, WHICH SENT GILBERT INTO ANOTHER TAILSPIN. A CONTRITE DIETRICH ARRANGED ROLES FOR GILBERT IN TWO OF HER 1936 FILMS, *DESIRE* AND *GARDEN OF ALLAH,* BUT HE DIED BEFORE HE COULD WORK ON THEM.

WHEN LEATRICE GILBERT FOUNTAIN INTERVIEWED DIRECTOR CLARENCE BROWN FOR HER BOOK ABOUT HER FATHER, *DARK STAR,* SHE ASKED HIM WHETHER MAYER HAD ENGINEERED GILBERT'S FAILURE IN TALKING FILMS. HIS RESPONSE: "LOUIS B. MAYER WAS A VERY GOOD FRIEND TO ME . . . . AND I DON'T BELIEVE IN SPEAKING BADLY ABOUT THE DEAD. TAKE IT FROM THERE."

THE BIG PARADE, 1925

A quintessential leading man with the perfect blend of elegance, sophistication, charm, and wit, he was for many the ultimate movie star that men wanted to be and women wanted to be with.

CARY GRANT

Cary Grant was his own greatest performance, a creature invented on screen from aspects of other actors he admired, including Douglas Fairbanks and Nöel Coward. With time, he assumed the role offscreen as well, rising from humble beginnings as a child of England's slums to become the epitome of class. In love with the theater and silent comedy from his early years, he ran away to join a troupe of comedians when he was fourteen, developing acrobatic skills he would use throughout his career. When they toured the United States in the twenties, he decided to stay and try his luck on Broadway, where he became a musical theater star. He was one of the many stage actors brought to Hollywood with the coming of sound. Under the new name of Cary Grant, he started at Paramount as a threat to Gary Cooper, but when Mae West had him cast as the man she invited to "come up some time and see me" in *She Done Him Wrong* (1933), he achieved leading man status in his own right. He started as a comic actor playing the con man hooked up with a cross-dressing Katharine Hepburn in *Sylvia Scarlett* (1936). Although the film bombed, glowing reviews for his sly, sarcastic performance gave him the courage to leave Paramount for freelance work. With the success of two sophisticated 1937 comedies, *Topper* and *The Awful Truth,* he became a star. Grant, however, won Oscar nods when he stepped out of character to play serious roles in *Penny Serenade* (1941) and *None but the Lonely Heart* (1944). He was a favorite with two of the era's greatest directors—Alfred Hitchcock (appearing in four of his films, starting with *Suspicion* in 1941) and Howard Hawks (starring in five of Hawks's films, starting with *Bringing up Baby* in 1938). Hitchcock brought Grant out of retirement in the fifties to make *To Catch a Thief* (1955), with Grace Kelly, and then gave the actor his biggest box office hit with *North by Northwest* (1959). In the fifties and sixties, Grant's leading ladies kept getting younger (Doris Day in *That Touch of Mink,* in 1962, and Audrey Hepburn in *Charade,* in 1963), but audiences didn't care. Grant did, however. After playing a fatherly role in 1966's *Walk, Don't Run,* he retired from the screen. For the rest of his life, he devoted himself to family (his only child, Jennifer, was born in 1966), charity work, and being Cary Grant, a role he played to perfection.

Born
Archibald Alexander Leach
January 18, 1904
Horfield, Bristol, England

Died
November 29, 1986
Davenport, Iowa,
of a stroke

Star Sign
Capricorn

Height
6'1½"

Wives and Child
Actress Virginia Cherill
(1934–1935, divorced)

Woolworth heiress
Barbara Hutton
(1942–1945, divorced)

Actress Betsy Drake
(1949–1962, divorced)

Actress Dyan Cannon
(1965–1968, divorced)
daughter, Jennifer

Publicist Barbara Harris
(1981–1986, his death)

Essential CARYGRANTFilms

ACADEMY AWARDS
Nominated for Best Actor
Penny Serenade
None but the Lonely Heart

Honorary Oscar in 1970 "for his unique mastery of the art of screen acting"

BRINGING UP BABY
(1938) RKO
In 1938, Grant seemed cast against type as a befuddled paleontologist under romantic assault from screwball heiress Katharine Hepburn in a film that, though a bomb when it was released, has become one of the screen's classic romantic comedies.

BRINGING UP BABY, 1938

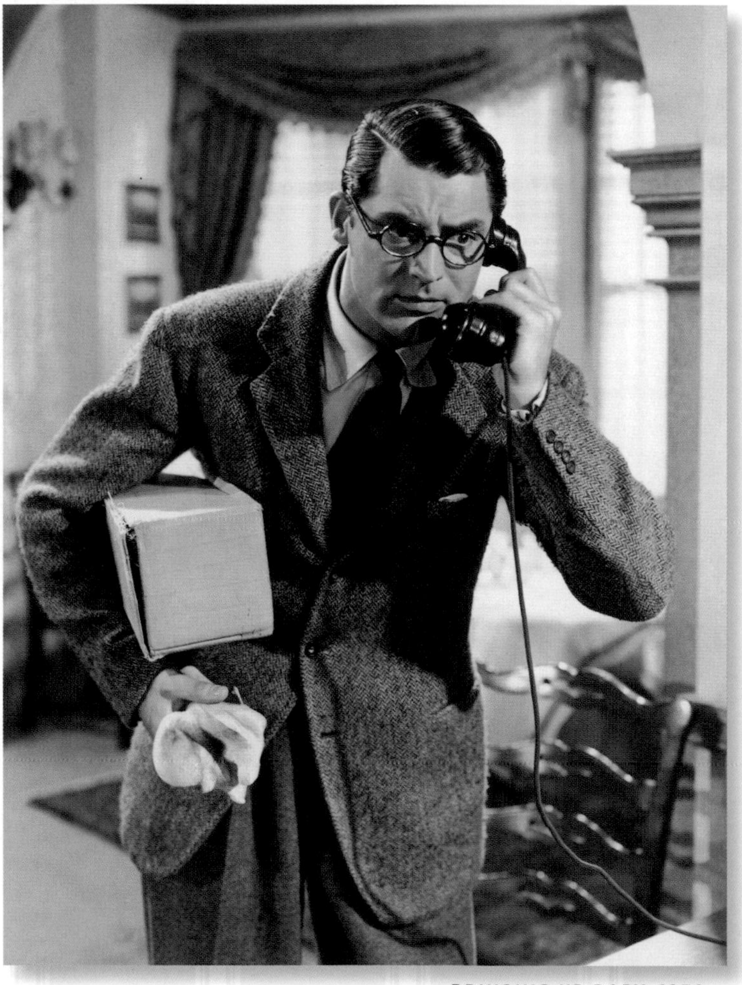

GUNGA DIN
(1939) RKO
Grant drew on his athletic skills and working-class background for this spirited adventure about a trio of British soldiers (Grant, Douglas Fairbanks Jr., and Victor McLaglen) in India taking on rebels.

NOTORIOUS
(1946) RKO
In one of Alfred Hitchcock's sexiest spy films, Grant stars as a U.S. agent who enlists a war criminal's daughter (Ingrid Bergman) to infiltrate a group of escaped Nazis living in South America, even if it means marrying their leader (Claude Rains).

AN AFFAIR TO REMEMBER
(1957) 20th Century-Fox
Grant and Deborah Kerr starred as a frustrated painter and a nightclub singer who fall in love during a romantic ocean voyage in a perennial favorite. It was directed by Leo McCarey, a remake from his own original *Love Affair* (1939), with Charles Boyer and Irene Dunne.

NORTH BY NORTHWEST
(1959) MGM
Director Alfred Hitchcock sent Grant on a deadly chase across the United States as an ad man who ends up playing a vital role in U.S. security when he's mistaken for a spy.

NORTH BY NORTHWEST, 1959

SIGNING AUTOGRAPHS, CIRCA 1942

BEHIND THE SCENES

THROUGHOUT FILMING OF *THE PHILADELPHIA STORY* (1940), GRANT WAS DISTURBED BY NEWS ABOUT THE LONDON BLITZ IN FROM ENGLAND AT THE BEGINNING OF WORLD WAR II. HE DONATED HIS ENTIRE SALARY FOR THAT FILM TO BRITISH WAR RELIEF AND THE RED CROSS.

GRANT OFTEN SAID THAT TWO ROLES CAPTURED HIS TRUE CHARACTER: THE GANGSTER IN *MR. LUCKY* (1943) AND THE COCKNEY DRIFTER IN *NONE BUT THE LONELY HEART* (1944). BOTH PRESENTED CHARACTERS WITH WORKING-CLASS BACKGROUNDS SIMILAR TO HIS, AND *MR. LUCKY* EVEN GAVE HIM A CHANCE TO DEMONSTRATE THE COCKNEY RHYMING SLANG OF HIS CHILDHOOD.

GRANT'S MARRIAGE TO WOOLWORTH HEIRESS BARBARA HUTTON GOT SOME PRETTY BAD PRESS. THE ACCUSATIONS THAT HE HAD MARRIED HER FOR HER MONEY LED TO THEIR BEING NICKNAMED "CASH AND CARY." ALTHOUGH THEY DIVORCED, GRANT REMAINED CLOSE TO HUTTON'S SON, LANCE REVENTLOW, REFERRING TO HIM AS "MY SON." WHEN THE YOUNG MAN DIED IN A PLANE CRASH, GRANT WAS DEVASTATED.

GRANT WAS UNCOMFORTABLE STARRING OPPOSITE AUDREY HEPBURN, WHO WAS TWENTY-FIVE YEARS HIS JUNIOR, IN *CHARADE* (1962) AND INSISTED THE SCRIPT BE CHANGED SO THAT SHE PURSUED HIM. HE ALSO INSERTED SEVERAL JOKING REFERENCES TO HIS AGE DURING FILMING.

He made cynicism big at the box office, overcoming typecasting as a genial good guy to find stardom as a wisecracking loner out to take the world for a ride.

WILLIAM
HOLDEN

Born
William Franklin Beedle Jr.
April 18, 1918
O'Fallon, Illinois

Died
November 16, 1981
Santa Monica, California,
of injuries from a fall

Star Sign
Aries

Height
5'11"

Wife and Children
Actress Brenda Marshall
(1941–1971, divorced)
sons, Peter and Scott
adopted daughter, Virginia

William Holden was Hollywood's "Golden Boy," literally shooting to stardom in only his third film. Haunted by inner demons, including his own disregard for his chosen profession, he grew from needing a few drinks to get through a day of shooting to developing a major drinking problem that would eventually take his life. Holden grew up in Pasadena, a model child except when he indulged in daredevil acts that revealed his rebellious side. Acting may have been one of those rebellions, something of which his conservative parents would have disapproved. While performing at the Pasadena Playhouse, he was spotted by a Paramount talent scout and signed up as part of the Golden Circle, a group of talented newcomers including Susan Hayward and Robert Preston. After just two bit parts, he won the title role in Columbia's film version of *Golden Boy* (1939) and then almost lost it when early rushes revealed his inexperience. Costar Barbara Stanwyck devoted her nights to coaching the young actor, who kept the role and also scored a major success in it. Columbia bought half his contract, and for the next several years he shuttled between minor pictures at both studios. Those films typecast him in what he called "Smiling Jim" roles, good guys with little edge or sex appeal. When Montgomery Clift turned down the role of a failed screenwriter turned gigolo in *Sunset Blvd.* (1950), however, writer-director Billy Wilder took a chance on Holden, whose performance made cynicism sexy. Another cynical role, in Wilder's World War II POW drama *Stalag 17* (1953), brought Holden an Oscar and made him one of the decade's top stars. Cynicism paid off again in *The Bridge on the River Kwai* (1957), and his deal for a share of the profits made him a millionaire several times over. In the sixties, Holden became involved in other interests, including a wildlife refuge in Kenya, often quipping that he was using his vocation to support his avocation. After a costly divorce from his wife of thirty years, he had several high-profile romances, including one with actress Stefanie Powers, eventually done in by his increasing dependence on alcohol. He managed to pull it together for a few more great performances, including the aging outlaw in *The Wild Bunch* (1969), the television news executive in *Network* (1976), and a fading film director in his last film, *S.O.B.* (1981).

Essential
WILLIAMHOLDENFilms

SUNSET BLVD.

(1950) Paramount
Holden starred for writer-director
Billy Wilder as a failed Hollywood
writer who falls into a sexual
relationship with deranged silent
star Gloria Swanson.

STALAG 17

(1953) Paramount
Wilder promised to find another
great role for Holden, and he did
when he cast him as a wisecracking
POW during World War II who may
or may not be the camp informant.

PICNIC

(1955) Columbia
In one of his sexiest performances,
Holden stars as a drifter who
steams up a small-town holiday
weekend, particularly when he
joins beauty queen Kim Novak for
a torrid dance.

THE BRIDGE ON
THE RIVER KWAI

(1957) Columbia
Holden's role as a conniving U.S.
sailor on a mission to stop British
POWs from building a railroad
bridge for the Japanese was
secondary to Alec Guinness's as
the POWs' commander, but Holden
was the name drawing audiences
into producer-director David Lean's
lavish production.

THE WILD BUNCH

(1969) Warner Bros.
Holden led a group of aging
outlaws out for one final score
in the last days of the Old West
in director Sam Peckinpah's
controversial, violent western.

THE BRIDGE ON THE RIVER KWAI, 1957

SUNSET BLVD., 1950

THE WILD BUNCH, 1969

BEHIND THE SCENES

TO REPAY BARBARA STANWYCK FOR SAVING HIS CAREER DURING THE FILMING OF *GOLDEN BOY* (1939), HOLDEN SENT HER A BOUQUET OF RED ROSES EVERY YEAR ON THE ANNIVERSARY OF THE FILM'S START DATE.

WRITER J. D. SALINGER NAMED THE PROTAGONIST OF *CATCHER IN THE RYE* HOLDEN CAULFIELD AFTER SEEING A MOVIE MARQUEE ADVERTISING THE FILM *DEAR RUTH* (1947), WITH WILLIAM HOLDEN AND JOAN CAULFIELD.

INITIALLY, HOLDEN DIDN'T WANT TO MAKE *THE BRIDGE ON THE RIVER KWAI* (1957), BECAUSE OF THE EXTENSIVE LOCATION SHOOT IN CEYLON AND THE FACT THAT HIS ROLE WOULD BE SECONDARY TO ALEC GUINNESS'S. KNOWING THEY NEEDED HIM FOR BOX OFFICE APPEAL, THE PRODUCERS FINALLY GOT HIM TO SIGN FOR THE FILM BY OFFERING HIM $50,000 A YEAR FOR THE REST OF HIS LIFE.

WHEN BARBARA STANWYCK ACCEPTED HER HONORARY OSCAR IN 1982, SHE HELD THE AWARD UP AND SAID, "THIS IS FOR YOU, MY GOLDEN BOY."

AFTER HOLDEN AND ERNEST BORGNINE PLAYED THE CAMPFIRE SCENE IN *THE WILD BUNCH* (1969), IN WHICH THEY DISCUSS THEIR FADING CAREERS AS OUTLAWS, DIRECTOR SAM PECKINPAH WAS CRYING TOO HARD TO YELL, "CUT!"

HOLDEN'S EFFORTS TO PRESERVE AFRICAN WILDLIFE AND EDUCATE THE PUBLIC ABOUT CONSERVATION ISSUES ARE SUSTAINED BY THE WILLIAM HOLDEN WILDLIFE FOUNDATION, AN ORGANIZATION CONTINUED AFTER HIS DEATH BY FORMER LOVE STEFANIE POWERS, WHO HAD DEVELOPED A PASSION FOR WILDLIFE DURING THEIR RELATIONSHIP, AND HIS PARTNERS IN THE MOUNT KENYA GAME RANCH.

The clown prince of Hollywood, he seldom got the girl but always got the laughs, making an art of self-deprecating quips in *Road* capers and tirelessly hitting the road for five decades to entertain America's armed forces.

BOB
HOPE

Quick with a quip, with a heart that put him on the right side of any battle, Bob Hope was one of the first stand-up comics to build his film career on a nonstop string of jokes, many of them topical, self-deflating, or both. When teamed with the more laid-back Bing Crosby, he became a box office giant. Comic teams were nothing new to the movies, but unlike their predecessors Laurel and Hardy and followers Martin and Lewis, Hope and Crosby were equals, each capable of winning Dorothy Lamour at the end of the road. Hope caught the theatrical bug early on, auditioning for amateur shows in Cleveland, Ohio, where the family had moved from London when he was four. He broke into vaudeville as a dancer but then moved into comedy, which led to Broadway stardom in the 1933 musical *Roberta*. Although he starred in seven comedy shorts during his Broadway years, it was success as the host of his own radio series that brought him to Hollywood, where he made his screen debut in *The Big Broadcast of 1938* (1938), introducing his signature song, "Thanks for the Memories." Hope's early films were a mixed bag, often featuring dramatic scenes that seemed beyond his range. His screen image finally fell into place when Paramount cast him as Paulette Goddard's cowardly hero in the comic thriller *The Cat and the Canary* (1939). One year later, he teamed with Crosby and Lamour for *Road to Singapore* (1940), launching one of Hollywood's most popular film series. The films' fast-paced, self-referential humor expanded the bounds of screen comedy and kept audiences coming back for six more entries. World War II brought Hope a new audience, as he started regular tours to entertain U.S. servicemen at home and abroad, putting himself at great risk to bring them a piece of home. In the fifties, he branched out into more serious roles like those in the biopics *The Seven Little Foys* (1955), in which he played vaudeville star Eddie Foy, and *Beau James* (1957), the life of New York mayor "Gentleman" Jimmy Walker. Old friend Lucille Ball was his last great screen partner, particularly in the adult comedy *The Facts of Life* (1960). As he began limiting his film appearances, Hope still maintained a rigorous schedule of entertaining the troops and headlining top-rated TV specials, while also hosting the Academy Awards a record eighteen times.

Born
Leslie Towns Hope
May 29, 1903
London, England

Died
July 27, 2003
Toluca Lake, California,
of pneumonia

Star Sign
Gemini

Height
5'11½"

Wife and Children
Singer Dolores Reade
(1934-2003, his death)
adopted daughters,
Linda Roberta Theresa
and Eleanor Avis "Nora"
adopted sons,
Anthony Reade and
William Kelly Francis

Essential
BOBHOPEFilms

ACADEMY AWARDS
Honorary Oscar in 1941
for "unselfish services to
the motion picture industry"

Honorary Oscar and life
membership in the Academy in
1945 "for his many services"

Honorary Oscar in 1953
for "his contribution to
the laughter of the world"

Jean Hersholt
Humanitarian Award
in 1950

Honorary Oscar in 1966
"for unique and
distinguished service"

THE CAT AND THE CANARY
(1939) Paramount
Bob Hope set the star image that
would serve him for the next sixty
years as he fought fear to help
beautiful heiress Paulette Goddard
survive a night in a spooky mansion.

ROAD TO SINGAPORE
(1940) Paramount
In their first *Road* picture, Hope
and Bing Crosby try to forget their
trouble with women, until they
run into the sarong-wearing
Dorothy Lamour.

ROAD TO UTOPIA
(1946) Paramount
Hope and Crosby head for Alaska
in one of their funniest *Road*
movies, this time playing vaudeville
performers caught up in the
gold rush and the usual battle for
Dorothy Lamour's affections.

THE PALEFACE
(1948) Paramount
Undercover agent Jane Russell
passed traveling dentist Hope off
as her husband and a crack shot
so she could ferret out a band of
gun runners.

THE SEVEN LITTLE FOYS
(1955) Paramount
In a rare biopic, Hope played the
famed vaudeville star who dealt
with his large brood by putting
them into the act, with James
Cagney in a guest shot as
George M. Cohan.

ROAD TO UTOPIA, 1946

BEHIND THE SCENES

HOPE'S SIXTY-ONE-YEAR CONTRACT WITH NBC WAS THE LONGEST WITH A SINGLE RADIO OR TELEVISION NETWORK IN SHOW BUSINESS HISTORY.

HOPE, WHO HAS EARNED 1,500 AWARDS FOR HIS WORK AS A PERFORMER AND A HUMANITARIAN, HOLDS A PLACE IN *THE GUINNESS BOOK OF RECORDS* AS THE MOST HONORED ENTERTAINER IN HISTORY.

ROAD TO ZANZIBAR (1941) WAS ORIGINALLY WRITTEN FOR FRED MACMURRAY AND GEORGE BURNS, WHO BOTH PASSED ON THE SCRIPT. ONLY THEN DID PARAMOUNT EXECUTIVES DECIDE TO MAKE IT A FOLLOW-UP TO HOPE, BING CROSBY, AND DOROTHY LAMOUR'S *ROAD TO SINGAPORE* (1940). WITH THE SECOND PICTURE, THE *ROAD* FILMS BECAME A SERIES.

INITIALLY, HOPE RESISTED THE IDEA OF TAKING HIS RADIO SHOW TO U.S. MILITARY BASES, FEARING IT WOULD BE TOO EXPENSIVE. FROM HIS FIRST CAMP SHOW IN 1941, HOWEVER, HE REALIZED HOW MUCH THE SERVICEMEN NEEDED THE TOUCH OF HOME—AND THE BEAUTIFUL FEMALE ENTERTAINERS—HE COULD BRING THEM.

THE SCENE IN *ROAD TO MOROCCO* (1942) IN WHICH THE CAMEL SPITS IN HOPE'S FACE WASN'T SCRIPTED. THE ANIMAL DID IT WHILE THE CAMERAS WERE ROLLING, AND HOPE'S AND CROSBY'S REACTIONS WERE SO FUNNY, IT STAYED IN THE FILM.

HOPE ENLISTED HIS RADIO WRITERS TO PUNCH UP HIS FILM SCRIPTS WITH EXTRA GAGS. HE TOLD THEM THE STUDIO HAD GIVEN HIM $5,000 TO PAY THEM, BUT WHEN MEL SHAVELSON WAS HIRED TO WRITE THE SCRIPT FOR *THE PRINCESS AND THE PIRATE* (1944), PRODUCER SAM GOLDWYN LET SLIP THE FACT THAT HOPE'S PRODUCERS ALWAYS GAVE HIM $10,000 FOR HIS WRITERS. HOPE WAS POCKETING HALF THE FEE HIMSELF.

THE PALEFACE (1948) WAS THE TOP-GROSSING COMIC WESTERN UNTIL SURPASSED BY *BLAZING SADDLES* IN 1974.

HOPE'S SIXTY-NINE-YEAR MARRIAGE IS CONSIDERED THE LONGEST IN HOLLYWOOD HISTORY.

A square-jawed, strapping hunk, he was one of the last great studio-created stars, projecting the illusion that he was every woman's ideal mate.

ROCK
HUDSON

Rock Hudson was a dream to his legions of fans and even to himself. He didn't think of himself as Rock Hudson, but rather as Roy Fitzgerald, the name he acquired when adopted by his stepfather. Behind the image of masculine beauty he projected was a deeply conflicted man who drank and smoked excessively to deal with his fear of being exposed as gay in an era when a whiff of sexual ambivalence could cost a young actor his career. Acting was something he had pursued since he worked as a movie theater usher back in Illinois. He had migrated to Hollywood after World War II and hung out at studio gates, hoping to attract attention. Before long, the strapping young man had an agent, a new name, and a contract at Universal Studios, where he would become one of the last studio-manufactured stars. Universal groomed him through classes and a series of small roles. When he was ready, they gave him his first starring role in a prestige picture, the remake of *Magnificent Obsession* (1954), and the film made him a star. He profited from a loan to Warner Bros. to work with Elizabeth Taylor and James Dean on *Giant* (1956), revealing untapped talents and winning his sole Oscar nomination. Then he shifted gears into romantic comedy, teaming with Doris Day for *Pillow Talk* (1959), the first of three comedies that would put him at the top of the box office charts. As the studio system faded, Hudson was smart enough to move into television for a six-year run on the series *McMillan and Wife* in the seventies. Television and musical theater tours kept him in the public eye, but when he signed for a recurring guest shot on the prime time soap *Dynasty* in 1984, coworkers noticed he was having problems remembering lines and speaking. His gaunt appearance on the premiere of Doris Day's cable show, *Doris Day's Best Friends*, in 1985 first alerted the press something was wrong. Then *Variety* columnist Army Archerd broke the news that Hudson had contracted the AIDS virus. At first, Hudson blamed his health problems on liver cancer, which he also had. When he finally admitted the truth, he was the first celebrity to publicly acknowledge that he had AIDS. His highly publicized illness and death put a human face on the disease that inspired other celebrities, including Taylor, to get involved in AIDS charities.

Born
Roy Harold Scherer Jr.
November 17, 1925
in Winnetka, Illinois

Died
October, 2, 1985
Beverly Hills, California,
of AIDS complications

Star Sign
Scorpio

Height
6'4"

Wife
Secretary Phyllis Gates
(1955–1958, divorced)

Essential
ROCKHUDSONFilms

ACADEMY AWARDS
Nominated for Best Actor
Giant

MAGNIFICENT OBSESSION

(1954) Universal-International
As it had for Robert Taylor in the thirties, this lush romance, about a playboy who finds the faith to become an accomplished neurosurgeon and save the woman he loves, made Rock Hudson a star.

WRITTEN ON THE WIND

(1956) Universal-International
In his third film for director Douglas Sirk, Hudson is an oilman caught in a tangled romantic web with alcoholic Robert Stack, the man's twisted sister (Dorothy Malone), and innocent outsider Lauren Bacall.

GIANT

(1956) Warner Bros.
As a Texas rancher trying to maintain the ways of the past, Hudson got to romance Elizabeth Taylor, trade blows with James Dean, and work with Oscar-winning director George Stevens.

PILLOW TALK

(1959) Universal-International
In the first of his romantic comedies, Hudson is a big-city wolf sharing a telephone party line with decorator Doris Day, the only woman who can tame him.

SECONDS

(1966) Paramount
Although this thriller initially failed at the box office, director John Frankenheimer's tale of an aging businessman (Hudson) who hires a mysterious organization to fake his death and rebuild him surgically has become a cult classic.

SECONDS, 1966

GIANT, 1956

BEHIND THE SCENES

ALTHOUGH HE GOT THE ACTING BUG EARLY, ROCK HUDSON NEVER LANDED ANY ROLES IN HIGH SCHOOL PLAYS BECAUSE HE COULDN'T REMEMBER LINES. IN HIS FILM DEBUT, *FIGHTER SQUADRON* (1948), IT TOOK HIM THIRTY-EIGHT TAKES TO GET HIS SOLE LINE RIGHT.

HUDSON GOT HIS SCREEN NAME FROM TALENT SCOUT HENRY WILLSON, WHO HAD ALSO NAMED TAB HUNTER AND RORY CALHOUN. ON MEETING THE FUTURE STAR, THE FIRST THING WILLSON THOUGHT OF WAS THE ROCK OF GIBRALTAR. THE "HUDSON" PART WAS INSPIRED BY THE RIVER.

HUDSON WAS ON LOCATION WITH ACTOR ROBERT STACK FOR *TARNISHED ANGELS* (1958) WHILE STACK'S WIFE WAS EXPECTING A BABY. HUDSON PERSONALLY ARRANGED FOR A DIRECT PHONE LINE BETWEEN THE HOSPITAL AND THE AIRPORT WHERE THEY WERE FILMING AND HAD A PLANE WITH THE BANNER "IT'S A GIRL!" FLY OVER THE SET WHEN HE GOT THE NEWS.

BOTH HUDSON AND DORIS DAY RECALLED THEIR WORKING RELATIONSHIP AS ONE FILLED WITH FUN AND MUTUAL ADMIRATION. ON THE SET OF THEIR FILMS, ROCK CALLED DORIS "EUNICE BLOTTER" BECAUSE IT AMUSED HIM; SHE REFERRED TO HIM AS "ROY HAROLD."

HUDSON'S FORMER COMPANION MARC CHRISTIAN WON A LAWSUIT AGAINST THE LATE ACTOR'S ESTATE ON THE GROUNDS THAT HUDSON HAD EXPOSED HIM TO AIDS WITHOUT WARNING HIM. HUDSON HAD TOLD HIS CLOSEST FRIENDS THAT HE HAD NOT ENGAGED IN SEXUAL RELATIONS WITH CHRISTIAN AFTER HIS DIAGNOSIS.

HUDSON AND ELIZABETH TAYLOR HAD BECOME CLOSE FRIENDS WHILE FILMING *GIANT* (1956), AND SHE WAS AT HIS BEDSIDE WHEN HE DIED. HIS DEATH LED TO HER INVOLVEMENT IN RAISING MILLIONS OF DOLLARS FOR AIDS-RELATED CHARITIES.

WITH DORIS DAY, CIRCA 1959

His impassive response to even the most outlandish situations gave his characters an ironic detachment, and "the Great Stone Face" weathered outrageous peril with soulful grace and comic agility.

BUSTER
KEATON

Born
Joseph Frank Keaton VI
October 4, 1895
Piqua, Kansas

Died
February 1, 1966
Los Angeles, California,
of lung cancer

Star Sign
Libra

Height
5'6"

Wives and Children
Actress Natalie Talmadge
(1921–1932, divorced)
sons, James and Robert

Nurse Mae Scriven
(1933–1936, divorced)

Dancer Eleanor Norris
(1940–1966, his death)

Buster Keaton learned early on that if he wanted audiences to laugh at his almost surreal slapstick routines, he would have to play them seriously. It was a trick he developed in vaudeville. Joining the family's very physical comedy act at five, he was routinely flung about the stage and sometimes into the audience. He stayed with the act until he was twenty-two, when his father's drinking threatened to make things a little too realistic. Turning down lucrative offers to star on stage, Keaton signed with movie comic and director Roscoe "Fatty" Arbuckle. He made his screen debut in *The Butcher Boy* (1917) and quickly learned the basics of film comedy. Arbuckle even gave him a chance to codirect. When his mentor moved into full-length features in 1920, Keaton's future brother-in-law, producer Joseph M. Schenck, gave him a shot at starring in his own shorts. In nineteen two-reelers made over the next three years—including *The Boat* (1921) and *Cops* (1922)—Keaton learned to make the camera his comic conspirator in a series of ever more intricate routines, often combining special effects with his own natural athletics. Keaton graduated to features in 1923, upping the scale of his gags to use an entire ship in *The Navigator* (1924) and a period train in *The General* (1927) as comic props. Though later generations would view these films as classics, their box office failure at the time prompted Schenck to sell Keaton's contract to MGM, where the comic lost much of his creative control. His MGM films were popular, but Keaton responded to increasing studio interference by drinking heavily, which cost him his family, his fortune, and his career; MGM fired him in 1933. He didn't fully recover until his third wife, dancer Eleanor Norris, got him to stop drinking for good. By this point, he could only find work writing gags at MGM, mostly for Red Skelton. Keaton made a comeback in the postwar years, however, starting with a 1947 performance at Cirque Medrano in Paris. Critic James Agee's influential 1949 article "Comedy's Greatest Era" and the discovery of several of his films, long thought lost, brought him back to prominence, leading to an honorary Oscar in 1959. Keaton finished his career playing bit parts in the Frankie Avalon–Annette Funicello beach films, frankly puzzled by the adulation of new generations of critics who hailed him as one of the screen's great directors.

Essential
BUSTERKEATONFilms

OUR HOSPITALITY

(1923) Metro
In his second feature, Buster Keaton expanded the scope of his work with the story of a nineteenth-century Southerner who falls for the daughter (his real-life wife, Natalie Talmadge) of a family feuding with his.

SHERLOCK JR.

(1924) Metro
Keaton played the film medium for laughs as a projectionist who deals with romantic problems by dreaming himself into the movie he's showing; in one memorable scene, he's stuck on screen as the film cuts among different settings.

THE GENERAL

(1927) United Artists
Confederate train engineer Keaton crosses enemy lines to rescue his lady love and his beloved locomotive (the General) from Union forces during the Civil War.

STEAMBOAT BILL JR.

(1928) United Artists
A riverboat captain (Ernest Torrence) fails to make a man of his college-student son (Keaton), but a funny—and frightening—cyclone does the trick for him.

THE CAMERAMAN

(1928) MGM
In his last picture made with any degree of artistic control, Keaton stars as an aspiring newsreel photographer out to impress girlfriend Marceline Day.

THE GENERAL, 1927

THE CAMERAMAN, 1928

BEHIND THE SCENES

KEATON WAS A PIONEER IN THE USE OF MULTIPLE EXPOSURES IN THE SHORT *THE PLAYHOUSE* (1921), IN WHICH HE PLAYS AN ENTIRE THEATER ORCHESTRA, THE CONDUCTOR, THE ACTORS ON STAGE, AND THE AUDIENCE—ONE SHOT FEATURES NINE KEATONS IN ONE FRAME. IN A TITLE CARD, ONE OF THE AUDIENCE MEMBERS SAYS, "THIS FELLOW KEATON SEEMS TO BE THE WHOLE SHOW."

ONE FALL IN *SHERLOCK JR.* (1924) WENT WRONG, BUT KEATON USED THE STUNT FOOTAGE IN THE FILM ANYWAY. TWO YEARS LATER, DURING A ROUTINE PHYSICAL, HE DISCOVERED THAT HE HAD BROKEN HIS NECK.

THE RAILROAD BRIDGE'S COLLAPSE IN *THE GENERAL* (1927) IS THE MOST EXPENSIVE SCENE EVER SHOT FOR A SILENT FILM.

KEATON MARRIED HIS SECOND WIFE, A NURSE, IN AN ALCOHOLIC HAZE. IT WAS WEEKS BEFORE HE SOBERED UP ENOUGH TO REALIZE THEY WERE MARRIED.

RED SKELTON OFFERED TO WORK WITHOUT SALARY IF MGM WOULD GIVE HIM A FREE HAND TO DEVELOP FILMS WITH KEATON, BUT STUDIO EXECUTIVES TURNED THEM DOWN. INSTEAD, THEY CAST SKELTON IN WATERED-DOWN REMAKES OF SUCH KEATON CLASSICS AS *THE GENERAL* (*A SOUTHERN YANKEE*, 1948) AND *THE CAMERAMAN* (*WATCH THE BIRDIE*, 1950).

ONE MGM STAR WHO BENEFITED FROM KEATON'S PRESENCE ON THE LOT WAS LUCILLE BALL, WHO DEVELOPED A GREAT DEAL OF THE COMIC TECHNIQUE SHE WOULD USE IN *I LOVE LUCY* BY STUDYING WITH HIM.

KEATON'S WIDOW, ELEANOR, BURIED HIM WITH A ROSARY IN ONE POCKET AND A DECK OF CARDS IN THE OTHER. "THAT WAY," SHE SAID, "WHEREVER HE WAS GOING, HE WAS READY."

Umbrella and lamppost have never been the same since this love-struck hoofer splashed his way into the hearts of moviegoers in *Singin' in the Rain,* creating an iconic movie moment and proving that real guys *do* dance.

GENE
KELLY

Born
Eugene Curran Kelly
August 23, 1912,
Pittsburgh, Pennsylvania

Died
February 2, 1996
Beverly Hills, California,
of complications
from two strokes

Star Sign
Leo

Height
5'7"

Wives and Children
Actress Betsy Blair
(1941–1957, divorced)
daughter, Kerry

Dancer Jeanne Coyne
(1960–1973, her death)
son, Timothy
daughter, Bridget

Writer Patricia Ward
(1990–1996, his death)

Where other dancers performed in evening wear, Gene Kelly danced in a polo shirt and khakis. He was at home hoofing it with children and cartoon figures or stomping in rain puddles. Pioneering in the use of real locations and special effects in musical numbers and the use of dance to express character, he stretched the genre's boundaries. The combination of dance classes and youthful athletics contributed to Kelly's unique style. After performing in vaudeville and nightclubs with his brother Fred, he landed some roles on Broadway, most notably as a would-be dancer in *The Time of Your Life* and the dancing heel in Rodgers and Hart's *Pal Joey*. The latter brought him film offers, leading to a contract with producer David O. Selznick. With no musicals on his plate, however, Selznick sold the contract to MGM, where Kelly made his screen debut opposite Judy Garland in *For Me and My Gal* (1942). Working with Garland and producer Arthur Freed made him see the potential for dance on film, but he wouldn't get to explore it fully until MGM loaned him to Columbia to partner with Rita Hayworth in *Cover Girl* (1944). His "Alter Ego Ballet" in that film, in which special effects allowed him to dance with himself, was his first use of film technique to extend the language of dance. Kelly got to carry his ideas further and make his directing debut (with Stanley Donen as codirector) in *On the Town* (1949), the first musical with numbers shot on location. Then, in director Vincente Minnelli's *An American in Paris* (1951), he staged a seventeen-minute dream ballet that allowed him to play out his character's conflicts in dance. He followed with possibly the greatest movie musical ever, *Singin' in the Rain* (1952), an energetic spoof of the early days of talking pictures costarring Debbie Reynolds and Donald O'Connor. Sadly, it was his last hit. Later films were hampered by cost-cutting and other forms of studio interference. After leaving MGM, he created acclaimed TV specials and directed films, the most well known being *Hello, Dolly!* (1969). But when his second wife died, his desire to care for their children meant turning down jobs away from home, including the chance to direct *Cabaret* (1972). *That's Entertainment* (1974) and its two sequels (1976 and 1994) brought his earlier work renewed attention, and he won the American Film Institute's Life Achievement Award in 1985.

Essential
GENE KELLY Films

ACADEMY AWARDS
Nominated for Best Actor
Anchors Aweigh

Honorary Oscar in 1952
for his achievements in the art
of choreography on film

FOR ME AND MY GAL
(1942) MGM
In his film debut, Gene Kelly
won strong reviews as a dancer
who'll use anybody, including
wife Judy Garland and partner
George Murphy, to get ahead.

COVER GIRL
(1944) Columbia
Kelly's role as a nightclub dancer
who almost loses girlfriend
Rita Hayworth to the world of
high fashion gave him his first
opportunity to use dance and film
together to express character.

ON THE TOWN
(1949) MGM
Joining Frank Sinatra and Jules
Munshin as a trio of sailors looking
for love during a whirlwind twenty-
four-hour leave, Kelly sang and
danced amid such New York
landmarks as the Statue of Liberty
and Rockefeller Center, making his
directing debut with Stanley Donen.

AN AMERICAN IN PARIS
(1951) MGM
As a painter trying to build a career
in Paris, Kelly is torn between
gamin Leslie Caron (in her film
debut) and wealthy sponsor Nina
Foch, all under Vincente Minnelli's
sophisticated direction.

SINGIN' IN THE RAIN
(1952) MGM
Kelly and codirector Donen go back
to the days of all-talking, all-singing,
all-dancing movies for this tale of a
silent screen star (Kelly) struggling
to build a new career in musicals
with the help of girlfriend Debbie
Reynolds and the hindrance of
temperamental star Jean Hagen.

SINGIN' IN THE RAIN, 1952

ANCHORS AWEIGH, 1945

WITH DIRECTOR VINCENTE MINNELLI,
AN AMERICAN IN PARIS, 1951

BEHIND THE SCENES

KELLY'S DANCE WITH HIMSELF IN *COVER GIRL* (1944) WAS THE FIRST TIME ANYBODY HAD ATTEMPTED TO PAN AND DOLLY DURING A DOUBLE-EXPOSURE SHOT.

IN MOST OF HIS FILMS, KELLY DANCED IN A PAIR OF MOCCASINS BUILT LIKE DANCE SLIPPERS SO THEY WOULD BE MORE SUPPLE. WHEN HE SWITCHED TO ROLLER SKATES FOR A TAP DANCE IN *IT'S ALWAYS FAIR WEATHER* (1955), HE PICKED THEM UP IN THE LOCAL HARDWARE STORE AND DIDN'T USE ANY SPECIAL DEVICES TO KEEP THEM ON HIS FEET.

AFTER KELLY'S SUCCESS IN *COVER GIRL*, MGM EXECUTIVES DECIDED HE WAS TOO VALUABLE TO BE LOANED TO OTHER STUDIOS. THAT DECISION COST HIM LEADING ROLES IN *SUNSET BLVD.* (1950), *GUYS AND DOLLS* (1955), AND *PAL JOEY* (1957).

TO PROVE THAT HIS IDEA FOR A DANCE WITH CARTOON CHARACTERS IN *ANCHORS AWEIGH* (1945) WAS FEASIBLE, KELLY WORKED OUT THE LOGISTICS WITH WALT DISNEY. HE WANTED TO USE MICKEY MOUSE IN THE NUMBER, BUT DISNEY WOULDN'T EVEN CONSIDER THE IDEA, SO MGM'S JERRY THE MOUSE GOT THE ROLE INSTEAD.

KELLY AND DIRECTOR VINCENTE MINNELLI WANTED TO FILM *BRIGADOON* (1954) ON LOCATION IN THE SCOTTISH HIGHLANDS, BUT PRODUCER ARTHUR FREED DECIDED THE PRECARIOUS SCOTTISH WEATHER WOULD MAKE LOCATION SHOOTING TOO EXPENSIVE AND DECIDED TO SHOOT IT ON A STUDIO SOUNDSTAGE. MANY CRITICS COMPLAINED ABOUT THE FILM'S STUDIO-BOUND FEEL, AND IT TURNED OUT A BOX OFFICE DISAPPOINTMENT.

KELLY AND STANLEY DONEN WERE HOLLYWOOD'S ONLY SUCCESSFUL DIRECTING TEAM, UNTIL THEY MADE *IT'S ALWAYS FAIR WEATHER*. HAVING DIRECTED SOLO BY THIS POINT, DONEN WANTED MORE CONTROL OVER THE FILM, WHICH KELLY WAS LOATH TO RELINQUISH. NOR DID IT HELP THAT DONEN'S WIFE, DANCER JEANNE COYNE, HAD FALLEN IN LOVE WITH KELLY. DONEN AND KELLY DID NOT SPEAK FOR FORTY YEARS.

He emerged as one of the screen's iciest tough guys, a handsome blond whose stoic face made him as fit to play cold-blooded killers as noble heroes.

ALAN
LADD

Sometimes it takes one role to put a performer over, particularly if he or she does not fit the Hollywood mold. That's what happened to Alan Ladd. Told his blond good looks weren't right for the movies, he turned to radio before hitting the big time with a role in Paramount's *This Gun for Hire* (1942). The character, a professional assassin, was a perfect fit for Ladd, whose performance heralded the arrival of a new breed of screen gangster—handsome, well dressed, and totally self-possessed. For audiences, his impassive gaze masked untold depths, which apparently was the case offscreen as well. At four, Ladd had watched his father die of a heart attack. Years later, his mother committed suicide in front of him. An undernourished, undersized child, he had turned to track and swimming to prove his manliness, but his dreams of competing for the United States in the 1932 Olympics were dashed by an injury. By that time, he had another dream—acting. Radio work brought him to the attention of agent Sue Carol, who eventually married him, though Ladd was nine years her junior. A showy supporting role in the World War II film *Joan of Paris* (1942) won him a test for the lead in *This Gun for Hire,* and Paramount promoted him to stardom. Ladd starred in a variety of tough-guy roles, and he was best suited to film noir, particularly when teamed with Veronica Lake in *The Glass Key* (1942) and *The Blue Dahlia* (1946). The fact that he was one of Paramount's top money-making stars often worked against him, however. Knowing any film starring him would turn a profit, studio management rarely thought of him for more prestigious projects. He only got his most acclaimed role, in director George Stevens's western *Shane* (1953), because nobody expected it to do well. By the time *Shane* became a hit, Ladd had left for Warner Bros., where he was consigned to a series of threadbare action films. Things seemed to be turning around, however, when he accepted a supporting part as fading western star Nevada Smith in *The Carpetbaggers* (1964). Advance word indicated it was the performance of his career, and there was talk of his starring in a prequel. Before the film could be released, however, Ladd died. His role in *Nevada Smith* (1966) ended up going to his successor in onscreen coolness, Steve McQueen.

Born
Alan Walbridge Ladd
on September 3, 1913
Hot Springs, Arkansas

Died
January 29, 1964
Palm Springs, California,
of an alcohol and
sedative overdose

Star Sign
Virgo

Height
5'6"

Wives and Children
Student
Marjorie Jane Harrold
(1936–1941, divorced)
son, Alan Jr.

Actress turned agent
Sue Carol
(1942–1964, his death)
daughter, Alana
son, David

Essential
ALAN**LADD**Films

THIS GUN FOR HIRE
(1942) Paramount
In his breakthrough role, Ladd starred as a paid assassin caught in a moral dilemma when he discovers his latest employer (Laird Cregar) is a traitor to the war effort.

TWO YEARS BEFORE THE MAST
(1946) Paramount
Ladd held his own against a shipful of character actors (including Howard Da Silva and William Bendix) as a callow playboy who grows up fast when he's shanghaied to serve under a sadistic captain.

THE BLUE DAHLIA
(1946) Paramount
Raymond Chandler wrote this story of a veteran (Ladd) suspected of killing his unfaithful wife, with Lake as the woman who tries to help him clear his name.

SHANE
(1953) Paramount
In George Stevens's western classic, Ladd starred as a mysterious gunman trying to escape his violent past until he's forced to face off with sadistic killer Jack Palance.

THE CARPETBAGGERS
(1964) Paramount
Ladd's final film casts him as a western star (supposedly modeled on Tom Mix) caught up in the tangled relationships of a ruthless tycoon (George Peppard) and the blonde bombshell (Carroll Baker) he turns into a star.

THE BLUE DAHLIA, 1946

SHANE, 1953

BEHINDTHESCENES

ONE OF ALAN LADD'S MOST RECOGNIZABLE BIT PARTS WAS AS A REPORTER IN ORSON WELLES' *CITIZEN KANE* (1941). HE'S EASY TO SPOT SMOKING A PIPE IN THE FINAL SCENES SET AT XANADU.

DETECTIVE WRITER RAYMOND CHANDLER ONLY AGREED TO WRITE *THE BLUE DAHLIA* (1946) BECAUSE HE WAS BLOCKED ON THE NOVEL HE WAS WRITING. WHEN THEY HAD TO STEP UP FILMING TO FREE LADD IN TIME FOR MILITARY SERVICE, CHANDLER NEEDED A STAFF OF SIX SECRETARIES (AND A LOT OF BOOZE) TO FINISH THE SCRIPT.

THE MANAGEMENT AT PARAMOUNT HAD SO LITTLE FAITH IN *SHANE* (1953) THAT THEY KEPT IT ON THE SHELF FOR TWO YEARS AFTER ITS COMPLETION. AT ONE POINT THEY EVEN TRIED SELLING THE FINISHED FILM TO ANOTHER STUDIO. TO THEIR SURPRISE, THE PICTURE GROSSED $20 MILLION.

LADD AND JUNE ALLYSON FELL IN LOVE WHILE FILMING THE KOREAN WAR DRAMA *THE MCCONNELL STORY* (1955) BUT FINALLY DECIDED THEY COULD NOT LEAVE THEIR FAMILIES FOR EACH OTHER. HE CALLED HER A FEW HOURS BEFORE HIS DEATH.

LADD FOUGHT UNSUCCESSFULLY FOR THE TITLE ROLE IN *LAWRENCE OF ARABIA* (1962). IT ULTIMATELY WENT TO PETER O'TOOLE.

LADD FATHERED A HOLLYWOOD DYNASTY OF HIS OWN. HIS SON DAVID AND DAUGHTER ALANA BOTH ACTED AS CHILDREN, AND DAVID'S DAUGHTER WITH CHERYL LADD, JORDAN, IS CURRENTLY PURSUING AN ACTING CAREER. LADD'S SON FROM HIS FIRST MARRIAGE, ALAN JR., IS ONE OF THE MOST SUCCESSFUL EXECUTIVES IN THE FILM BUSINESS. DURING HIS TIME AS PRESIDENT OF 20TH CENTURY-FOX, HE WAS RESPONSIBLE FOR *STAR WARS* (1977) AND *ALIEN* (1979). HE WON A BEST PICTURE OSCAR FOR *BRAVEHEART* (1995).

THIS GUN FOR HIRE, 1942

Behind the glistening white smile and impressive physique, his magnetic tough guys possessed an unexpected sensitivity.

BURT
LANCASTER

Burt Lancaster himself said it best: "Most people seem to think I'm the kind of guy who shaves with a blowtorch. Actually, I'm bookish and worrisome." He was one of the most physical of Hollywood stars, a quality honed during his adolescent study of gymnastics and an early career in the circus. Until he had his first heart attack in 1980, he worked out daily. And the focus he brought to training his body carried into his acting, giving his work an impressive and sometimes frightening intensity. It was easy to believe that this man could win over the powerful characters played by Katharine Hepburn in *The Rainmaker* (1957) and Anna Magnani in *The Rose Tattoo* (1955). But there also was a brain behind the swagger, making him an action hero with a soul and, in later films like *The Leopard* (1963) and *Atlantic City* (1980), an aging tough guy reflecting on past glories. After an impressive screen debut as the doomed boxer in *The Killers* (1946), Lancaster built a solid career combining action films like *The Crimson Pirate* (1952) with serious dramas like *All My Sons* (1948) and *Come Back, Little Sheba* (1952). After an Oscar nomination for *From Here to Eternity* (1953), he seized control of his career, joining his agent, Harold Hecht, to create a production company responsible for many of his most ambitious films as well as the Oscar-winning *Marty* (1955). Lancaster was at a box-office peak in the early sixties, thanks to *Birdman of Alcatraz* (1962) and his Oscar-winning performance in *Elmer Gantry* (1960). But with his interest shifting to more mature roles, he stepped away from Hollywood to star in director Luchino Visconti's Italian epic *The Leopard*. Badly cut on its initial U.S. release, the film failed with critics and at the box office (it was much better received in a 1990 restored version), and his career never really recovered, despite such hits as *The Professionals* (1966) and *Airport* (1970). As he grew older, Lancaster realized he didn't have to get the girl to get a good picture and won some of his best reviews for *Atlantic City* (1980), in which he loved and lost Susan Sarandon. The 1980 heart attack slowed him down considerably, though he still won accolades for his performance in the Scottish comedy *Local Hero* (1983). He finished his career working opposite Sidney Poitier as a racist lawyer in *Separate but Equal* (1990).

Born
Burton Stephen Lancaster
November 2, 1913
New York, New York

Died
October 20, 1994
Century City, California,
of a heart attack

Star Sign
Scorpio

Height
6'2"

Wives and Children
Acrobat June Ernst
(1935–1946, divorced)

Stenographer Norma Anderson
(1946–1969, divorced)
son, William Henry
daughters, Susan Elizabeth,
Joanna, and Sighle
adopted son, James Stephen

Film coordinator
Susie Scherer
(1991–1994, his death)

Essential
BURTLANCASTERFilms

ACADEMY AWARDS
Won Best Actor
Elmer Gantry

Nominated for Best Actor
From Here to Eternity
Birdman of Alcatraz
Atlantic City

FROM HERE TO ETERNITY
(1953) Columbia
The surfside clinch between army sergeant Lancaster and his commanding officer's wife (Deborah Kerr) is one of the screen's most famous love scenes and only one of the highlights in this tense drama about Hawaiian life on the brink of World War II.

SWEET SMELL OF SUCCESS
(1957) United Artists
Lancaster turns his intensity to evil as a power-mad gossip columnist (modeled on Walter Winchell) who enlists venal press agent Tony Curtis to break up his sister's romance with a young musician.

ELMER GANTRY
(1960) United Artists
In an adaptation of Sinclair Lewis' controversial novel, Lancaster is a bogus fire-and-brimstone preacher whose past sins could destroy his newfound success.

BIRDMAN OF ALCATRAZ
(1962) United Artists
His intensity confined to a small prison cell, Lancaster offers a surprisingly thoughtful performance in the true story of a convicted murderer who rehabilitated himself through his study of bird life.

ATLANTIC CITY
(1980) Paramount
Lancaster had the role of a lifetime as an aging mob flunky obsessed with a romantic waitress (Susan Sarandon) against the backdrop of a city fighting to survive.

SWEET SMELL OF SUCCESS, 1957

FROM HERE TO ETERNITY, 1953

ELMER GANTRY, 1960

BEHINDTHESCENES

BURT LANCASTER WAS NICKNAMED "MOM" ON THE SET OF *FROM HERE TO ETERNITY* (1953) BECAUSE WHEN MONTGOMERY CLIFT AND FRANK SINATRA WERE OUT DRINKING ALL NIGHT, HE WAS THE ONE WHO GOT THEM SOBERED UP IN TIME FOR THEIR CALLS. FOR YEARS AFTERWARD, SINATRA SENT HIM A GREETING CARD ON MOTHER'S DAY.

ON MANY OF HIS FILMS, LANCASTER DEMANDED AN EXERCISE BAR BE PUT UP SO HE COULD USE IT IN HIS DAILY FITNESS REGIMEN.

LANCASTER WAS DUBBED THE INDUSTRY'S ALL-TIME "OSCAR BRIDESMAID" BECAUSE OF THE NUMBER OF PERFORMERS WHO WON THE AWARD WORKING WITH HIM, INCLUDING FRANK SINATRA AND DONNA REED IN *FROM HERE TO ETERNITY*, ANNA MAGNANI IN *THE ROSE TATTOO* (1955), MAXIMILIAN SCHELL IN *JUDGMENT AT NUREMBERG* (1961), AND HELEN HAYES IN *AIRPORT* (1970).

WHEN *ELMER GANTRY* (1960) CAME OUT, LANCASTER RECEIVED A LETTER FROM A CHILDHOOD FRIEND TELLING HIM THE TITLE ROLE WAS THE CLOSEST TO THE YOUNG LANCASTER OF ANY CHARACTER HE'D PLAYED.

A LIFELONG LIBERAL, LANCASTER'S CAMPAIGNING FOR GEORGE MCGOVERN'S 1972 PRESIDENTIAL BID EARNED HIM A PLACE ON RICHARD NIXON'S ENEMIES LIST.

LANCASTER'S SON BILL IS A SCREENWRITER AND BASED HIS SCRIPT FOR *THE BAD NEWS BEARS* (1976) ON HIS OWN YOUTHFUL EXPERIENCES BEING COACHED BY HIS FATHER IN LITTLE LEAGUE. THE ROLE PLAYED BY WALTER MATTHAU IS LOOSELY BASED ON LANCASTER.

LANCASTER WON HIS AWARD-WINNING ROLE IN *ATLANTIC CITY* (1980) BECAUSE FIRST CHOICE ROBERT MITCHUM HAD JUST HAD A FACE-LIFT AND LOOKED TOO YOUNG.

He could do zany or tragic with equal success, but he's best remembered for his comic, put-upon Everyman characters.

JACK
LEMMON

The best career advice Jack Lemmon ever got came from his father, a baker who told him, "The day I don't find romance in a loaf of bread, I'm going to quit." Fortunately for film fans, Lemmon found the romance in acting throughout a career that lasted over half a century.He never stopped taking chances. Established as a comic actor, he defied the naysayers to deliver a harrowing performance as an alcoholic in *Days of Wine and Roses* (1962). Rather than coast on variations of his most popular film characters, he took chances as the tragic nuclear-power-plant executive in *The China Syndrome* (1979), an American businessman searching for his son in revolution-torn Chile in *Missing* (1982), and a desperate businessman in *Glengarry Glen Ross* (1992). In later years, he even returned to Broadway, most notably for the demanding role of James Tyrone in Eugene O'Neill's *Long Day's Journey Into Night* (opposite Kevin Spacey, who would become a close friend).

To each project he brought an unfailingly positive energy that made him one of the industry's most beloved actors. Lemmon started his career on Broadway and in live television before signing with Columbia Pictures. He made his debut working with the best, starring opposite Judy Holliday for director George Cukor in *It Should Happen to You* (1954). A year later, he won his first Oscar, for *Mister Roberts* (1955). Lemmon started one of his most important working partnerships when director Billy Wilder cast him in *Some Like It Hot* (1959), followed by *The Apartment* (1960). Wilder would also pair Lemmon with his most popular costar, Walter Matthau, in *The Fortune Cookie* (1966). They would team for ten films in all, including such hits as *The Odd Couple* (1968) and *Grumpy Old Men* (1993). In addition, Matthau would play the title role in the only film Lemmon directed, *Kotch* (1971). To the end, Lemmon kept accepting roles, large and small, whenever a project interested him. He won an Emmy playing the acting teacher dying of Lou Gehrig's disease in *Tuesdays with Morrie* (1999) and made his last film appearance, as the uncredited narrator, in *The Legend of Bagger Vance* (2000) for the chance to work with director Robert Redford and make a film about golf. His father's last words were, "Spread a little sunshine." For the rest of Lemmon's life, one of his on-set mantras was, "I'm spreading a little sunshine through the day," something he always managed to do.

Born
John Uhler Lemmon III
February 8, 1925
Newton, Massachusetts

Died
June 27, 2001
Los Angeles, California,
of cancer

Star Sign
Aquarius

Height
5'9"

Wives and Children
Actress Cynthia Stone
(1950–1956, divorced)
son, Christopher

Actress Felicia Farr
(1962-2001, his death)
daughter, Courtney

Essential
JACKLEMMONFilms

IT SHOULD HAPPEN TO YOU

(1954) Columbia
In his film debut, Jack Lemmon plays a documentary filmmaker in love with a fame-hungry woman (Judy Holliday) who rents a billboard just to see her name on it.

SOME LIKE IT HOT

(1959) United Artists
Roaring Twenties musicians Lemmon and Tony Curtis go on the lam disguised as women but have trouble keeping up their masquerade when they meet beautiful singer Marilyn Monroe in director Billy Wilder's film, named the funniest movie of all time in an American Film Institute poll.

THE APARTMENT

(1960) United Artists
In his first Everyman role and his second film with Wilder, Lemmon stars as an ambitious businessman out to advance his career by loaning his apartment to the higher-ups for their affairs, until the boss leaves behind rejected girlfriend Shirley MacLaine.

THE ODD COUPLE

(1968) Paramount
Working for the second time with frequent costar and close friend Walter Matthau, Lemmon played Felix, the ultimate neatnik, in this adaptation of Neil Simon's stage classic that inspired the hit television series.

GLENGARRY GLEN ROSS

(1992) New Line
For this adaptation of David Mamet's Pulitzer Prize—winning play, Lemmon joins an impressive all-star cast—including Al Pacino, Kevin Spacey, Ed Harris, Alan Arkin, and Alec Baldwin—as a desperate real estate salesman fighting to keep his job.

THE APARTMENT, 1960

THE ODD COUPLE, 1968

SOME LIKE IT HOT, 1959

BEHIND THE SCENES

BEFORE THE START OF EVERY SCENE HE PLAYED ON CAMERA, LEMMON WOULD SAY, "IT'S MAGIC TIME."

IN *SOME LIKE IT HOT* (1959), LEMMON PLAYS WITH MARACAS WHILE ANNOUNCING HIS ENGAGEMENT TO OSGOOD FIELDING III (JOE E. BROWN) BECAUSE IN PREVIEWS, THE SCENE—ORIGINALLY SHOT WITHOUT THE INSTRUMENTS—HAD GENERATED SO MUCH LAUGHTER, THE AUDIENCE MISSED MOST OF THE LINES. THE SCENE WAS RESHOT WITH THE ADDED BUSINESS TO ALLOW PAUSES IN DIALOGUE FOR LAUGHS.

IN OVER SEVENTY MOVIES, LEMMON ONLY PLAYED ONE DEATH SCENE—IN *THE CHINA SYNDROME* (1979).

WHEN VING RHAMES WON A GOLDEN GLOBE FOR *DON KING: ONLY IN AMERICA* (1997), HE WAS SO CONVINCED IT SHOULD HAVE GONE TO LEMMON FOR *12 ANGRY MEN* (1997), HE CALLED HIM TO THE PODIUM AND TRIED TO GIVE IT TO HIM. WHEN LEMMON WON THE AWARD FOR *TUESDAYS WITH MORRIE* (1999), HE QUIPPED, "IN THE SPIRIT OF VING RHAMES, I'M GOING TO GIVE THIS AWARD TO JACK LEMMON."

He was a master of physical comedy, throwing his milquetoast, bespectacled characters into ever more dangerous situations in pursuit of love and laughs.

HAROLD
LLOYD

Harold Lloyd discovered the key to his personal brand of comedy while walking to the studio one morning. He was amazed to see a crowd of onlookers focusing their attention on a man scaling the side of a building. That was the seed for the creation of his "thrill comedies," in which he scaled buildings (*Safety Last!*, 1923) or raced to the rescue on the top of a speeding bus (*Girl Shy*, 1924). His comic daredevil act made him the best paid of all silent-comedy stars. Lloyd had started acting at age twelve, when he joined a stock company in Omaha. Moving to San Diego, he started doing extra work in the movies, where he befriended fellow extra Hal Roach. When Roach founded his own film studio, he made the twenty-year-old his star. At first, Lloyd was a pale imitation of Charles Chaplin's Little Tramp, playing a mischievous character named Lonesome Luke. But the star didn't want to be a second-best anything. Over Roach's objections, he created a character he dubbed "Glasses," an enterprising but timid young man in oversize horn-rim glasses whose job or love life gets him into ever more dangerous scrapes. On his first appearance in 1917, "Glasses" was a hit. Lloyd took the character into features for 1921's *A Sailor-Made Man*, a hit that led to a string of classics, including *Safety Last!* and *The Freshman* (1925). Lloyd resisted the coming of sound, convinced he wouldn't be as funny with dialogue, and he turned out to be right. From his first sound film, 1929's *Welcome Danger*, his box office draw went into a decline. Dissatisfied, he tried changing the formula, but even films he thought worked, like *Movie Crazy* (1932) and *The Milky Way* (1936), were box office duds. He cut back to one film every two years, then simply drifted away from filmmaking. An attempted comeback to work with director Preston Sturges on *The Sin of Harold Diddlebock* (1947) was another disappointment, particularly when producer Howard Hughes cut the film almost beyond recognition. Because of his early retirement, conservative lifestyle, and wealth, Lloyd didn't generate headlines like his contemporaries and was largely forgotten until he released *Harold Lloyd's World of Comedy* (1962), a compilation of some of his funniest work. Since he retained full ownership of most of his films, his family has carefully managed their release on home video, building a new generation of fans.

Born
Harold Clayton Lloyd
April 20, 1893
Burchard, Nebraska

Died
March 8, 1971
Beverly Hills, California,
of prostate cancer

Star Sign
Aries

Height
5'10"

Wife and Children
Actress Mildred Davis
(1923–1969, her death)
daughter, Mildred Gloria
son, Harold Clayton Jr.
adopted daughter,
Marjorie Elizabeth "Peggy"

Essential
HAROLD LLOYD Films

ACADEMY AWARDS
Honorary Oscar in 1953
to a "master comedian
and good citizen"

GRANDMA'S BOY
(1922) Hal Roach
When his grandmother gives him a magic amulet, a timid young man (Harold Lloyd) takes on one dangerous challenge after another. Originally intended as a serious drama, Lloyd and his writers went back into production to add more gags and to turn it into a comedy when test audiences kept laughing at the film's early preview.

SAFETY LAST!
(1923) Pathé
The image of Lloyd hanging from the hands of a giant clock is one of the most famous in film history; it's all part of his scheme to convince the girl he loves that he runs the department store where he works as a clerk.

THE FRESHMAN
(1925) Pathé
Lloyd's misguided efforts to win popularity in college include attending a party in a suit that starts falling apart and playing in a slapstick football game.

THE KID BROTHER
(1927) Paramount
In his favorite film, Lloyd is a small-town sheriff's cowardly son who sets out to clear his father's name (and win the girl) after a robbery.

SPEEDY
(1928) Paramount
As a young taxi driver, Lloyd gives a ride to baseball great Babe Ruth, then leads a campaign to save the local streetcar line for his girlfriend's father in a film shot on location in Manhattan and Coney Island.

SPEEDY, 1928

SAFETY LAST!, 1923

PHOTOGRAPHING A MODEL, 1955

BEHINDTHESCENES

A 1919 ACCIDENT WITH A PROP BOMB THAT TURNED OUT TO BE THE REAL THING COST HAROLD LLOYD THE THUMB AND FOREFINGER ON HIS RIGHT HAND. HE DID HIS MOST DANGEROUS STUNTS WITH ONLY SEVEN FINGERS AND ONE THUMB (HIDING HIS HAND WITH A GLOVE AND PROSTHETIC).

LLOYD'S FAMOUS SCENE CLIMBING THE CLOCK TOWER IN *SAFETY LAST!* (1923) WAS SHOT ON A FAKE BUILDING ERECTED ON THE ROOF OF A SKYSCRAPER, WITH A MATTRESS ON THE ROOF TO SERVE AS A SAFETY NET. THAT DIDN'T MAKE IT ANY SAFER. TO TEST THE SCENE, LLOYD HAD A DUMMY DROPPED FROM THE CLOCK FACE TO THE MATTRESS, WHERE IT BOUNCED OFF BEFORE PLUMMETING TO THE STREET BELOW.

FOR MOST OF HIS SILENT FILMS, LLOYD HAD THREE LEADING LADIES. HE STARTED WITH BEBE DANIELS IN 1916, BUT SHE LEFT HIM THREE YEARS LATER TO STAR FOR CECIL B. DEMILLE. HE LIKED HIS SECOND LEADING LADY, MILDRED DAVIS, SO MUCH HE MARRIED HER. JOINING HIM IN 1924'S *GIRL SHY!* WAS JOBYNA RALSTON, WHO WOULD REMAIN HIS COSTAR THROUGH 1927'S *KID BROTHER*.

AN INNOVATOR IN FILM TECHNOLOGY, LLOYD PARTICIPATED IN THE FIRST EXPERIMENTS WITH TWO-COLOR TECHNICOLOR, WITH TEST FOOTAGE SHOT AT GREEN ACRES, HIS BEVERLY HILLS ESTATE.

LLOYD EXPERIMENTED WITH 3-D PHOTOGRAPHY, SHOOTING BOTH LANDSCAPES AND EROTIC PHOTOS OF STARLETS.

With a successful career on both stage and screen, he ventured far beyond his successful romantic roles to tackle an extraordinary range of challenging, often anguished characters with sublime craftsmanship and nuance.

FREDRIC
MARCH

Fredric March is one of those rare actors whose career bridged the glamorous days of the Hollywood studios and the world of independent productions grounded in gritty realism. From callow youth to swashbuckling hero to drawing room comedian to grizzled old man, he could play anything with such a complete conviction that audiences never saw the actor behind the character. At an early age, March could mimic passersby on the street. He also was acting in school plays through most of his student years, but to please his family he went for a career in banking until a sudden illness almost killed him, convincing him to pursue his dream of acting. After smaller roles on Broadway, he landed in a touring production of *The Royal Family,* playing a takeoff of stage legend John Barrymore so well, even Barrymore liked it. When the production hit Los Angeles in 1928, it won him a contract with Paramount, though at first he seemed typecast as a young Barrymore. Not only did he re-create his stage role in *The Royal Family of Broadway* (1930), but he also took on one of Barrymore's most famous roles in *Dr. Jekyll and Mr. Hyde* (1932). When those films made him a star, March went freelance and never signed another long-term contract. He would still accept Barrymore-style roles like alcoholic has-been Norman Maine in *A Star Is Born* (1937) if the script was good, but he also stretched to play the fast-talking newspaper reporter in *Nothing Sacred* (1938) and the legendary author in *The Adventures of Mark Twain* (1944). By the late thirties, March was one of the highest-paid people in the United States, but, rather than capitalize on his screen successes, he took off for Broadway. For the rest of his career, he alternated stage work in such classics as Thornton Wilder's *The Skin of Our Teeth* and Eugene O'Neill's *Long Day's Journey Into Night* with screen appearances. After a two-year absence from films, he played a returning veteran in *The Best Years of Our Lives* (1946), scoring another Oscar. By now, he was moving into character roles, with an acclaimed performance as Willie Loman in the film version of Arthur Miller's *Death of a Salesman* (1951) and a fiery re-creation of the Scopes Monkey Trial, opposite Spencer Tracy, in *Inherit the Wind* (1959). March ended his distinguished film career with another classic, playing optimistic bar owner Harry Hope in O'Neill's *The Iceman Cometh* (1973).

Born
Ernest Frederick McIntyre Bickel
August 31, 1897
Racine, Wisconsin

Died
April 14, 1975
Los Angeles, California,
of prostate cancer

Star Sign
Virgo

Height
5'10"

Wives and Children
Actress Ellis Baker
(1924–1927, divorced)

Actress Florence Eldridge
(1927–1975, his death)
adopted daughter, Penelope
adopted son, Anthony

Essential
FREDRICMARCHFilms

DR. JEKYLL AND MR. HYDE

(1932) Paramount
In one of the sexiest renderings of Robert Louis Stevenson's classic tale of the conflict between good and evil, Fredric March starred as the doctor who unleashes his own immorality.

A STAR IS BORN

(1937) United Artists
William Wellman wrote and directed the original version of the classic Hollywood exposé, with March as fading star Norman Maine and Janet Gaynor (ironically, she was the one making the comeback) as the innocent he turns into a star.

THE BEST YEARS OF OUR LIVES

(1946) RKO
With Dana Andrews and real-life amputee Harold Russell, March captured the spirit of the postwar generation in this tale of veterans trying to readjust to civilian life, with March trying to reconnect with a family (including wife Myrna Loy and daughter Teresa Wright) that's grown up while he was away.

DEATH OF A SALESMAN

(1951) Columbia Pictures
March took on one of the great characters in American drama, Willie Loman, for this tale of an aging salesman reliving past failures while trying to cope with an uncertain future.

INHERIT THE WIND

(1960) United Artists
In a role modeled on famed orator William Jennings Bryan, March locks horns with Spencer Tracy in a still timely tale of the conflict over teaching evolution.

A STAR IS BORN, 1937

NOTHING SACRED, 1937

BEHIND THE SCENES

AFTER CHANGING HIS NAME FROM ERNEST BICKEL TO FREDRIC MARCH, HE SENT A NOTE TO THEATRICAL AGENTS ON NEW YEAR'S DAY OF 1924 ANNOUNCING, "THIS IS 1924, I WON'T BE BICKEL ANYMORE. FREDRIC MARCH IS NOW MY NAME, WISHING EVERYONE THE SAME. HAPPY NEW YEAR!"

DIRECTOR ROUBEN MAMOULIAN FOUGHT TO CAST MARCH IN *DR. JEKYLL AND MR. HYDE* (1931), OVER OBJECTIONS THAT MARCH WAS TOO LIGHTWEIGHT FOR THE ROLE, BECAUSE HE CONSIDERED MARCH THE ONLY ACTOR AT PARAMOUNT WHO COULD DO JUSTICE TO BOTH CHARACTERS.

MARCH WON HIS FIRST OSCAR IN A RARE TIE (WITH WALLACE BEERY FOR *THE CHAMP*, 1931). NOTING THAT THEY HAD BOTH ADOPTED CHILDREN RECENTLY, HE QUIPPED, "IT SEEMS A LITTLE ODD THAT WE WERE BOTH GIVEN AWARDS FOR THE BEST MALE PERFORMANCE OF THE YEAR."

THE FAMOUS SCENE IN *NOTHING SACRED* (1937), IN WHICH MARCH PLAYS A REPORTER WHO EXCHANGES SLUGS WITH CAROLE LOMBARD, RESULTED IN BOTH STARS ENDING UP AT THE LOCAL HOSPITAL WITH CUTS AND BRUISES.

A LIFELONG LIBERAL, MARCH ALMOST LOST THE CHANCE TO STAR IN *THE BEST YEARS OF OUR LIVES* (1946) BECAUSE OF SUSPICIONS THAT HE WAS A COMMUNIST. WHEN HE AND ELDRIDGE WERE LISTED AS COMMUNISTS IN THE MAGAZINE *COUNTER-ATTACK*, THEY SUED FOR LIBEL AND WON.

ONE OF THE BIGGEST MISTAKES OF MARCH'S CAREER WAS TURNING DOWN THE LEADING ROLE IN THE ORIGINAL BROADWAY RUN OF ARTHUR MILLER'S *DEATH OF A SALESMAN.* HE MADE UP FOR IT BY AGREEING TO STAR IN THE FILM VERSION.

DR. JEKYLL AND MR. HYDE, 1932

He was an uncomplicated good guy whose lack of pretense and wholesome good looks embodied an ideal of American innocence and frontier spirit.

JOEL
MCCREA

Born
Joel Albert McCrea
November 5, 1905
South Pasadena, California

Died
October 20, 1990
Woodland Hills, California,
of pulmonary complications

Star Sign
Scorpio

Height
6'3"

Wife and Children
Actress Frances Dee
(1933–1990, his death)
sons, Joel Dee,
David, and Peter

The image of the good-hearted westerner came naturally to Joel McCrea. His paternal grandfather was a stagecoach driver, and the California native started raising horses at an early age. While he was still in school, he found work as a horse wrangler on silent serials and later did extra work after studying at the Pasadena Playhouse. When he moved into leading roles at RKO Pictures, the studio first tried to market him as a sex symbol, frequently stripping him to the waist in films like *Bird of Paradise,* with Dolores Del Rio, and *The Most Dangerous Game* (both 1932). His leading ladies saw him in the same vein: Del Rio kept inviting him over for back rubs, and Constance Bennett wanted to marry him. But McCrea wanted a less complicated life. When he fell in love with Frances Dee while filming *The Silver Cord* (1933), their fifty-seven-year marriage would become a Hollywood rarity. Even that didn't hold his leading ladies at bay, however. During the filming of *Barbary Coast* (1935), Miriam Hopkins hoped to steal him for herself, which may have added some extra sizzle to their love scenes. But then, everyone seemed to love Joel McCrea. After directing him in *The Lost Squadron* (1932), Gregory La Cava took a liking to him and tailored a role as a mental patient in *Private Worlds* (1935) to fit his strengths, which led to a contract with independent producer Samuel Goldwyn. High-profile Goldwyn films like *Barbary Coast* and *Dead End* (1937) made him a bigger star. When Gary Cooper turned down director Alfred Hitchcock's *Foreign Correspondent* (1940), the film helped cement McCrea's status as an all-American hero. Moving to Paramount, he forged a strong working relationship with writer-director Preston Sturges, who displayed McCrea's comic talents in *Sullivan's Travels* (1941) and *The Palm Beach Story* (1942). With the success of *The More the Merrier* (1943), he could write his own ticket, and he moved into his favorite genre, the western, for the rest of his career. After retiring from the screen in 1959, McCrea came back for director Sam Peckinpah's *Ride the High Country* (1962), costarring another western legend, Randolph Scott. After that, he made only sporadic screen appearances. Wise investments in oil, livestock, and real estate made him one of the screen's wealthiest actors and freed him to pursue the two careers he considered most important—family man and gentleman rancher.

Essential
JOELMCCREAFilms

FOREIGN CORRESPONDENT
(1940) United Artists
Joel McCrea scored a hit in this Alfred Hitchcock picture, as the innocent abroad, a U.S. reporter thrust into international intrigue while covering Europe on the brink of war.

SULLIVAN'S TRAVELS
(1941) Paramount
In the film often hailed as writer-director Preston Sturges's best, McCrea starred as a comedy director who lives a hobo's life to research poverty for his first serious picture.

THE PALM BEACH STORY
(1942) Paramount
McCrea was the eye of a screwball storm in his second film for Sturges, a fast-paced comedy of mismatched couples as he and estranged wife Claudette Colbert romance an eccentric and very wealthy brother and sister (Rudy Vallee and Mary Astor).

THE MORE THE MERRIER
(1943) Columbia
The wartime housing shortage in Washington, D.C., inspired this romantic comedy about a woman (Jean Arthur) caught in a compromising situation when she rents part of her apartment to an elderly man (Charles Coburn), who takes in McCrea as a third roommate and then plays Cupid for the younger pair.

RIDE THE HIGH COUNTRY
(1962) MGM
McCrea and Randolph Scott made film history in Sam Peckinpah's trail-blazing western about old friends who clash while escorting a gold shipment through treacherous country.

THE PALM BEACH STORY, 1942

WITH VERONICA LAKE ON THE SET OF *SULLIVAN'S TRAVELS*, 1941

CIRCA 1940s

BEHINDTHESCENES

ONE OF JOEL MCCREA'S MOST IMPORTANT HOLLYWOOD FRIENDSHIPS WAS WITH WILL ROGERS. NOT ONLY DID ROGERS HELP HIM LAND A ROLE IN HIS OWN FILM *LIGHTNIN'* (1930), HE TOLD THE YOUNG MAN, "SAVE HALF OF WHAT YOU MAKE, AND LIVE ON JUST THE OTHER HALF." FOLLOWING ROGERS'S ADVICE, MCCREA BECAME ONE OF THE WEALTHIEST MEN IN HOLLYWOOD.

WHEN HE FINISHED WORK ON *SULLIVAN'S TRAVELS* (1941), MCCREA PRESENTED DIRECTOR-WRITER PRESTON STURGES WITH A WATCH ENGRAVED, "FOR THE FINEST DIRECTION I'VE EVER HAD." THEY WOULD WORK TOGETHER ON TWO MORE FILMS, *THE PALM BEACH STORY* (1942) AND *THE GREAT MOMENT* (1944).

WHEN MCCREA TURNED DOWN THE LEAD IN *KING KONG* (1933), ARGUING THAT THE ACTORS WOULD TAKE A BACK SEAT TO THE SPECIAL EFFECTS, HE HELPED THE PRODUCERS CAST HIS ROLE WHEN HE SUGGESTED BRUCE CABOT, THEN THE DOORMAN AT A POPULAR HOLLYWOOD NIGHT SPOT, TO INTERVIEW FOR THE FILM.

ONE REASON THAT HOLLYWOOD'S BIGGEST DIVAS LOVED WORKING WITH MCCREA WAS HIS HEIGHT. WHENEVER THEY PLAYED A SCENE WITH HIM, THEY HAD TO LOOK UP, WHICH WIPED AWAY LITTLE THINGS LIKE DOUBLE CHINS AND OTHER SIGNS OF AGING THAT MAKEUP COULDN'T ALWAYS HIDE.

Speed was a way of life for the king of cool, who answered to nobody in roles marked by fierce independence and raw intensity.

STEVE
MCQUEEN

Steve McQueen turned blue eyes, a killer smile, and a ton of attitude into his ticket to stardom, creating a new breed of big-screen rebel, perfect for the swinging sixties. Like predecessors Humphrey Bogart and Robert Mitchum, he lived by his own code. Like Gary Cooper and Alan Ladd, he practiced a minimalist approach to acting that barely registered. The Nazis could send him back to the POW camp, the mob could kill all his witnesses, the towering inferno could blaze out of control—but it didn't matter as long as he had a job to do. The ride wasn't always easy for McQueen, who came from a broken home and might have gone into a life of crime had not eighteen months in a juvenile detention facility scared him straight. After a variety of odd jobs, he started studying acting in New York, where small theater roles led to an unbilled film debut in *Somebody up There Likes Me* (1956), starring Paul Newman. His first starring role was as the troubled teen who defeats *The Blob* (1958). He got some much needed exposure from a two-year run on the TV western *Wanted: Dead or Alive,* but McQueen's big break came when a short-lived feud between Frank Sinatra and Sammy Davis Jr. cost the latter a role in *Never So Few* (1959). McQueen took Davis's place, making a good impression on director John Sturges, who cast him in two star-making pictures, *The Magnificent Seven* (1960) and *The Great Escape* (1963). His onscreen stock continued to rise with popular roles as a crusading cop in *Bullitt,* a sexy bank thief in *The Thomas Crown Affair* (both 1968), and a heroic fire chief in *The Towering Inferno* (1974). He also took time for more dramatic fare, winning an Oscar nomination for *The Sand Pebbles* (1966) and teaming with Dustin Hoffman for the prison story *Papillon* (1973). McQueen was big enough to survive the scandal when he stole Ali MacGraw, his costar in *The Getaway* (1972), from her husband, Paramount head Robert Evans, whose studio was producing the film. Then he took a four-year break from filmmaking, returning for the personal project *An Enemy of the People* (1978), almost unrecognizable behind a heavy beard. He finished his career with two more action films, *Tom Horn* and *The Hunter* (both 1980), before dying of cancer later that year.

Born
Terence Steven McQueen
March 24, 1930
Beech Grove, Indiana

Died
November 7, 1980
Juarez, Mexico,
of lung cancer

Star Sign
Aries

Height
5'9"

Wives and Children
Singer-actress Neile Adams
(1956–1971, divorced)
daughter, Terri Leslie
son, Chadwick Stephen

Actress Ali MacGraw
(1973–1978, divorced)

Model Barbara Minty
(1980, his death)

Essential
STEVEMCQUEENFilms

THE MAGNIFICENT SEVEN

(1960) United Artists
In this western remake of the classic Japanese film *Seven Samurai* (1955), Steve McQueen shot to stardom as the most sardonic of a group of gunfighters hired to defend a Mexican village from marauding bandits.

THE GREAT ESCAPE

(1963) United Artists
McQueen was part of a group of POWs who staged a daredevil breakout from a supposedly escape-proof prison camp in a film inspired by real events during World War II.

THE THOMAS CROWN AFFAIR

(1968) United Artists
In his favorite film, McQueen was a slick millionaire who seduces insurance investigator Faye Dunaway to cover up his involvement in a bank robbery.

BULLITT

(1968) Warner Bros.
McQueen led a breakneck car chase through San Francisco as a cop who defies his superiors to find out who killed his partner and the witness they were guarding.

PAPILLON

(1973) Allied Artists
McQueen escapes again (and again) as a legendary criminal who devoted his life to breaking out of an island prison camp in French Guyana, with Dustin Hoffman as his accomplice.

ALI MACGRAW AND STEVE MCQUEEN DURING FILMING OF *PAPILLON*, 1973.

BULLITT, 1968

BEHIND THE SCENES

INITIALLY, MCQUEEN'S SHOOTING SCHEDULE FOR *WANTED: DEAD OR ALIVE* KEPT HIM OUT OF *THE MAGNIFICENT SEVEN* (1960). HE DELIBERATELY CRASHED HIS CAR AND DID HIS SCENES FOR THE FILM WHILE PRODUCTION ON THE TV SERIES WAS SUSPENDED WHILE HE "RECOVERED."

MCQUEEN DID ALL HIS MOTORCYCLE STUNTS FOR *THE GREAT ESCAPE* (1963) EXCEPT THE SIXTY-FOOT JUMP OVER THE FENCE. HE ALSO STOOD IN FOR ONE OF HIS NAZI PURSUERS, GETTING THE RARE CHANCE TO CHASE HIMSELF ON SCREEN.

INFIDELITY INDIRECTLY SAVED MCQUEEN'S LIFE. BECAUSE OF A ROMANTIC ASSIGNATION, HE PASSED ON A DINNER INVITATION FROM SHARON TATE THE NIGHT HER HOUSE WAS INVADED BY MEMBERS OF THE MANSON FAMILY. WHEN THE STORY BROKE, MCQUEEN STARTED CARRYING A GUN.

A PASSIONATE AUTO RACER, MCQUEEN COMPETED FOR TEAM USA IN THE INTERNATIONAL SIX DAY TRIALS IN EAST GERMANY AND PATENTED A RACING-CAR SEAT.

ALTHOUGH HE WAS A HEAVY SMOKER, MCQUEEN'S LUNG CANCER WAS NOT THE TYPE NORMALLY ASSOCIATED WITH THAT HABIT. IT WAS A VARIETY USUALLY CAUSED BY ASBESTOS EXPOSURE, PROBABLY FROM THE ASBESTOS-INSULATED SUITS HE WORE WHEN RACING.

TWO PROJECTS MCQUEEN WAS PLANNING WHEN HE DIED: *FIRST BLOOD* (1982), WHICH WENT TO SYLVESTER STALLONE, AND *THE BODYGUARD* (1992), EVENTUALLY FILMED WITH KEVIN COSTNER. THE LATTER WOULD HAVE COSTARRED MCQUEEN WITH DIANA ROSS, BUT THE INTERRACIAL ROMANCE WAS CONSIDERED TOO CONTROVERSIAL DURING HIS LIFETIME.

He made blasé sexy with his take-it-or-leave-it insolence and sleepy eyes while his offscreen antics added to his image as a tough guy rebel.

ROBERT
MITCHUM

Robert Mitchum couldn't have become a star had he been working in Hollywood at any time except the post—World War II era. Neither conventionally handsome nor a convincing proponent of family values, he started his career with villainous roles, including a convincing psycho in the low-budget classic *When Strangers Marry* (1944). But when audiences began to tire of Hollywood homilies, paving the way for the vicious world of film noir, his laid-back, deceptively effortless acting made him the perfect hero for a new era. His pre-Hollywood life could have been a film noir. After losing his father when he was a toddler, Mitchum took to the road at sixteen, riding the rails, boxing, and even doing time on a Georgia chain gang. He was working at Lockheed Aircraft in California when his sister got him involved with a local theater group. That led to unbilled movie roles in parts so small he managed to make eighteen films in 1943. He signed with RKO to star in westerns, but a loan-out for *The Story of G.I. Joe* (1945), which brought him his only Oscar nomination, convinced the studio to put him into bigger roles. With the growing popularity of film noir, Mitchum shot to stardom as a sardonic soldier in *Crossfire* (1947) and defined the genre in the film noir *Out of the Past* (1947). Then he was arrested for smoking marijuana. The scandal would have destroyed any other career, but it just enhanced Mitchum's antisocial image. Leaving the studio in 1954, Mitchum scored personal triumphs as a psychotic preacher in *The Night of the Hunter* (1955) and a marine stranded with a nun (Deborah Kerr) in *Heaven Knows, Mr. Allison* (1957). Mitchum upheld his image by dismissing his own acting in interviews, obscuring the hard work behind his best performances to the extent that even impressive characterizations like his Australian sheepherder in *The Sundowners* (1960) and the vengeance-crazed ex-con in *Cape Fear* (1962) were ignored by Oscar voters. Not one to let age slow him down, Mitchum scored a surprise hit as an aging, philosophical Philip Marlowe in *Farewell, My Lovely* (1975) and helped drive ratings in the miniseries *The Winds of War* (1983) and its sequel, *War and Remembrance* (1988). Even as his health was failing, Mitchum continued to work, playing an aging gunman opposite Johnny Depp in director Jim Jarmusch's *Dead Man* (1995).

Born
Robert Charles Durman Mitchum
August 6, 1917
Bridgeport, Connecticut

Died
July 1, 1997
Santa Barbara, California,
of lung cancer and emphysema

Star Sign
Leo

Height
6'1½"

Wife and Children
Student Dorothy Spencer
(1940–1997, his death)
sons, James and Christopher
daughter, Petrine

Essential
ROBERT**MITCHUM**Films

ACADEMY AWARDS
Nominated for
Best Supporting Actor
The Story of G.I. Joe

OUT OF THE PAST
(1947) RKO
Mitchum starred as a private eye mixed up with ruthless gang boss Kirk Douglas and his seductive, murderous moll (Jane Greer) in a film noir classic.

THE NIGHT OF THE HUNTER
(1955) United Artists
Mitchum took a stab at villainy in this American gothic tale of a murderous preacher after the widow (Shelley Winters) and children of a deceased bank robber, the only directing effort for actor Charles Laughton.

HEAVEN KNOWS, MR. ALLISON
(1957) 20th Century–Fox
John Huston directed Mitchum and Deborah Kerr as a marine and a nun fighting their attraction while marooned on a Pacific island during World War II.

THE SUNDOWNERS
(1960) Warner Bros.
Mitchum went Down Under with costars Deborah Kerr and Peter Ustinov and director Fred Zinnermann for this tale of a migrant sheepherder who risks his savings to buy his wife a home.

CAPE FEAR
(1962) Universal-International
Blaming lawyer Gregory Peck for sending him to prison, sadistic ex-con Mitchum terrorizes the man and his family in a suspense classic remade by Martin Scorsese in 1991 with Robert De Niro in Mitchum's role.

OUT OF THE PAST, 1947

THE NIGHT OF THE HUNTER, 1955

BEHIND THE SCENES

AN ACCOMPLISHED WRITER BEFORE HE GOT INTO ACTING, MITCHUM OFTEN CONTRIBUTED NEW MATERIAL TO HIS FILM'S SCRIPTS. WHEN NICHOLAS RAY TOOK OVER DIRECTION OF *MACAO* (1952), WITH JANE RUSSELL, MITCHUM WROTE ALL THE SCENES THEY RESHOT.

MITCHUM DIRECTED THE CHILD ACTORS IN *THE NIGHT OF THE HUNTER* (1955), BECAUSE DIRECTOR CHARLES LAUGHTON DIDN'T LIKE CHILDREN.

THE NIGHT OF THE HUNTER WAS A FLOP ON ITS INITIAL U.S. RELEASE BUT A HUGE HIT IN EUROPE, GRADUALLY BUILDING UP A CULT FOLLOWING IN THE STATES AS WELL. FILMMAKERS HAVE COPIED MITCHUM'S TATTOOED KNUCKLES, READING "LOVE" AND "HATE," IN EVERYTHING FROM SPIKE LEE'S *DO THE RIGHT THING* (1989) TO AN EPISODE OF *THE SIMPSONS*.

FOR ONE SCENE IN *HEAVEN KNOWS, MR. ALLISON* (1957), MITCHUM HAD TO CRAWL REPEATEDLY OVER SHARP CORAL. WHEN DIRECTOR JOHN HUSTON WAS SHOCKED AT HOW BADLY CUT UP HIS LEGS WERE, MITCHUM SIMPLY SAID, "YOU WORK, YOU SUFFER."

ALTHOUGH HE RARELY SANG IN HIS FILMS, MITCHUM RECORDED SEVERAL SONGS, INCLUDING THE FOLK-INSPIRED NUMBERS HE PERFORMED IN *RACHEL AND THE STRANGER* (1948), AN ALBUM OF CALYPSO NUMBERS INSPIRED BY HIS WORK ON THE CARIBBEAN LOCATION OF *FIRE DOWN BELOW* (1957), AND "THE BALLAD OF THUNDER ROAD," THE THEME FROM HIS 1958 FILM *THUNDER ROAD*. THE LATTER WAS ACTUALLY A BIG HIT.

WHILE MITCHUM WAS IN JAPAN FILMING *THE YAKUZA* (1975), SOME REAL-LIFE JAPANESE GANGSTERS OFFERED TO TAKE CARE OF ANYONE WHO GAVE HIM A HARD TIME.

MITCHUM IS SURVIVED BY THREE GENERATIONS OF ACTORS, SONS JAMES AND CHRISTOPHER, GRANDCHILDREN BENTLEY AND CARRIE, AND GREAT-GRANDCHILDREN CAPPY AND GRACE VAN DIEN.

More interested in the quality of his work than in box office success, he was a master of screen biography, immersing himself in the lives of history's most driven men with an unsurpassed vigor and intensity.

PAUL
MUNI

Paul Muni never wanted to be a star. In fact, he turned his nose up at the notion: "I think 'star' is what you call actors who can't act." Acting was his life's blood, and at the height of his stardom in the thirties, he was revered as one of the greatest. His unerring talent for humanizing his characters brought him success as one of the screen's most vicious gangsters and some of history's most famous men. For most of his roles, he transformed his appearance so completely, he was dubbed "the New Lon Chaney." The child of actors, he rose to prominence at New York's Yiddish Art Theater, debuting there at the age of twelve in the role of an eighty-year-old man. He made his Broadway debut in 1926, the first time the thirty-two-year-old actor had performed in English. Stage work brought him to Fox, where he won an Oscar nomination for his film debut in *The Valiant* and then played seven characters, including Napoleon and Franz Schubert, in *Seven Faces* (both 1929). When other screen offers didn't meet his expectations, he returned to Broadway and scored a major hit in *Counsellor at Law*. Muni returned to Hollywood in 1932, starring as a vicious gangster in *Scarface: The Shame of the Nation* and an escaped convict in *I Am a Fugitive from a Chain Gang*. Warner Bros. was so impressed, they signed him to a long-term contract, publicizing him as the screen's greatest actor. In 1936, Muni convinced them to take a chance on a historical biography, *The Story of Louis Pasteur*, and the studio that had forged most of its hits with stories ripped from the headlines suddenly found box office gold in the past. Muni won an Oscar for his performance and went on to play historical figures in *The Life of Emile Zola* (1937) and *Juarez* (1939). Dissatisfied with life in Hollywood, he chose not to renew his contract, returning to the screen only occasionally for such roles as Frederick Chopin's teacher in *A Song to Remember* (1945) and the reincarnated gangster in *Angel on My Shoulder* (1946). Mostly, he focused his energies on stage work. In 1956, he had his biggest stage success as the crusading lawyer based on Clarence Darrow in *Inherit the Wind*. After one more film role, the aging doctor in *The Last Angry Man* (1959), failing eyesight and other health problems forced him to retire.

Born
Meshilem Meier Weisenfreund
September 22, 1895
Lemberg, Austria-Hungary
(now Lviv, Ukraine)

Died
August 25, 1967
Montecito, California,
of heart trouble

Star Sign
Virgo

Height
5'10"

Wife
Bella Finkel
(1921–1967, his death)

Essential
PAULMUNIFilms

SCARFACE: THE SHAME OF THE NATION

(1932) United Artists
In the most brutal of the era's gangster films, Paul Muni played a character modeled on equal parts Al Capone and Cesare Borgia as he killed his way to the top of the crime world with the help of trusty sidekick George Raft and loving (almost too loving) sister Ann Dvorak.

I AM A FUGITIVE FROM A CHAIN GANG

(1932) Warner Bros.
Based on a true story so explosive its original author had to visit Hollywood incognito, the film starred Muni as a jobless man who discovers that criminal justice in the South is little different from slavery.

THE STORY OF LOUIS PASTEUR

(1936) Warner Bros.
In his first great biographical role, Muni starred as the crusading scientist who fought derision in his native land to proving his medical theories.

THE GOOD EARTH

(1937) MGM
Muni starred as the Chinese peasant whose life is changed by his silently suffering wife (Luise Rainer), a revolution, and a still impressive re-creation of a locust attack in this adaptation of Pearl S. Buck's classic novel.

ANGEL ON MY SHOULDER

(1946) United Artists
In a rare comic performance, Muni starred as a gangster whose early death prompts the Devil (Claude Rains) to make mischief by putting his soul into the body of a judge, only to have his new identity turn the former criminal into a model citizen.

SCARFACE: THE SHAME OF THE NATION, 1932

I AM A FUGITIVE FROM A CHAIN GANG, 1932

BEHIND THE SCENES

MUNI HAD TO WEAR LIFTS AND PADDING TO GIVE HIM AN APELIKE APPEARANCE IN *SCARFACE: THE SHAME OF THE NATION* (1932).

MUNI'S MOVE INTO DARKNESS AFTER SAYING "I STEAL," HIS FINAL LINE IN *I AM A FUGITIVE FROM A CHAIN GANG* (1932), WAS AN ACCIDENT. THE LIGHT OVER HIS HEAD BLEW OUT JUST AS HE HAD FINISHED THE LINE, AND DIRECTOR MERVYN LEROY KEPT IT IN THE FILM.

SEX APPEAL PLAYED AS STRONG A ROLE AS ACTING IN CONVINCING WARNER BROS. TO SIGN MUNI TO A CONTRACT. WHEN THE HANDSOME ACTOR INSISTED ON WEARING ELABORATE MAKEUP FOR EACH CHARACTER HE PLAYED, STUDIO HEAD JACK WARNER QUIPPED, "WHY ARE WE PAYING HIM SO MUCH MONEY, WHEN WE CAN'T FIND HIM?"

WHEN MGM'S IRVING G. THALBERG OFFERED HIM THE ROLE OF WANG LUNG IN *THE GOOD EARTH* (1937), MUNI PROTESTED, "I'M ABOUT AS CHINESE AS HERBERT HOOVER." THE SAME COULD BE SAID FOR MOST OF THE CAST, WHICH INCLUDED GERMAN LUISE RAINER AND AMERICANS WALTER CONNELLY AND CHARLIE GRAPEWIN.

IN ADDITION TO HIS ACTING SKILLS, MUNI PLAYED THE VIOLIN, OFTEN USING IT TO RELAX BETWEEN TAKES. HE DID HIS OWN PLAYING IN THE FILM *WE ARE NOT ALONE* (1939).

ON THE SET OF *THE GOOD EARTH*, 1937

This blue-eyed matinee idol refused to be typecast, pursuing challenging roles that ultimately made him a both a box office draw and a critical success.

PAUL
NEWMAN

Born
Paul Leonard Newman
January 26, 1925
Shaker Heights, Ohio

Star Sign
Aquarius

Height
5'9"

Wives and Children
Actress Jackie Witt
(1949–1958, divorced)
son, Scott
daughters, Susan
and Stephanie

Actress Joanne Woodward
(1958–)
daughters, Elinor,
Melissa, and Claire

Paul Newman became a sex symbol in spite of himself. Warner Bros. initially assigned him romantic roles, but on his own he sought out projects that went against the grain. Although primarily interested in artistic challenges, he has turned his aspirations into box office dynamite, emerging as one of the screen's most compelling and seductive rebel heroes. Matching his artistic integrity is one of Hollywood's strongest records of public service. Yet Newman would be the last to paint himself a saint. As he once said, "I'd like to be remembered as a guy who tried." He started trying to act in college after he was booted from the football team. Stage and television work in the early fifties brought him a contract at Warner Bros., where he made a heavily panned screen debut in *The Silver Chalice* (1954). However, his second film, *Somebody up There Likes Me* (1956), established him as one of the screen's hottest young actors. That was one of two roles Newman inherited when James Dean died. The other, Brick in *Cat on a Hot Tin Roof* (1958), made him a star. Once free of his Warner Bros. contract, he built his box office power with gritty roles like the pool shark in *The Hustler* (1961) and the sexy, amoral rancher in *Hud* (1963), then reached a peak as the rebellious convict in *Cool Hand Luke* (1967). When his wife, actress Joanne Woodward, couldn't interest Hollywood in a novel she wanted to film, Newman stepped in to produce and direct (for the first time) *Rachel, Rachel* (1968), winning the New York Film Critics Circle Award for his work. Directing didn't cut back on his performance schedule, though. He and Robert Redford virtually invented the buddy picture with *Butch Cassidy and the Sundance Kid* (1969), followed by *The Sting* (1973). By this point, Newman had developed an effortless approach to acting that gave his characters an easy, lived-in quality. His work was often too subtle to put him in the winner's circle at the Oscars. After six unsuccessful nominations, the Academy voted him a special award for his body of work in 1985. A year later, he won the Oscar for re-creating his role from *The Hustler* in *The Color of Money*. Since then, he has continued to find new artistic challenges and new ways to do his part—or, as he put it, "extend himself as a human being—someone who isn't complacent, who doesn't cop out."

Essential
PAUL**NEWMAN**Films

SOMEBODY UP THERE LIKES ME
(1956) MGM
Paul Newman established his credentials as "the new Marlon Brando" playing boxer Rocky Graziano, who rose from a life of crime to become the middleweight champion.

THE HUSTLER
(1961) 20th Century-Fox
In the film that made him the screen's sexiest rebel, Newman starred as an up-and-coming pool champion caught between crooked manager George C. Scott and sympathetic prostitute Piper Laurie.

HUD
(1963) Paramount
As "the man with the barbed wire soul," Newman betrayed everybody foolish enough to care about him—including father Melvyn Douglas, nephew Brandon De Wilde, and housekeeper Patricia Neal.

BUTCH CASSIDY AND THE SUNDANCE KID
(1969) 20th Century-Fox
In the film that defined the buddy movie, Newman and Robert Redford starred as two outlaws whose exploits mirror the youthful rebellions that occurred during the era in which it was made.

THE VERDICT
(1982) 20th Century-Fox
Alcoholic lawyer Newman got it together long enough to save his career in a daring malpractice case pitting him against slick corporate attorney James Mason.

BUTCH CASSIDY AND THE SUNDANCE KID, 1969

COOL HAND LUKE, 1967

WITH JOANNE WOODWARD, 1956

BEHIND THE SCENES

PAUL NEWMAN WAS SO ASHAMED OF HIS SCREEN DEBUT IN *THE SILVER CHALICE* (1954) THAT WHEN IT AIRED ON LOS ANGELES TELEVISION TEN YEARS LATER, HE TOOK OUT AN AD IN THE TRADE PAPERS APOLOGIZING FOR THE FILM. TO HIS DISAPPOINTMENT, THE AD HELPED THE TELECAST ACHIEVE RECORD RATINGS.

TO PLAY MIDDLEWEIGHT CHAMPION ROCKY GRAZIANO IN *SOMEBODY UP THERE LIKES ME* (1956), NEWMAN SPENT TWO WEEKS LIVING WITH THE CHAMP TO GET HIS SPEECH AND PHYSICAL MANNERISMS DOWN PAT. HE WOULD DO SIMILAR RESEARCH ON MOST OF HIS FILM ROLES.

EARLY IN HIS CAREER, NEWMAN WAS MISTAKEN FOR MARLON BRANDO SO OFTEN, HE STARTED SIGNING AUTOGRAPHS IN HIS NAME.

NEWMAN'S MOST CONSISTENT COLLABORATOR IS HIS WIFE, JOANNE WOODWARD. THEY HAVE COSTARRED IN TEN FILMS, STARTING WITH *THE LONG HOT SUMMER* (1958) AND RUNNING THROUGH *MR. & MRS. BRIDGE* (1990), AND HE HAS DIRECTED HER IN ALL BUT ONE OF THEIR FILMS TOGETHER.

THAT'S REALLY NEWMAN AND ROBERT REDFORD LEAPING OFF THE CLIFF IN *BUTCH CASSIDY AND THE SUNDANCE KID* (1969), BUT THEY FELL ONLY SIX FEET, LANDING ON A MATTRESS ON THE LEDGE BELOW THEM.

WHEN HIS ONLY SON, SCOTT, DIED FROM AN ACCIDENTAL OVERDOSE OF PILLS AND LIQUOR, NEWMAN FOUNDED THE SCOTT NEWMAN FOUNDATION TO FINANCE ANTIDRUG EDUCATION EFFORTS. AN OFFSHOOT, THE ROWDY RIDGE GANG CAMP, HELPS MOTHERS AND THEIR CHILDREN DEAL WITH DRUG ABUSE.

IN 1982, NEWMAN FOUNDED NEWMAN'S OWN, A LINE OF FOODS INCLUDING SALAD DRESSINGS, PASTA SAUCES, POPCORN, AND ORGANIC FOODS WHOSE SALES HAVE FUNDED OVER $150 MILLION IN CHARITABLE DONATIONS. HE WOULD LATER QUIP, "THE EMBARRASSING THING IS THAT MY SALAD DRESSING IS OUTGROSSING MY FILMS."

His name has become synonymous with virtuosity for stage and screen accomplishments that are revered among fellow actors, including groundbreaking interpretations, as actor and director, of Shakespeare.

LAURENCE
OLIVIER

Laurence Olivier didn't just create characters; he created "the universe in the palm of his hands," one of his own definitions of acting. Graced with the ability to disappear inside even the showiest role, he transformed himself into a series of unforgettable characters. Through the course of his career, he moved from romantic lead to cultured villain to grand old man with little concern for billing or salary. Olivier started acting at fifteen, debuting as Kate in a boys' school production of *The Taming of the Shrew*. He first hit Hollywood in the early thirties, but after the embarrassment of being fired from *Queen Christina* (1933) after one meeting with Greta Garbo (she preferred casting former lover John Gilbert), he returned to England, where he began building his reputation as a classical actor. He also rose to stardom as a romantic lead in British films like the adventure *Fire over England* (1936), on which he met future wife Vivien Leigh, and the romantic comedy *The Divorce of Lady X* (1938). That brought him back to Hollywood for *Wuthering Heights* (1939), which made him a movie star in the United States. After hits in *Rebecca* (1940) and *Pride and Prejudice* (1941), Olivier returned to England during World War II to focus on stage work. His films of Shakespeare's plays, starting with *Henry V* in 1945 and moving to his Oscar-winning work on *Hamlet* in 1948, were the first to garner both box office success and critical acclaim. He took a chance on a grittier character when he starred as a faded song-and-dance man in *The Entertainer,* both on stage and in a 1960 film version. The production also introduced him to future wife Joan Plowright. Despite a memorable villainous role in *Spartacus* (1960), he continued focusing most of his attentions on stage work, especially his artistic leadership of the National Theatre in London, which eventually named its main facility the Olivier Theatre. When health problems made stage work impossible in the seventies, he turned increasingly to the screen and television, giving acclaimed performances as a fugitive Nazi in *Marathon Man* (1976) and, in his last major role, *King Lear* in a 1983 television production. When he died, he became only the second actor in history (following Edmund Kean) to be interred in Westminster Abbey. In 1984, the Society of London Theatre renamed its annual awards, the most prestigious in England, the Oliviers.

Born
Laurence Kerr Olivier
May 22, 1907
Dorking, Surrey, England

Died
July 11, 1989
Steyning, West Sussex, England,
of complications from
a muscle disorder

Star Sign
Gemini

Height
5'10½"

Wives and Children
Actress Jill Esmond
(1930–1940, divorced)
son, Tarquin

Actress Vivien Leigh
(1940–1960, divorced)

Actress Joan Plowright
(1961–1989, his death)
son, Richard Kerr
daughters, Agnes Margaret
and Julie Kate

Essential
LAURENCE**OLIVIER**Films

WUTHERING HEIGHTS

(1939) Samuel Goldwyn
Laurence Olivier shot to stardom
in the United States playing the
romantically obsessed Heathcliff
to Merle Oberon's Cathy in director
William Wyler's romantic
adaptation of the classic tale
of love on the English moors.

PRIDE AND PREJUDICE

(1940) MGM
In Jane Austen's comedy of
manners, Olivier was the prickly
Mr. Darcy, too proud to admit his
love for beautiful country girl
Greer Garson.

HENRY V

(1944) Two Cities Films Ltd.
Partly intended as a wartime
morale-booster for the British,
this Technicolor adaptation of the
Shakespearean play was a radical
adaptation that showcased Olivier's
directing talents.

HAMLET

(1948) Universal
Olivier's unorthodox, psycho-
analytical approach to the
melancholy Dane may have upset
the purists, but it won him an Oscar
and a new generation of fans.

THE ENTERTAINER

(1960) Continental
In his first film with future wife Joan
Plowright (cast as his daughter),
Olivier starred as a faded variety
star who will use anyone he can to
make sure the show goes on.

WUTHERING HEIGHTS, 1939

WITH VIVIEN LEIGH, 1940

BEHIND THE SCENES

WHEN LAURENCE OLIVIER FIRST ARRIVED IN HOLLYWOOD IN THE EARLY THIRTIES, THE STUDIO HEADS SAW HIM AS THE NEXT RONALD COLMAN. ONE SUGGESTED CHANGING HIS NAME TO LARRY OLIVER.

PRODUCER SAMUEL GOLDWYN COMPLAINED LOUDLY TO DIRECTOR WILLIAM WYLER ABOUT OLIVIER'S LACK OF PASSION IN EARLY RUSHES OF *WUTHERING HEIGHTS* (1939). OLIVIER OVERHEARD THE EXCHANGE AND, IN HIS NEXT SCENE, INSTEAD OF JUST BEATING ON A WINDOW, PUT HIS FISTS THROUGH THE PLATE GLASS. GOLDWYN NEVER COMPLAINED AGAIN.

WITH MANY BRITISH STUNTMEN OFF AT WAR, OLIVIER NOT ONLY HAD TO DO HIS OWN STUNTS ON *HENRY V*, HE ALSO HAD TO TEACH STUNT WORK TO THE EXTRAS, LEAVING HIM WITH TWO FRACTURED SHOULDERS.

UNTIL ROBERTO BENIGNI WON FOR *LIFE IS BEAUTIFUL* IN 1999, OLIVIER WAS THE ONLY ACTOR TO DIRECT HIMSELF IN AN OSCAR-WINNING PERFORMANCE.

HAMLET (1948) IS THE ONLY SHAKESPEAREAN ADAPTATION TO WIN THE OSCAR FOR BEST PICTURE, AND OLIVIER IS THE ONLY ACTOR TO WIN FOR PERFORMING A SHAKESPEAREAN ROLE.

WHEN *SPARTACUS* (1960) WAS RESTORED AFTER OLIVIER'S DEATH, THE PRODUCERS WANTED TO PUT BACK IN A SCENE CUT BY THE CENSORS IN WHICH OLIVIER ATTEMPTS TO SEDUCE TONY CURTIS. WITH THE SOUNDTRACK LOST, THEY GOT PERMISSION FROM OLIVIER'S WIDOW, JOAN PLOWRIGHT, TO HAVE ANTHONY HOPKINS IMITATE OLIVIER AND REDUB THE DIALOGUE.

OLIVIER WAS NEVER SATISFIED WITH HIS SUCCESS. THE ACTOR WHOSE CAREER HE MOST ENVIED WAS CARY GRANT.

He shot to screen fame playing T. E. Lawrence, the first and most vivid of many wild-eyed visionaries he would bring to life with delightful eccentricity and a devilish gleam.

PETER
O'TOOLE

As T. E. Lawrence, Peter O'Toole approached the daunting task of forging relations with the Bedouins in Arabia with the simple statement "it's going to be fun." Fun is exactly what O'Toole has brought audiences in four decades of work. Whether commanding the epic worlds of *Lawrence of Arabia* (1962) and *The Last Emperor* (1987) or revealing the more personal crises of a boys' school teacher in *Goodbye, Mr. Chips* (1969), he has brought to life an unparalleled string of visionaries trying to remake the world in their own images. O'Toole dropped out of school at fourteen for a job as a copy boy, though he spent most of his time going to movies and plays. During a tour of the nation's theaters, he was so moved by Michael Redgrave's performance in *King Lear* that it inspired him to become an actor. He was already building a solid theatrical career, while making minor film appearances, when he beat out a strong field of contenders, including Marlon Brando and Albert Finney, for the title role in director David Lean's *Lawrence of Arabia*. The acclaimed epic made him an overnight sensation but also became his personal cross, as he spent the rest of his life looking for a suitable follow-up. That search led him to great roles, particularly England's King Henry II in *The Lion in Winter* (1968) and a demented British lord in *The Ruling Class* (1972). In the seventies, O'Toole's career was sidelined when health problems, eventually proven to stem from stomach cancer, were mistaken for the product of excessive drinking. After making a full recovery and quitting drinking, he made a triumphant comeback as the egotistical director in *The Stunt Man* (1980), followed by his comic turn as a drunken movie star in *My Favorite Year* (1982). Throughout his career, O'Toole continued to seek new challenges onstage, tackling some of Shakespeare's greatest roles and bringing his performance as Henry Higgins in *Pygmalion* to Broadway. Although he has never won an Oscar, despite seven nominations (a record shared with Richard Burton), he received an honorary Oscar in 2003. O'Toole has also published the first two volumes of a projected three-part autobiography, *Loitering with Intent*, hailed for being as much fun as their subject.

Born
Peter Seamus O'Toole
August 2, 1932
Connemara, County Galway, Ireland

Star Sign
Leo

Height
6'3"

Wife and Children
Actress Sian Phillips
(1959–1979, divorced)
daughters, Kate and Pat

Son, Lorcan
born out of wedlock to
actress Karen Brown

Essential
PETER O'TOOLE Films

LAWRENCE OF ARABIA

(1962) Columbia Pictures
In his star-making role, Peter O'Toole embodied the enigmatic military leader who united the Arabs against the Turks in World War I, with scenes directed by David Lean in the desert locations where they originally happened.

THE LION IN WINTER

(1968) AVCO Embassy
O'Toole and Katharine Hepburn sparred memorably as British royals fighting and scheming to determine who will be heir to the throne, with Anthony Hopkins as one of the contenders.

GOODBYE, MR. CHIPS

(1969) MGM
A kinder, gentler, though no less visionary, O'Toole starred in this musical remake of the 1939 classic about an eccentric Latin teacher who became a boys' school favorite under the influence of his loving wife (Petula Clark).

THE RULING CLASS

(1972) AVCO Embassy
O'Toole demonstrated astonishing range as a demented British lord who believes he is Jesus until a failed insanity cure leaves him convinced he's Jack the Ripper.

MY FAVORITE YEAR

(1982) MGM
O'Toole's hard-drinking matinee idol, modeled on equal parts John Barrymore and Errol Flynn, wreaked havoc on the set of a live television comedy in director Richard Benjamin's comic hit, based on Mel Brooks's experiences writing for Sid Caesar.

THE LION IN WINTER, 1968

LAWRENCE OF ARABIA, 1962

HOW TO STEAL A MILLION, 1966

BEHINDTHESCENES

AS A TRIBUTE TO HIS IRISH HERITAGE, O'TOOLE ALWAYS WEARS SOMETHING GREEN, USUALLY HIS SOCKS.

AT THE URGING OF PRODUCER SAM SPIEGEL AND DIRECTOR DAVID LEAN, O'TOOLE HAD A NOSE JOB BEFORE GOING INTO PRODUCTION ON *LAWRENCE OF ARABIA* (1962) SO HE COULD LOOK MORE LIKE T. E. LAWRENCE. IT WAS ACTUALLY HIS SECOND: HE HAD GOTTEN THE FIRST EARLY IN HIS FILM CAREER.

AFTER NINE MONTHS OF SHOOTING *LAWRENCE OF ARABIA* (1962) IN THE DESERT, O'TOOLE WAS WORKING ON THE FILM'S SPANISH LOCATION WHEN HE WAS SUMMONED TO SAM SPIEGEL'S YACHT, WHERE THE PRODUCER TORE HIS PERFORMANCE APART. IN RETALIATION, O'TOOLE CLIMBED UP THE YACHT'S ANCHOR CHAIN IN THE MIDDLE OF THE NIGHT AND STOLE SPIEGEL'S CIGARS.

O'TOOLE IS ONE OF ONLY FOUR ACTORS (THE OTHERS ARE PAUL NEWMAN, BING CROSBY, AND AL PACINO) TO RECEIVE TWO OSCAR NOMINATIONS FOR PLAYING THE SAME CHARACTER—IN HIS CASE, KING HENRY II IN *BECKET* (1964) AND *THE LION IN WINTER* (1968).

IN 2003, O'TOOLE MADE HEADLINES BY INITIALLY REFUSING THE LIFETIME ACHIEVEMENT OSCAR THE ACADEMY HAD VOTED FOR HIM TO RECEIVE, PROTESTING THAT HE STILL HAD A CHANCE TO WIN THE AWARD COMPETITIVELY AND ASKING THEM TO WAIT UNTIL HE WAS EIGHTY. HE LATER ACCEPTED, CLAIMING HE HAD THOUGHT THE ACADEMY WAS MERELY ASKING HIM IF HE'D ACCEPT THE AWARD IF IT WERE GIVEN.

Tall, sturdy, and urbane, he was a quiet but powerful force of moral decency, who brought nobility to his portraits of gentleman heroes.

GREGORY
PECK

Decency was Gregory Peck's stock in trade. The innate integrity behind his work made him an ideal father figure, even while he was still a matinee idol. Audiences trusted him long before he delivered his favorite performance as noble small-town lawyer Atticus Finch in *To Kill a Mockingbird* (1962). When he departed from that persona, it made his few villainous roles all the more effective. When he played an honest businessman brought down by corporate chicanery in *Other People's Money* (1991), it was hard not to see it as an affront to the nation itself. A child of divorce, Peck spent much of his childhood going to the movies. After doing one play in college (his first experience with *Moby Dick*), he got the acting bug and took off for New York, where he made his Broadway debut in 1942. Although all his Broadway shows were failures, solid notices won him a contract shared by producer David O. Selznick and 20th Century-Fox. He started on screen as a star in the World War II drama *Days of Glory* (1944), then won his first Oscar nomination as the noble priest in *The Keys of the Kingdom* (1944). Because of his height and natural good looks, he was viewed early on as the new Gary Cooper, something female fans caught on to quickly. When he starred opposite Ingrid Bergman in director Alfred Hitchcock's *Spellbound* (1945), moviegoers' reactions drowned out dialogue during many of his close-ups. As a contract player, Peck scored in westerns like *Duel in the Sun* (1946), social dramas like *Gentleman's Agreement* (1947), and war films like *Twelve O'Clock High* (1949). He proved his ability to deliver the goods as a comic star in *Roman Holiday* (1953), opposite Audrey Hepburn. When his long-term contracts expired in the fifties, he went freelance, increasingly attracted only to projects that intrigued him, like his favorite film *To Kill a Mockingbird*. However, finding roles as enticing as Atticus Finch proved difficult. His acting career waning, Peck tried his hand at producing in the early 1970s, only to make an unexpected comeback in the surprise hit *The Omen* (1976). He made his television debut, appropriately cast as Abraham Lincoln, in the 1982 miniseries *The Blue and the Gray*. Peck remained active despite declining health. At the time of his death, there was even talk of his starring in a remake of director Ingmar Bergman's Swedish classic *Wild Strawberries* (1959).

Born
Eldred Gregory Peck
April 5, 1916
La Jolla, California

Died
June 12, 2003
Los Angeles, California,
of natural causes

Star Sign
Aries

Height
6'3"

Wives and Children
Hairdresser and makeup artist
Greta Konen
(1942–1954, divorced)
sons, Jonathan, Stephen,
and Carey Paul

Journalist Veronique Passani
(1955–2003, his death)
son, Anthony
daughter, Cecilia

Essential
GREGORYPECKFilms

DUEL IN THE SUN

(1946) Selznick
Peck went bad—and it made
him even sexier—to play an
unscrupulous cowboy who shot
his own brother for love of
seductive serving girl Pearl Chavez
(Jennifer Jones).

GENTLEMAN'S AGREEMENT

(1947) 20th Century–Fox
In this controversial Oscar winner,
Peck starred as a journalist who
puts his family at risk by pretending
to be Jewish to write an exposé of
anti-Semitism.

TWELVE O'CLOCK HIGH

(1949) 20th Century–Fox
Peck faced almost unendurable
pressure as a general trying to whip
a bomber unit into shape during
the early days of World War II.

ROMAN HOLIDAY

(1953) Paramount
Taking a chance on love, Peck
scored a hit in this romantic
comedy as a journalist who takes in
runaway princess Audrey Hepburn
to land a story about her getaway.

TO KILL A MOCKINGBIRD

(1962) Universal-International
In his favorite film, Peck starred as
a quiet crusader, a small-town
lawyer and single father defending
a black man charged with rape in
thirties Alabama.

TO KILL A MOCKINGBIRD, 1962

ROMAN HOLIDAY, 1953

BEHINDTHE**SCENES**

WHILE TAKING DANCE CLASSES WITH MARTHA GRAHAM IN NEW YORK, GREGORY PECK SUSTAINED A BACK INJURY THAT WOULD KEEP HIM OUT OF WORLD WAR II. ONCE HE BECAME A STAR, STUDIO PUBLICISTS INSISTED HE SAY IT WAS A COLLEGE SPORTS INJURY, NOT WANTING HIM TO ADMIT TO HAVING STUDIED DANCE.

IN *ROMAN HOLIDAY* (1953), PECK IMPROVISED THE MOMENT IN WHICH HE PRETENDS TO HAVE LOST HIS HAND IN "THE MOUTH OF TRUTH." AUDREY HEPBURN'S SCREAMS OF HORROR, FOLLOWED BY DELIGHTED LAUGHTER, WERE REAL.

NOVELIST HARPER LEE WAS SO IMPRESSED BY PECK'S PERFORMANCE AS ATTICUS FINCH, A CHARACTER SHE HAD MODELED ON HER FATHER, IN *TO KILL A MOCKINGBIRD* (1962), SHE GAVE THE ACTOR HER FATHER'S WATCH.

AS PRESIDENT OF THE MOTION PICTURE ARTS AND SCIENCES IN 1968, PECK WAS THE ONE WHO DECIDED TO POSTPONE THE OSCAR PRESENTATIONS AFTER MARTIN LUTHER KING JR.'S ASSASSINATION.

GOVERNOR PECK: IT ALMOST HAPPENED IN 1970, WHEN THE DEMOCRATIC PARTY TRIED TO GET HIM TO COUNTER RONALD REAGAN'S REELECTION BID.

ACCIDENTS HAUNTED THE PRODUCTION OF *THE OMEN* (1976). BOTH PECK'S AND SCREENWRITER DAVID SELTZER'S FLIGHTS TO ENGLAND WERE STRUCK BY LIGHTNING. WHEN THEY MOVED TO ISRAEL FOR LOCATION SHOOTING, PECK HAD TO CHANGE HIS FLIGHT PLANS, AND THE FLIGHT HE HAD ORIGINALLY BOOKED CRASHED, KILLING ALL ON BOARD.

The first black actor to win the Oscar for Best Actor and the first top box office star of color, he blazed a trail into the Hollywood mainstream with his charismatic portrayals of intelligent, self-possessed men of profound dignity.

SIDNEY
POITIER

It seemed fitting that the night Sidney Poitier received his honorary Oscar in 2002, Halle Berry became the first African American to win a Best Actress Oscar and Denzel Washington only the second to win Best Actor (Poitier had been the first). Poitier's battles against racism had paved the way for their careers. He did it through the sheer quality of his acting, creating a gallery of very human, often fallible characters that reinforced the positive messages of the civil rights movement. Poitier was raised in the Bahamas and moved to New York at eighteen, sleeping in a bus station men's room until he could earn a living. On a whim, he auditioned for the American Negro Theatre, where he was soundly rejected. Instead of giving up, he worked as a janitor there in exchange for acting classes. On his second audition, he got in, quickly working his way up to leading roles on Broadway. These led to a brief tenure in Hollywood, where he made his screen debut locking horns with racist gangster Richard Widmark in *No Way Out* (1950). Poitier's early battles for civil rights and his support of such blacklisted artists as Paul Robeson and Canada Lee made him politically suspect, forcing director Richard Brooks to fight to cast him in *Blackboard Jungle* (1955). When the film became a hit, however, Poitier started landing better screen roles, including the escaped convict in *The Defiant Ones* (1958), for which he became the first black male nominated for an acting Oscar. A Broadway success in *A Raisin in the Sun*, followed by its 1961 film version, further raised his stock in Hollywood. When *Lilies of the Field* became the sleeper hit of 1963, it brought him a Best Actor Oscar. Then three box office smashes in 1967—*In the Heat of the Night; To Sir, With Love;* and *Guess Who's Coming to Dinner*—made Poitier the nation's top-grossing star. He broke new ground writing the story for and starring in the romantic comedy *For Love of Ivy* (1968) and directing himself and Harry Belafonte in the western *Buck and the Preacher* (1972). In the eighties, Poitier cut back on acting to focus on his directing career but came back for selected projects like the miniseries *Separate but Equal* (1991), in which he played future U.S. Supreme Court justice Thurgood Marshall, and the 1997 television movie *Mandela and De Klerk,* in which he played Nelson Mandela.

Born
Sidney Poitier
February 20, 1927
Miami, Florida

Star Sign
Pisces

Height
6'2½"

Wives and Children
Model-dancer
Juanita Hardy
(1952–1975, divorced)
daughters, Beverly, Pamela,
Sherry, and Gina

Actress Joanna Shimkus
(1976–)
daughters, Anika
and Sydney

Essential
SIDNEYPOITIERFilms

ACADEMY AWARDS
Won Best Actor
Lilies of the Field

Nominated for Best Actor
The Defiant Ones

Honorary Oscar in 2002 "for his
extraordinary performances
and unique presence"

A RAISIN IN THE SUN
(1961) Columbia
In the film version of Lorraine
Hansberry's pioneering play,
Poitier starred as a man fighting
to make a better life for his family
in the Chicago slums.

LILIES OF THE FIELD
(1963) United Artists
Poitier scored a surprise hit as
an unemployed construction
worker dragooned into building
a chapel for a group of European
nuns transplanted to the
American Southwest.

TO SIR, WITH LOVE
(1967) Columbia
Between engineering jobs, Poitier
took a teaching position in the
London slums, fighting to get his
students on the right path.

IN THE HEAT OF THE NIGHT
(1967) United Artists
On a trip to his hometown,
African American police detective
Poitier joined forces with Southern
cop Rod Steiger to investigate a
racially inflammatory murder case
in the Oscar-winning film that
inspired two sequels and a hit
television series.

GUESS WHO'S COMING TO DINNER
(1967) Columbia
Poitier and fiancée seek the
blessing of her parents, played
by Spencer Tracy and Katharine
Hepburn, for their interracial
marriage.

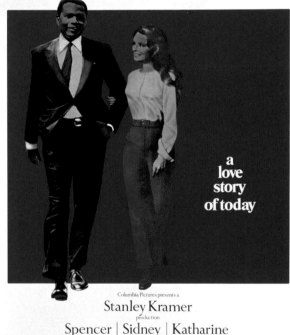

a
love
story
of today

Columbia Pictures presents a
Stanley Kramer
production
Spencer | Sidney | Katharine
Tracy | Poitier | Hepburn

guess who's coming to dinner
and introducing
Katharine Houghton
Music by De Vol · Written by William Rose · Produced and directed by Stanley Kramer
Technicolor®
Columbia Pictures

GUESS WHO'S COMING TO DINNER, 1967

LILIES OF THE FIELD, 1963

BEHIND THE SCENES

THE TWENTY-TWO-YEAR-OLD POITIER LIED ABOUT HIS AGE, CLAIMING TO BE TWENTY-SEVEN, WHEN HE READ FOR DIRECTOR-WRITER JOSEPH L. MANKIEWICZ FOR HIS FIRST FILM, *NO WAY OUT* (1950).

WHEN RICHARD BROOKS CAST POITIER IN *BLACKBOARD JUNGLE* (1955), MGM'S LAWYERS DEMANDED THE ACTOR SIGN A LOYALTY OATH BECAUSE OF HIS POLITICAL ACTIVITIES. POITIER IGNORED THEIR REQUESTS, AND THEY EVENTUALLY LEFT HIM ALONE.

TONY CURTIS INSISTED THAT POITIER BE GIVEN TOP BILLING ON *THE DEFIANT ONES* (1958).

POITIER TOOK A CUT IN SALARY AND WORKED FOR A PERCENTAGE TO GET *LILIES OF THE FIELD* (1963) MADE. DIRECTOR RALPH NELSON HAD TO PUT UP HIS HOUSE AS COLLATERAL TO GET FINANCING.

COLUMBIA HAD SO LITTLE FAITH IN *TO SIR, WITH LOVE* (1967) THEY KEPT IT ON THE SHELF FOR A YEAR. THEY FINALLY SNUCK IT INTO A THEATER IN WESTWOOD, CALIFORNIA, WHERE IT BECAME A RUNAWAY HIT. WHEN THEY POLLED TO FIND OUT WHY, THEY GOT ONE OVERWHELMING RESPONSE: PEOPLE HAD COME TO SEE POITIER.

LET'S DO IT AGAIN (1975), WHICH POITIER DIRECTED AND STARRED IN, WAS THE HIGHEST-GROSSING FILM DIRECTED BY A BLACK MAN UNTIL SPIKE LEE'S *JUNGLE FEVER* IN 1991.

Suave, streetwise, and never far from a cocktail shaker, he cornered the market on debonair irony as the ultimate gentleman sleuth in the *Thin Man* films.

WILLIAM
POWELL

Nobody could nurse a scotch or make wry faces over the stupidity of others like William Powell. He could deliver a withering bon mot while also making fun of himself, creating characters who were both sophisticated and totally unpretentious. With his most popular costar, Myrna Loy, Powell created an unprecedented image of marriage as a meeting of minds as well as hearts. They traded good-natured barbs and stood together against a world of fools, snobs and, in the *Thin Man* films, killers. Suavity was hardly in his blood; his father was an accountant who wanted Powell to become an attorney. But after a few weeks of law school, he switched to the American Academy of Dramatic Art in New York. From 1912 to 1922, he struggled to build a stage career, finally hitting pay dirt as a dying romantic in 1922's *Spanish Love*. Strong reviews led to his screen debut as one of Moriarty's henchmen in *Sherlock Holmes* (1922), starring John Barrymore. That set the pace for most of his silent roles, as he menaced everyone from Lillian and Dorothy Gish in *Romola* (1924) to Emil Jannings in *The Last Command* (1928), much of the time under contract to Paramount. Sound proved a boon to Powell, whose comic delivery has often been called impeccable, and he finally became a star playing urbane sleuth Philo Vance in *The Canary Murder Case* (1929). Disappointed with his other roles at Paramount, he jumped ship for Warner Bros. in 1932, then moved to MGM, where he scored first time out in *Manhattan Melodrama* (1934), the first film to pair him with his perfect leading lady, Myrna Loy. Director W. S. Van Dyke reteamed them for *The Thin Man* (1934), a surprise hit that made them top stars. Powell had grown close to Jean Harlow making *Reckless* in 1935, but after two divorces was afraid to take another chance on marriage. When she died suddenly in 1937, he was overcome with grief. Then a bout with rectal cancer took him off the screen for a year, and his career never fully recovered. In the late forties, Powell left MGM to freelance, scoring a hit as the authoritarian patriarch in *Life with Father* (1947). After that he made only sporadic film appearances, including a role in support of Marilyn Monroe and Lauren Bacall in *How to Marry a Millionaire* (1953). He retired from the screen after playing Doc in *Mister Roberts* (1955).

Born
William Horatio Powell
July 29, 1892
Pittsburgh, Pennsylvania

Died
March 5, 1984
Palm Springs, California,
of cardiac arrest

Star Sign
Leo

Height
6'

Wives and Child
Actress Eileen Wilson
(1915–1930, divorced)
son, William David

Actress Carole Lombard
(1931–1933, divorced)

Actress Diana Lewis
(1940–1984, his death)

Essential
WILLIAMPOWELLFilms

THE LAST COMMAND
(1928) Paramount)
In one of his best villainous roles, William Powell costarred for director Josef von Sternberg as a Russian émigré turned film director who found himself directing old enemy Emil Jannings, a onetime Czarist general who began working as a movie extra.

THE THIN MAN
(1934) MGM
In the film that launched the hit movie series, retired police detective Nick Charles (Powell) and his wealthy wife, Nora (Myrna Loy), took on their first murder case because she wanted to find out how exciting his old job was.

MY MAN GODFREY
(1936) Universal
In one of the best of all screwball comedies, dizzy socialite Carole Lombard hired hobo Powell as the family butler, not realizing a secret from his past could change her life.

LIBELED LADY
(1936) MGM
Blessed with one of the most complicated plots in Hollywood history, the film teams Powell and Myrna Loy with newspaper editor Spencer Tracy and his eternally jilted fiancée for raucous screwball comedy.

LIFE WITH FATHER
(1947) Warner Bros.
In this adaptation of the long-running Broadway hit, Powell starred as a 19th-century gentleman who thought he ruled the roost at home, little knowing how thoroughly wife Irene Dunne was in charge.

THE THIN MAN, 1934

MY MAN GODFREY, 1936

BEHINDTHE**SCENES**

ALTHOUGH HIS FATHER REFUSED TO FINANCE HIS ACTING CAREER—POWELL STUDIED IN NEW YORK THANKS TO A LOAN FROM HIS AUNT—WHEN POWELL BECAME A STAR, HE BUILT HIS PARENTS A NEW HOME IN CALIFORNIA AND HIRED HIS FATHER AS HIS BUSINESS MANAGER.

ONE OF THE REASONS POWELL LEFT PARAMOUNT WAS THEIR REFUSAL TO PROMISE HE'D NEVER AGAIN HAVE TO WORK WITH DIRECTOR JOSEF VON STERNBERG, WHO HAD A HABIT OF PICKING ON ACTORS.

POWELL SURPRISED HOLLYWOOD BY MAINTAINING FRIENDLY RELATIONS WITH BOTH HIS EX-WIVES. HE EVEN CONTINUED DATING CAROLE LOMBARD AFTER THEIR SPLIT. SHE TOLD AN INTERVIEWER, "WE MADE BETTER FRIENDS THAN WE DID AS MARRIEDS, AND NOW, FREE OF MARRIAGE, WE CAN ENJOY THE FRIENDSHIP FULLY, WITHOUT TIES OR OBLIGATIONS."

POWELL MARRIED MGM STARLET DIANA LEWIS ONLY SIX WEEKS AFTER THEY MET, AND THEY WOULD STAY TOGETHER UNTIL HIS DEATH FORTY-FOUR YEARS LATER.

AFTER WORKING WITH POWELL AND MYRNA LOY ON *MANHATTAN MELODRAMA* (1934), DIRECTOR W. S. VAN DYKE PROPOSED TEAMING THEM AS THE CRIME-SOLVING COUPLE IN *THE THIN MAN* (1934), ONLY TO BE OPPOSED BY MGM STUDIO HEAD LOUIS B. MAYER, WHO DIDN'T THINK THEY HAD THE BOX OFFICE PULL. VAN DYKE HAD TO AGREE TO MAKE THE FILM IN TWO WEEKS TO KEEP PRODUCTION COSTS DOWN IF HE WANTED TO WORK WITH THE TWO UNTESTED STARS.

POWELL AND LOY WERE SUCH A SUCCESSFUL SCREEN TEAM, PEOPLE OUTSIDE HOLLYWOOD ASSUMED THEY REALLY WERE MARRIED. NOT ONLY DID THEY GET FAN MAIL ASKING FOR MARITAL ADVICE, BUT WHEN THEY WENT TO SAN FRANCISCO FOR LOCATION SHOOTING ON *AFTER THE THIN MAN* (1936), WITH POWELL'S LOVE JEAN HARLOW ALONG FOR THE RIDE, THEY DISCOVERED THEY'D BEEN BOOKED INTO THE BRIDAL SUITE. THE LADIES SHARED THE SUITE, WHILE POWELL HAD TO SETTLE FOR A SMALL ROOM SEVERAL FLOORS BELOW.

Playing roles of many nationalities, he started his career as one of Hollywood's most versatile character actors before carving a niche for himself as a larger-than-life man of the earth.

ANTHONY
QUINN

Born
Antonio Rudolfo Oaxaca Quinn
April 21, 1915
Chihuahua, Mexico

Died
June 3, 2001
Boston, Massachusetts,
of pneumonia and respiratory
complications during a
battle with throat cancer

Star Sign
Taurus

Height
6'2"

Wives and Children
Actress Katherine DeMille
(1937–1965, divorced)
sons, Christopher and Duncan
daughters, Christina,
Kathleen, and Valentina

Costume designer
Iolanda Addoloi
(1966–1997, divorced)
sons, Francesco Daniele,
Daniele Antonio,
and Lawrence Alexander

Secretary Kathy Benvin
(1997–2001, his death)
daughter, Antonia
son, Ryan

Three other children
born out of wedlock

Anthony Quinn was one of the screen's biggest men, both in height and in the size of his characters' emotions. In a way, his expansive presence was also his curse. After his triumph in *Zorba the Greek* (1964), he had a hard time scaling back for less mythic roles. But when a film needed an earthy embodiment of the life force, Quinn was the perfect choice. He had pretty earthy roots to begin with: His Irish soldier-of-fortune father and Mexican mother had fought with Pancho Villa before moving to Los Angeles. A speech defect requiring surgery led Quinn to take acting lessons, opening the door to a new career. He conned his way into a small role in Cecil B. DeMille's *The Plainsman* (1936) and then developed his craft through other films at Paramount, most often as a villain. That typecasting continued to dog him through contracts at Warner Bros., 20th Century–Fox, and RKO. To expand his acting horizons, Quinn turned to the stage. After he spent two years touring and playing Broadway in *A Streetcar Named Desire,* the play's director, Elia Kazan, brought him back to Hollywood for an Oscar-winning role as Marlon Brando's brother in *Viva Zapata!* (1952). With nothing of the same caliber offered in Hollywood, Quinn took off for Italy, working for next to nothing as the traveling strongman in Federico Fellini's *La Strada* (1954). The film made him an international star, but before its U.S. release, he accepted a six-minute part in *Lust for Life* (1956). It would become one of the smallest roles to win an Oscar. After prestigious assignments in *Lawrence of Arabia* and *Requiem for a Heavyweight* (both 1962), he landed his signature role, as the free-spirited, life-loving *Zorba the Greek*. The role made him a fortune and brought him an Oscar nomination. It would stick with him the rest of his life, with many of his subsequent performances dismissed as "Zorba the Pope," "Zorba the Hillbilly" or, quite simply, "Zorba the Quinn." In the early eighties, he stopped trying to escape from the role, going on tour and then playing almost a year on Broadway in a revival of the musical *Zorba*. In 1991, Quinn showed how delicate his acting could be as Maureen O'Hara's amorous neighbor in *Only the Lonely,* their first film together since 1955's *The Magnificent Matador*.

Essential
ANTHONY QUINN Films

VIVA ZAPATA!

(1952) 20th Century–Fox
As the brother of Mexican revolutionary Emiliano Zapata (Marlon Brando), Quinn stole scene after scene with his blustery characterization.

LA STRADA

(1954) Trans-Lux
Quinn shot to international stardom as the traveling strongman who bought a simple-minded waif (director Federico Fellini's wife, Giulietta Masina) to help with his act, only to find her a threat to his masculine bravado.

REQUIEM FOR A HEAVYWEIGHT

(1962) Columbia
As a down-and-out boxer trying to find a better life, Quinn gave one of his most restrained performances, helped greatly by a cast including Mickey Rooney, Jackie Gleason, and Julie Harris.

ZORBA THE GREEK

(1964) International Classics
Quinn was a sensation as the life-loving peasant who taught young Englishman Alan Bates how to live—and dance.

THE SECRET OF SANTA VITTORIA

(1969) United Artists
In one of his few later roles to stand up in comparison to Zorba, Quinn starred as an Italian small-town mayor who conspired to hide the local treasure—a million bottles of wine—from the Nazis during World War II.

LA STRADA, 1954

ZORBA THE GREEK, 1964

BACK TO BATAAN, 1945

BEHIND THE SCENES

IN HIGH SCHOOL, QUINN WON A COMPETITION TO STUDY WITH LEGENDARY ARCHITECT FRANK LLOYD WRIGHT, WHO CONVINCED HIM TO HAVE AN OPERATION AND THERAPY FOR A SPEECH PROBLEM. ALTHOUGH HE THOUGHT QUINN HAD THE MAKINGS OF A GOOD ARCHITECT, WHEN SPEECH CLASSES LED TO AN ACTING CAREER, HE GAVE THE YOUNG MAN HIS BLESSING.

QUINN WON HIS ROLE IN *THE PLAINSMAN* (1936) BY PRETENDING TO BE A PUREBLOODED CHEYENNE WHO SPOKE NO ENGLISH. HE BLEW HIS COVER WHEN HE TOLD DIRECTOR CECIL B. DEMILLE HE WAS STAGING A SCENE INCORRECTLY. WHEN THE AUTOCRATIC DIRECTOR AGREED WITH HIM, THE INCIDENT MADE QUINN FAMOUS ON THE PARAMOUNT LOT, LEADING TO MORE ROLES.

WHEN QUINN WON BEST SUPPORTING ACTOR FOR 1952'S *VIVA ZAPATA!* THE SAME NIGHT DEMILLE WON BEST PICTURE FOR *THE GREATEST SHOW ON EARTH,* IT MARKED THE ONLY TIME FATHER-IN-LAW AND SON-IN-LAW BOTH WON OSCARS IN THE SAME YEAR.

ardo *LA STRADA* (1954) COULD HAVE MADE QUINN A WEALTHY MAN HAD HE NOT LISTENED TO HIS AGENT. GIVEN A ONE-THIRD OWNERSHIP OF THE PICTURE, HE LET HIS AGENT CONVINCE HIM THE FILM WOULD BE A FAILURE AND SOLD HIS SHARE FOR $15,000.

QUINN'S CHARACTER IN *BACK TO BATAAN* (1945), ANDRES BONIFACIO, WAS NAMED AFTER THE LEADER OF THE PHILIPPINES' LATE-19TH-CENTURY REVOLT AGAINST SPAIN.

QUINN'S DANCE IN *ZORBA THE GREEK* WAS IMPROVISED DURING FILMING BECAUSE THE ACTOR HAD BROKEN HIS FOOT, MAKING THE ORIGINAL, MORE ATHLETIC STAGING IMPOSSIBLE.

This atypical leading man proved his staying power in a versatile fifty-year career, beginning with the snarling, cigar-chomping underworld big shots that became a mobster prototype for the screen.

EDWARD G.
ROBINSON

Edward G. Robinson summed up his career the best: "Some people have youth, some have beauty—I have menace." Short, chubby, and far from conventionally attractive, he was the least likely candidate for screen stardom. When he conquered the mobs as *Little Caesar* (1930), he also conquered the box office, launching a movie career that would last for more than four decades. However monstrous the character, he could capture his soul, startling audiences with the depths of pain and insecurity lurking beneath even the hardest surfaces. Robinson, the son of Romanian Jews, was torn between law and rabbinical studies when he fell in love with acting. A hit as a gangster in Broadway's *The Racket* brought him to Hollywood's attention, but although he played a few gangster roles in his earliest films, none had the dimension of Rico Bandello in *Little Caesar,* a character he saw as something out of Greek tragedy. The film brought him a contract with Warner Bros., but it also typecast him. Though he played a wide variety of roles there—including the fight manager in *Kid Galahad* (1937), the crusading researcher in *Dr. Ehrlich's Magic Bullet* (1940), and the sadistic captain in *The Sea Wolf* (1941)—he remained best known for his gangster parts. After leaving Warner Bros., Robinson gladly accepted a third-billed role in director Billy Wilder's *Double Indemnity* (1944), followed by two classic films noir teaming him with Joan Bennett and director Fritz Lang, *The Woman in the Window* and *Scarlet Street* (both 1945). Known as one of Hollywood's softest touches, Robinson had to pay for his generosity when 11 of the more than 300 charities he had helped turned up on a list of Communist front organizations. It took him four years to clear his name, and by the time he could work again, Hollywood was in the throes of change, and he had a hard time finding good roles. Among his many character parts, one of the best was the wily cardsharp in *The Cincinnati Kid* (1965), a film reuniting him with onetime Warner Bros. star Joan Blondell. Health problems forced Robinson to pass on the role of Dr. Zaius in *Planet of the Apes* (1968), and he died two weeks after filming a supporting role in *Soylent Green* (1973). Two months later, the Academy of Motion Picture Arts and Sciences presented him with a posthumous honorary Oscar, appropriately on the night *The Godfather* won Best Picture.

Born
Emanuel Goldenberg
December 12, 1893
Bucharest, Romania

Died
January 26, 1973
Hollywood, California,
of cancer

Star Sign
Sagittarius

Height
5'5"

Wives and Child
Actress Gladys Lloyd
(1927–1956, divorced)
son, Emmanuel Jr.

Designer Jane Robinson
(1958–1973, his death)

Essential
EDWARD G.ROBINSONFilms

ACADEMY AWARDS
Honorary Oscar in 1973
to "a player, a patron of the arts,
and a dedicated citizen"

LITTLE CAESAR
(1931) Warner Bros.
Edward G. Robinson shot to stardom—and helped generations of impressionists get laughs—with his performance as a ruthless hood who would stop at nothing to become king of the mobsters.

DOUBLE INDEMNITY
(1944) Paramount
Robinson moved into character roles, almost stealing the show, as an insurance investigator doggedly pursuing murderous widow Barbara Stanwyck and his colleague and best friend, Fred MacMurray, in Billy Wilder's influential film noir.

THE WOMAN IN THE WINDOW
(1945) RKO
In the first of two films noir with Joan Bennett, Dan Duryea, and director Fritz Lang, Robinson stars as a college professor whose obsession with a woman's portrait leads to a moment of weakness that could destroy his life.

OUR VINES HAVE TENDER GRAPES
(1945) MGM
Robinson couldn't have gotten farther from his gangster roles than when he played a gentle Norwegian farmer trying to help daughter Margaret O'Brien grow up in rural Wisconsin.

KEY LARGO
(1948) Warner Bros.
Returning to Warner Bros. and gangster roles, Robinson starred as a deported gangster trying to sneak back into the country during a Florida hurricane, if only he could get past Humphrey Bogart.

LITTLE CAESAR, 1931

SMART MONEY, 1931

BEHIND THE SCENES

DOUBLE INDEMNITY (1944) ORIGINALLY ENDED WITH A TWENTY-MINUTE SEQUENCE DEPICTING THE TRIAL AND EXECUTION OF WALTER NEFF (FRED MACMURRAY), BUT IT MADE THE FILM TOO LONG. EVEN THOUGH HE THOUGHT THAT VERSION CONTAINED SOME OF HIS BEST WORK IN THE PICTURE, ROBINSON HAD TO SHOOT A NEW ENDING, WITH MACMURRAY DYING AFTER CONFESSING TO HIM.

ROBINSON WAS A FAMED ART COLLECTOR, STARTING WHEN HE PURCHASED A PAINTING FOR $2 IN 1913. HE HAD TO SELL MOST OF HIS COLLECTION (TO GREEK SHIPPING MAGNATE STAVROS NIARCHOS) TO COVER THE SETTLEMENT WHEN HE DIVORCED HIS FIRST WIFE IN 1956 BUT GRADUALLY REBUILT IT BEFORE HIS DEATH.

ROBINSON'S ROLE AS A NAZI HUNTER IN DIRECTOR ORSON WELLES'S *THE STRANGER* (1946) WAS ORIGINALLY WRITTEN FOR AGNES MOOREHEAD, BUT RKO'S MANAGEMENT INSISTED ON A BIGGER BOX OFFICE NAME.

ROBINSON WAS ALMOST TOTALLY DEAF WHEN HE MADE HIS LAST FILM, *SOYLENT GREEN* (1973). HE NEEDED SEVERAL TAKES ON EACH SCENE TO GET THE DIALOGUE RHYTHMS RIGHT SO HE COULD COME IN ON CUE AND OFTEN KEPT ACTING AFTER DIRECTOR RICHARD FLEISCHER YELLED "CUT!"

KNOWING ROBINSON WAS ON HIS DEATHBED, THE ACADEMY OF MOTION PICTURE ARTS AND SCIENCE'S GOVERNORS HAD HIS HONORARY OSCAR PRESENTED TO HIM EARLY. HE EVEN WROTE THE ACCEPTANCE SPEECH HIS WIFE WOULD READ ON THE TELEVISED CEREMONIES.

Just over five feet tall, he filled the screen with larger-than-life energy and spunk, performing inspired duets with Judy Garland and topping the box office charts as everybody's favorite kid brother in MGM's Andy Hardy films.

MICKEY
ROONEY

Born
Joe Yule Jr.
on September 23, 1920,
Brooklyn, New York.

Star Sign
Virgo

Height
5'3"

Wives and Children
Actress Ava Gardner
(1942–1943, divorced)

Beauty queen Betty Jane Rase
(1944–1948, divorced)
sons, Joe Yule Jr. and Timothy

Actress Martha Vickers
(1949–1952, divorced)
son, Teddy

Model
Elaine Mahnken/Elaine Devry
(1952–1958, divorced)
son, Jimmy
daughter, Jonelle

Actress Carolyn Mitchell
(1958–1966, her death)
daughters, Kelly Ann,
Kerry, and Kimmy Sue
son, Kyle

Realtor Marge Lane
(1967, divorced)

Secretary Carolyn Nockett
(1969–1974, divorced)

Singer Jan Chamberlain (1978–)

Mickey Rooney has had the longest career in film history, seventy-nine years and counting. He was one star who did it all—singing, dancing, acting, playing drums and piano, and writing songs (he also writes fiction, paints abstract art, and campaigns for animal rights). And he did it with a boundless energy that personified youthful high spirits, even when he started playing character roles, proving that the magic behind Andy Hardy could still work in films like *The Black Stallion* (1979). Rooney came from a show business family, appearing on the stage for the first time at age eighteen months. He hit Hollywood to audition for the Our Gang series but instead won the role of young mischief maker Mickey McGuire in over sixty shorts released between 1927 and 1936. Rooney started attracting attention as Puck in *A Midsummer Night's Dream,* first at the Hollywood Bowl, then in Warner Bros.' 1935 film version. That led to a contract with MGM, where he rose to stardom in 1937 with the Andy Hardy films. As the rambunctious small-town boy, he moved from high school to college and through a series of chaste romantic encounters with such up-and-coming actresses as Judy Garland, Lana Turner, and Esther Williams. Rooney starred in fifteen Andy Hardy films and one short over a ten-year period. As his popularity soared, MGM put him into other vehicles built around his youthful energy, including *Boys Town* (1938), *National Velvet* (1944), and the "barnyard musicals" costarring good friend Garland. He was the nation's top box office star from 1939 until 1942. After the war, however, his career started slipping as he committed the one seemingly unpardonable sin in his fans' eyes—he grew up. His later films were a mixed bag, though there were occasional triumphs, including an Oscar-nominated performance in *The Bold and the Brave* (1956), the Emmy-winning television drama *The Comedian*, a role as Anthony Quinn's trainer in *Requiem for a Heavyweight* (1962), and an inspired turn as silent-star Dick Van Dyke's sidekick in *The Comic* (1969). His biggest comeback came in 1979, when he played the aging horse trainer in *The Black Stallion*. He followed with a smash Broadway run with Ann Miller in the 1980 musical *Sugar Babies* and an Emmy-winning performance as a mentally challenged man in *Bill* (1981). Since then he has toured with his eighth wife, singer Jan Chamberlain, and provided voices for animated films and television shows.

Essential
MICKEYROONEYFilms

LOVE FINDS ANDY HARDY

(1938) MGM

In the fourth Andy Hardy film, Rooney got stuck taking Lana Turner to the Christmas dance while girlfriend Ann Rutherford was out of town and amorous girl-next-door Judy Garland pined—and sang—in the background.

BOYS TOWN

(1938) MGM

As the most troubled boy Spencer Tracy's Father Flanagan tried to reform, Rooney did his best to disprove the man's contention that "there's no such thing as a bad boy."

THE HUMAN COMEDY

(1943) MGM

MGM studio head Louis B. Mayer considered this film his personal favorite. Rooney delivered one of his best performances as the small-town telegraph boy in William Saroyan's tale of life on the home front during World War II.

NATIONAL VELVET

(1944) MGM

Teaming with Elizabeth Taylor, Rooney starred in one of the greatest animal films of all time, playing a traveling horse trainer who helped a young girl prepare her beloved Pi for England's Grand National.

THE BLACK STALLION

(1979) United Artists

When young Kelly Reno was marooned on a desert island with a mysterious Arabian horse, Rooney, again playing a horse trainer, helped him ready the animal for the racetrack after their rescue.

NATIONAL VELVET, 1944

BABES IN ARMS, 1939

WITH AVA GARDNER, 1942

BEHIND THE SCENES

ACCORDING TO HOLLYWOOD LEGEND, WALT DISNEY NAMED MICKEY MOUSE AFTER ROONEY.

THE ANDY HARDY FILMS ORIGINATED IN AN ATTEMPT TO CAPITALIZE ON THE SUCCESS OF *AH, WILDERNESS!* (1935), WHICH HAD STARRED LIONEL BARRYMORE, SPRING BYINGTON, ERIC LINDEN, CECELIA PARKER AND, IN A SMALL ROLE, ROONEY. THEY STARRED IN THE FIRST HARDY FILM, *A FAMILY AFFAIR* (1937), BUT WHEN STUDIO HEAD LOUIS B. MAYER DECIDED TO DO A SERIES ABOUT THE FAMILY, HE REPLACED BARRYMORE AND BYINGTON WITH THE LESS EXPENSIVE LEWIS STONE AND FAY HOLDEN, DUMPED LINDEN, AND ELEVATED ROONEY TO STARDOM.

AFTER PERFORMING ROD SERLING'S 1957 TELEVISION DRAMA "THE COMEDIAN" LIVE ON *PLAYHOUSE 90*, ROONEY RECEIVED A TELEGRAM READING, "THANKS FOR THE ACTING LESSON, PAUL MUNI."

COMMENTING ON HIS MANY MARRIAGES AND HIS ABILITY TO STAY FRIENDLY WITH MOST OF HIS EX-WIVES, ROONEY ONCE QUIPPED, "THERE'S A MICKEY ROONEY'S FORMER WIVES MARCHING BAND."

The scrawny songster dubbed "The Voice" initially parlayed his singing success into film musicals, but he developed a talent worthy of the challenging, serious roles that marked his later career.

FRANK
SINATRA

Frank Sinatra made some of his greatest contributions to the screen playing desperate loners like the drug addict in *The Man with the Golden Arm* (1955) and the tormented veteran in *The Manchurian Candidate* (1962). Through all of the media in which he worked—recordings, concerts, television, and films—he developed the image of a swinger whose coolness masked his isolation and a troubled past. Sinatra started out singing in his native Hoboken. He made it to the big time in 1939 when he signed with the Harry James Orchestra, followed by even greater exposure singing with bandleader Tommy Dorsey. Female fans, dubbed "bobby-soxers," mobbed his earliest concerts. Sinatra made his first film appearances playing Frank Sinatra, most notably as Michèle Morgan's singing suitor in *Higher and Higher* (1943). Then he moved to MGM, where he played Gene Kelly's innocent sidekick in three films, most notably *On the Town* (1949). The scandal when he left his wife and children for Ava Gardner, coupled with a throat hemorrhage that almost destroyed his voice, put his career on the skids until he won the Oscar for his role in *From Here to Eternity* (1953). Now a respected dramatic actor, he tackled such ambitious roles as a would-be presidential assassin in *Suddenly* (1954), a junkie in *The Man with the Golden Arm*, and a writer exploring the seamy side of life in *Some Came Running* (1958). When Humphrey Bogart died, Sinatra inherited leadership of a group of drinking buddies called the Rat Pack. Sinatra's version was an entertainment powerhouse as he, Dean Martin, Sammy Davis Jr., Peter Lawford, and Joey Bishop joined forces for nightclub and television appearances and such films as *Ocean's Eleven* (1960) and *Robin and the Seven Hoods* (1964). Through Lawford, he forged a close relationship with future president John F. Kennedy, at whose urging he made the political thriller *The Manchurian Candidate*. The film pointed the way to later roles as a hard-nosed detective in *Tony Rome* (1967) and *The Detective* (1968). Although he announced his retirement in 1971, he was back on the concert stage within two years. Music—most notably the 1993 *Duets* album, which paired him with such current chart toppers as Luther Vandross, Barbra Streisand, and Bono—dominated his final years, while the 1988 reissue of *The Manchurian Candidate* reminded audiences of his acting artistry.

Born
Francis Albert Sinatra
December 12, 1915
Hoboken, New Jersey

Died
May 14, 1998
Los Angeles, California,
of heart disease,
kidney disease,
and bladder cancer

Star Sign
Sagittarius

Height
5'8½"

Wives and Children
Nancy Barbato
(1939–1951, divorced)
daughters, Nancy
and Christina
son, Frank Jr.

Actress Ava Gardner
(1951–1957, divorced).

Actress Mia Farrow
(1966–1968, divorced)

Former showgirl
Barbara Blakely Marx
(1976–1998, his death)

Essential
FRANK**SINATRA**Films

ON THE TOWN

(1949) MGM
In his best boy-next-door role, Sinatra was one of three sailors (with Gene Kelly and Jules Munshin) looking for love during a whirlwind twenty-four-hour leave in New York that paired him up with cab driver Betty Garrett.

FROM HERE TO ETERNITY

(1953) Columbia
Sinatra made one of the biggest comebacks in show business history as Maggio, the tough private standing up for best friend Montgomery Clift in this all-star, Oscar-winning production from director Fred Zinnemann.

THE MAN WITH THE GOLDEN ARM

(1955) United Artists
Any doubts about Sinatra's acting ability were dispelled when he starred as a card dealer trying to kick his heroin habit with the help of stripper Kim Novak.

SOME CAME RUNNING

(1958) MGM
Sinatra gave a rare glimpse of his vulnerable side as a World War II veteran who defies his hypocritical family to become a writer, with fellow Rat Packer Dean Martin and Rat Pack mascot Shirley MacLaine both costarring with him for the first time.

THE MANCHURIAN CANDIDATE

(1962) United Artists
Sinatra starred as a former POW dodging enemy agents as he tried to find out what happened to him and fellow prisoner Laurence Harvey behind enemy lines.

ON THE TOWN, 1949

WITH DEAN MARTIN AND SAMMY DAVIS JR., CIRCA 1960s

CIRCA 1940s

BEHINDTHESCENES

SINATRA WAS SO THIN THAT THE SEAT OF HIS SAILOR'S UNIFORM IN *ON THE TOWN* (1949) HAD TO BE PADDED.

NOT NATURALLY FUNNY, SINATRA HAD MOST OF HIS "AD LIBS" FOR APPEARANCES WITH THE RAT PACK WRITTEN BY CLOSE FRIEND DEAN MARTIN.

SINATRA SIGNED TO PLAY TERRY MALLOY IN *ON THE WATERFRONT* (1954) BUT THEN WAS OUSTED IN FAVOR OF MARLON BRANDO, LEADING HIM TO FILE A SUCCESSFUL LAWSUIT AGAINST COLUMBIA PICTURES. LATER, HE BEAT OUT BRANDO FOR ROLES IN *THE MAN WITH THE GOLDEN ARM* (1955) AND *PAL JOEY* (1957).

IN THE LATE FIFTIES, SINATRA ANNOUNCED PLANS TO STAR IN AND PRODUCE *THE EXECUTION OF PRIVATE SLOVIK,* THE TRUE STORY OF THE ONLY U.S. SOLDIER EXECUTED FOR DESERTION DURING WORLD WAR II. HE HIRED BLACKLISTED WRITER ALBERT MALTZ TO WRITE THE SCRIPT, BUT WHEN JOHN WAYNE MOUNTED A PRESS CAMPAIGN AGAINST THE FILM, SINATRA DROPPED HIS PLANS.

SINATRA WAS NOTORIOUS FOR LOSING PATIENCE AFTER ONE TAKE. WHEN DIRECTOR JOHN FRANKENHEIMER WAS PRAISED FOR AN OUT-OF-FOCUS SHOT OF THE STAR IN *THE MANCHURIAN CANDIDATE,* HE HAD TO ADMIT IT WAS AN ACCIDENT LEFT IN THE FILM BECAUSE HE DIDN'T WANT TO ASK SINATRA TO DO A SECOND TAKE.

WHEN THIRD WIFE MIA FARROW REFUSED TO WALK OUT ON *ROSEMARY'S BABY* (1968), WHICH WAS RUNNING BEHIND SCHEDULE, SO SHE COULD COSTAR WITH HIM IN *THE DETECTIVE* (1968), SINATRA HAD DIVORCE PAPERS DELIVERED TO HER ON THE FILM'S SET.

With his stammering delivery and gangly physique, he gave audiences a boyishly likable rooting interest, often playing average guys struggling to do the right thing when pushed to the limits.

JAMES
STEWART

Numerous television airings of *It's a Wonderful Life* (1946), particularly at the holidays, have made James Stewart seem a member of most people's families. That the film stands up to repeated viewings is a tribute to his ability to appear "unusually usual" (in the words of director W. S. Van Dyke) as everything from eternally tongue tied small-town boys to ruthless, often obsessed heroes. Stewart was himself a small-town boy. While studying architecture at Princeton, he allowed classmate Josh Logan to talk him into joining his University Players summer theater troupe in Cape Cod, where he met lifelong friend Henry Fonda. He learned his craft on Broadway before signing with MGM, where he made his feature debut in *The Murder Man* (1935), starring Spencer Tracy. MGM didn't know what to do with him at first; they even cast him as a villain in *After the Thin Man* (1936). It was director Frank Capra at Columbia Pictures who made him a star in *You Can't Take It with You* (1938) and *Mr. Smith Goes to Washington* (1939). After his Oscar-winning role as the reporter who falls for Katharine Hepburn in *The Philadelphia Story* (1940), Stewart signed up for World War II service. He came back a more mature personality, as demonstrated in his first postwar film, Capra's *It's a Wonderful Life*. Although it lost money on its initial release, television and revival-house screenings have made it one of his most recognizable roles. Stewart's MGM contract had run out during the war, and on his own, he explored a wide variety of roles, from the driven western heroes of *Winchester '73* (1950) and *The Naked Spur* (1953) to the whimsical comedy of *Harvey* (1950). After making *Rope* (1948), *Rear Window* (1954), and *The Man Who Knew Too Much* (1956) with director Alfred Hitchcock, Stewart played against his all-American charm in *Vertigo* (1958), an eerie tale of romantic obsession. Stewart also scored a hit as the eccentric, jazz-loving, small-town lawyer in *Anatomy of a Murder* (1959). Few of his later films offered as much range, however, as he was increasingly typecast as slow-talking, unsophisticated characters. Only the desert-survival adventure *Flight of the Phoenix* (1965), the poignant John Wayne western *The Shootist* (1976), and a return to Broadway for *Harvey* offered him real acting challenges. Stewart finished his career with cameo roles and voice-over work, most notably a cameo as Wylie Burp in 1991's *An American Tail: Feivel Goes West*.

Born
James Maitland Stewart
May 20, 1908
Indiana, Pennsylvania

Died
July 2, 1997
Los Angeles, California,
of a pulmonary embolism
following respiratory problems

Star Sign
Taurus

Height
6'3½"

Wife and Children
Former model
Gloria Hatrick McLean
(1949–1994, her death)
daughters, Judy and Kelly
adopted sons,
Ronald and Michael

Essential
JAMESSTEWARTFilms

MR. SMITH GOES TO WASHINGTON
(1939) Columbia
The role of a naive senator going up against a corrupt political machine headed by Claude Rains was the first to suggest the depths of James Stewart's dramatic talents.

THE SHOP AROUND THE CORNER
(1940) MGM
In the most fondly remembered of his four films with Margaret Sullavan, they starred for director Ernst Lubitsch as workplace enemies who didn't realize they'd fallen in love through anonymous letters.

THE PHILADELPHIA STORY
(1940) MGM
Stewart garnered his only Oscar win for his role as a cynical tabloid reporter who crashes socialite Katharine Hepburn's wedding with the assistance of her ex-husband (Cary Grant), only to find himself falling for the bride-to-be.

IT'S A WONDERFUL LIFE
(1946) RKO
The American dream hit rock bottom for Stewart in Frank Capra's tale of a small-town banker who consistently sacrificed himself for those around him without realizing how much good he was doing.

VERTIGO
(1958) Paramount
In a film often hailed as one of Alfred Hitchcock's greatest, Stewart is a detective who becomes obsessed with a mysterious woman (Kim Novak) who he is hired to follow.

MR. SMITH GOES TO WASHINGTON, 1939

IT'S A WONDERFUL LIFE, 1946

BEHINDTHESCENES

ONE OF STEWART'S FAVORITE LEADING LADIES WAS MARGARET SULLAVAN, WHOM HE HAD MET WORKING WITH THE UNIVERSITY PLAYERS. WHEN HE WAS NEW IN HOLLY-WOOD, SHE GAVE HIM A CAREER BOOST BY DEMANDING HIM AS HER LEADING MAN IN *NEXT TIME WE LOVE* (1936). THEY WOULD RETEAM FOR THREE MORE FILMS, INCLUDING *THE SHOP AROUND THE CORNER* (1940).

TO SOUND SUITABLY HOARSE FOR HIS FILIBUSTER SCENE IN *MR. SMITH GOES TO WASHINGTON* (1939), STEWART DRIED OUT HIS THROAT WITH BICARBONATE OF SODA.

STEWART SENT HIS OSCAR FOR *THE PHILADELPHIA STORY* (1940) HOME TO HIS FATHER, WHERE IT STOOD IN THE WINDOW OF THE FAMILY'S INDIANA, PENNSYLVANIA, HARDWARE STORE FOR TWENTY-FIVE YEARS.

WHILE FILMING THE LONG SHOT OF HIS PRAYER IN *IT'S A WONDERFUL LIFE* (1946), STEWART WAS SO MOVED, HE BEGAN SOBBING FOR REAL. RATHER THAN RISK LOSING THE INTENSITY BY SHOOTING ADDITIONAL TAKES, DIRECTOR FRANK CAPRA CREATED CLOSE-UPS BY ENLARGING FRAMES OF THE LONG SHOT.

STEWART DISTINGUISHED HIMSELF SERVING WITH THE U.S. ARMY AIR CORPS DURING WORLD WAR II. YEARS LATER, HE RETIRED FROM THE U.S. AIR FORCE RESERVE AS A BRIGADIER GENERAL, THE HIGHEST MILITARY RANK EVER EARNED BY A FILM STAR. ON HIS RETURN FROM WORLD WAR II, STEWART HAD A CLAUSE INSERTED IN MOST OF HIS FILM CONTRACTS PROHIBITING THE PRODUCTION COMPANIES FROM MENTIONING HIS MILITARY SERVICE IN ANY PUBLICITY.

BY THE TIME STEWART MADE HIS THIRD ALFRED HITCHCOCK FILM, *THE MAN WHO KNEW TOO MUCH* (1956), HE KNEW HOW THE DIRECTOR WORKED AND WAS CONSTANTLY REASSURING THE CAST OVER PROBLEMS WITH REWRITES. HE ALSO KNEW THAT HE AND DORIS DAY WOULD NEED TO REHEARSE ON THEIR OWN FOR THEIR MOST DIFFICULT SCENE, IN WHICH HE TELLS HER THEIR SON HAS BEEN KIDNAPPED. AS A RESULT, THEY GOT THE SCENE ON THE FIRST TAKE.

Rising above his youthful good looks, he shone in action films as well as romances, bringing gallantry and a robust, take-charge enthusiasm to three decades of work.

ROBERT
TAYLOR

Robert Taylor would have been the first to admit he was never the world's greatest actor. Originally signed at MGM because of his good looks, he gradually developed an innate decency that made him one of the screen's most appealingly masculine leading men. Although his heroes often lacked complexity, they were always grounded in a bedrock of traditional values, which may account for his staying power at MGM, where he was under contract for twenty-four years, longer than almost any other leading actor. The rugged action star grew up a mama's boy in Nebraska. To please his hypochondriac mother, he enrolled in California's Pomona College to study music. He also got involved with student theatrical productions, where an MGM talent scout spotted him. He signed with the studio in 1934, though at first they seemed mostly interested in showcasing his good looks in a series of thankless roles. That paid off, however, when he took his shirt off in *Society Doctor* (1935) and started getting more fan mail. Later that year, a loan to Universal for the hit romance *Magnificent Obsession*, with Irene Dunne, made him a star. MGM responded by casting him opposite other top leading ladies, including Greta Garbo in *Camille* (1937), Joan Crawford in *The Gorgeous Hussy* (1936), and Barbara Stanwyck in *His Brother's Wife* (1936) and *This Is My Affair* (1937). Stanwyck would become his constant companion offscreen, helping him grow up and hone his talents, and they married in 1939. Feeling the need to get beyond his pretty-boy image, Taylor asked for tougher roles, which he got, stating with 1938's *A Yank at Oxford*. Subsequent roles as a British army officer in *Waterloo Bridge* (1940), a glamorous gangster in *Johnny Eager* (1942), and a rugged marine in *Bataan* (1943) strengthened his new, more robust image. Like many male stars who served in World War II, Taylor had trouble reestablishing his career afterward. It took the historical epic *Quo Vadis?* (1951) to put him back on top, though rumors of his on-set dalliances with an Italian starlet ended his marriage to Stanwyck. After more historical hits, including *Ivanhoe* (1952), Taylor left MGM in 1958 and turned to television, where he starred for three years in the hit series *The Detectives*. He finished his career as host of the series *Death Valley Days*, replacing friend Ronald Reagan when the latter went into politics.

Born
Spangler Arlington Brugh
August 5, 1911
Filley, Nebraska

Died
June 8, 1969
Santa Monica, California,
of lung cancer

Star Sign
Leo

Height
5'11½"

Wives and Children
Actress Barbara Stanwyck
(1939–1951, divorced)

Actress Ursula Thiess
(1954–1969, his death)
son, Terrence
daughter, Theresa

Essential
ROBERT**TAYLOR**Films

CAMILLE
(1937) MGM
This prestige picture featured Robert Taylor as Greta Garbo's youthful lover, though it also inspired jokes about his being prettier than his leading lady.

A YANK AT OXFORD
(1938) MGM
Taylor created a new, manlier image as a young American student whose brashness alienated his classmates at the famed British school until his athletic skills made him a hero.

WATERLOO BRIDGE
(1940) MGM
In his favorite film, Taylor starred as a British army officer involved in a doomed romance with ballerina Vivien Leigh.

JOHNNY EAGER
(1942) MGM
Ads proclaimed that Taylor and Lana Turner were "hotter 'n T-N-T" when they starred as a glamorous gangster and the society girl he started to ruin (her father is the district attorney) and ends up loving.

QUO VADIS?
(1951) MGM
As a Roman centurion converted by beautiful Christian slave Deborah Kerr while Nero (Peter Ustinov) prepared to burn Rome, Taylor enjoyed his first big postwar hit, opening the way for more historical epics in his future.

WATERLOO BRIDGE, 1940

WITH BARBARA STANWYCK, CIRCA 1930s

JOHNNY EAGER, 1942

BEHINDTHESCENES

TAYLOR'S WIDOW'S PEAK WAS A STUDIO CREATION. IT WAS PART OF THE MGM HAIRDRESSING DEPARTMENT'S ATTEMPT TO CAPITALIZE ON HIS GOOD LOOKS.

WATERLOO BRIDGE (1940) IS ONE OF THE MOST POPULAR U.S.-MADE FILMS IN CHINA. STUDENTS OFTEN WATCH THE FILM TO PRACTICE THEIR ENGLISH.

TAYLOR WAS ONE OF THE "FRIENDLY WITNESSES" TESTIFYING AT THE START OF THE HOUSE UN-AMERICAN ACTIVITIES COMMITTEE'S HEARINGS ABOUT ALLEGED COMMUNIST INFILTRATION OF THE MOTION PICTURE INDUSTRY AND IS ONE OF THE ONLY HOLLYWOOD FIGURE TO BE FILMED NAMING NAMES.

AFTER TAYLOR'S RETIREMENT FROM MGM, THE STUDIO RECHRISTENED ITS WRITERS' HEADQUARTERS THE ROBERT TAYLOR BUILDING. IN 1989, AFTER LORIMAR PRODUCTIONS HAD BOUGHT THE BACK LOT, A GROUP OF WRITERS PETITIONED SUCCESSFULLY TO HAVE HIS NAME REMOVED FROM THE BUILDING BECAUSE OF HIS INVOLVEMENT IN THE ANTI-COMMUNIST WITCH-HUNT OF THE LATE FORTIES AND EARLY FIFTIES.

He played forthright, good-hearted individualists with such ease that he seemed not to be acting, whether in dark dramas or the crackling romantic comedies that paired him with his longtime offscreen companion, Katharine Hepburn.

SPENCER
TRACY

Spencer Tracy was one of the screen's great independents. As a child, he struck out on his own several times, running away from home at seven, joining the navy at seventeen, and quitting college to become an actor after starring in a few school productions. A three-year association with George M. Cohan bolstered his Broadway career, but he didn't think he had a future in movies until director John Ford spotted him playing a death row prisoner in *The Last Mile* and insisted Fox cast him in his own prison film, *Up the River* (1930). Tracy was so unhappy with most of his films there, however, that he grew increasingly rebellious, until the studio fired him. MGM production head Irving G. Thalberg came to the rescue but saw him initially only as a second lead. When Tracy almost stole *San Francisco* (1936) from stars Clark Gable and Jeanette MacDonald, the studio started developing vehicles for him. With his performance as Father Flanagan in *Boys Town* (1938), he became a star in his own right. Tracy found his perfect screen partner when Katharine Hepburn requested he be cast as her leading man in *Woman of the Year* (1942). Through nine films together, his craggy stubbornness was the perfect foil for her fussiness as they matched wits in a series of sophisticated battles of the sexes including *Adam's Rib* (1949) and *Pat and Mike* (1952). Offscreen, they became constant companions, though, out of respect for his wife, they kept their relationship as discreet as possible. Tracy moved effortlessly into older roles, playing the frustrated fathers in *Father of the Bride* (1950) and *The Actress* (1953) to perfection. He proved he could handle an action film— at fifty-five—in the modern western *Bad Day at Black Rock* (1955), his last MGM film. By the sixties, Tracy had become a walking symbol of integrity, as reflected by his performances in producer-director Stanley Kramer's *Inherit the Wind* (1960) and *Judgment at Nuremberg* (1961). Plagued by health problems, he was off screen for four years before making one last film with Hepburn, *Guess Who's Coming to Dinner* (1967). When he spoke of his deep love for her in the film, fans couldn't help thinking he was talking about their offscreen relationship as well. Seventeen days after finishing the film, he passed away. It was the end of an era.

Born
Spencer Bonaventure Tracy
April 5, 1900
Milwaukee, Wisconsin

Died
June 10, 1967
Beverly Hills, California,
of a heart attack

Star Sign
Aries

Height
5'10½"

Wife and Children
Actress Louise Treadwell
(1923–1967, his death)
son, John
daughter, Susy

Longtime companion actress
Katharine Hepburn
(1941–1967, his death)

Essential
SPENCER TRACY Films

FURY
(1936) MGM
Tracy gave the first hint of his potential as a film star in director Fritz Lang's tale of a man believed dead at the hands of a lynch mob who then watched in secret as his "killers" stood trial.

WOMAN OF THE YEAR
(1942) MGM
In their first film together, Tracy and Katharine Hepburn set the chemistry that would dominate in all their pairings, starring as a craggy sports columnist and a sophisticated political correspondent who married in haste and repented in hilarity.

ADAM'S RIB
(1949) MGM
Tracy and Hepburn starred as married attorneys on opposite sides of a controversial women's rights case, with Judy Holliday as the defendant and George Cukor directing.

FATHER OF THE BRIDE
(1950) MGM
Tracy mixed psychological comedy with physical humor as the beleaguered father who watched in horror as daughter Elizabeth Taylor's wedding grew more and more elaborate.

BAD DAY AT BLACK ROCK
(1955) MGM
Tracy headed up an impressive cast, including Robert Ryan and Walter Brennan, as a one-armed veteran who uncovered deadly secrets when he tried to bring a dead soldier's medals to the man's Japanese-American parents.

WOMAN OF THE YEAR, 1942

FATHER OF THE BRIDE, 1950

BEHIND THE SCENES

WHEN THE TRACYS LEARNED THEIR SON, JOHN, WAS DEAF, HIS WIFE BECAME A TIRELESS WORKER ON BEHALF OF DEAF CHILDREN AND THEIR FAMILIES, FOUNDING THE JOHN TRACY CLINIC IN 1943. BEING TRACY'S WIFE OPENED A LOT OF DOORS FOR HER, WHICH IS ONE REASON TRACY AND HEPBURN KEPT THEIR RELATIONSHIP UNDER WRAPS FOR OVER THIRTY YEARS.

THE SUCCESS OF *BOYS TOWN* (1938) GAVE AUDIENCES THE IMPRESSION THAT THE HOME FOR BOYS DIDN'T NEED ANY MORE MONEY, AND DONATIONS FELL OFF TREMENDOUSLY. TRACY HAD TO GO ON THE RADIO AND MAKE A PERSONAL APPEAL TO KEEP THE PLACE RUNNING.

TRACY WAS THE FIRST MAN TO WIN BACK-TO-BACK OSCARS FOR BEST ACTOR, A FEAT NOT DUPLICATED UNTIL TOM HANKS WON IN 1993 AND 1994.

WRITER GARSON KANIN, A LONGTIME FRIEND OF TRACY AND HEPBURN, ONCE ASKED TRACY WHY HE ALWAYS INSISTED ON TOP BILLING IN HIS FILMS WITH HER, REMINDING HIM, "LADIES FIRST." TRACY SHOT BACK, "THIS IS A MOVIE, CHOWDERHEAD, NOT A LIFEBOAT!"

TRACY WAS ALWAYS DIRECTOR VINCENTE MINNELLI'S FIRST CHOICE TO STAR IN *FATHER OF THE BRIDE* (1950), BUT WHEN STUDIO PRODUCTION HEAD DORE SCHARY PROMISED JACK BENNY A CHANCE TO TEST FOR THE ROLE, TRACY TURNED THE PICTURE DOWN, CONVINCED MINNELLI DIDN'T WANT HIM. THE DIRECTOR FINALLY ARRANGED A MEETING THROUGH HEPBURN, AT WHICH HE TOLD TRACY THAT THE FILM WOULD BE A MINOR PICTURE WITHOUT HIM BUT A CLASSIC WITH HIM. THAT WAS ALL HE'D NEEDED TO HEAR.

BECAUSE OF TRACY'S ILL HEALTH, NOBODY WOULD INSURE *GUESS WHO'S COMING TO DINNER* (1967). HEPBURN AND KRAMER HAD TO PUT UP THEIR SALARIES AS COLLATERAL TO CAST HIM IN THE FILM.

THE PHILADELPHIA STORY (1940) WAS ALMOST THE FIRST FILM TO TEAM TRACY AND KATHARINE HEPBURN. WHEN SHE FIRST SOLD MGM THE RIGHTS TO HER BROADWAY HIT, SHE REQUESTED CLARK GABLE TO PLAY HER EX-HUSBAND AND TRACY FOR THE JOURNALIST WHO FALLS FOR HER. BOTH STARS WERE TIED UP ON OTHER PICTURES, SO THE ROLES WENT TO CARY GRANT AND JAMES STEWART RESPECTIVELY.

Recognized as the first male sex symbol, he mesmerized female moviegoers with his exotic brand of illicit romance—only to leave his fans devastated by his unexpected death at the age of 31.

RUDOLPH
VALENTINO

Born
Rudolfo Alfonzo
Raffaelo Pierre Filibert
Guglielmi di Valentina
d'Antonguolla
May 6, 1895
Castellaneta, Italy

Died
August 23, 1926
New York, New York,
of a perforated ulcer
and blood poisoning

Star Sign
Taurus

Height
5'10"

Wives
Actress Jean Acker
(1919–1923, divorced)

Designer Natacha Rambova
(1923–1926, divorced)

The tango was Rudolph Valentino's ticket to the big time. The Latin dance, with its dominant, almost threatening male, was a perfect mirror of his star image as the "sex menace," as apt to throw a woman across the room as to make love to her. Valentino learned the dance hanging out with a wild crowd in Paris shortly after graduating from college in his native Italy. When he relocated to the United States, it was the dance that helped him establish a career in vaudeville after work as a landscaper, waiter, gigolo, and petty thief. He introduced the dance to the screen in his star-making vehicle, *The Four Horsemen of the Apocalypse* (1921) and toured vaudeville theaters performing it with his second wife, former dancer Natacha Rambova. Valentino had started his film career playing villains, eventually catching the eye of screenwriter June Mathis. When director Rex Ingram was looking for a new personality to play the tempestuous gaucho in *The Four Horsemen of the Apocalypse,* she recommended Valentino, and his tango scene made him a star. The film, Hollywood's first $1 million production, saved Metro Pictures from bankruptcy, but the studio didn't know what to do with this new breed of star and dropped his contract. Moving to Paramount, Valentino scored his biggest hits with *The Sheik* (1921) and *Blood and Sand* (1922). Then he made the mistake of letting Rambova take charge of his career. Although an accomplished designer in her own right, her influence on *Monsieur Beaucaire* and *A Sainted Devil* (both 1924) turned him into an androgynous pretty boy, costing him dearly at the box office and reviving suspicions that he was homosexual. When he signed with United Artists, the contract stipulated that Rambova have no involvement in his productions, which triggered a rift between the two. Nonetheless, Valentino revived his career by moving toward swashbuckling adventure with his first UA production, *The Eagle* (1925). But he was heartbroken when Rambova filed for divorce. Valentino was publicizing his next film, *The Son of the Sheik* (1926), when he fell ill in New York and died of an infection following surgery for a bleeding ulcer. His funeral was one of the biggest events in film history, with 80,000 mourners causing a near riot in New York. For years afterward, a mysterious woman in black placed flowers on his grave every year, on the anniversary of his death.

Essential
RUDOLPH VALENTINO Films

THE FOUR HORSEMEN OF THE APOCALYPSE
(1921) Metro
In the film that made him a star, Valentino played a free-living artist romancing married woman Alice Terry (the wife of director Rex Ingram) until World War I tore his family apart.

CAMILLE
(1921) Metro
With daring, stylized sets designed by Natacha Rambova, this modernized adaptation of the classic romance starred Valentino as the young innocent caught up in courtesan Alla Nazimova's decadent world.

THE SHEIK
(1921) Paramount
Lust drove desert chieftain Valentino to kidnap British socialite Agnes Ayres, but love sends him to her rescue when she's taken captive by an outlaw band in the film that made Valentino—and the word *sheik*—household words.

BLOOD AND SAND
(1922) Paramount
Valentino rose from poverty to stardom in the bullring, only to risk his reputation when he left wife Lila Lee for fiery temptress Nita Naldi.

THE EAGLE
(1925) United Artists
Russian army officer Valentino became a masked outlaw to avenge the theft of his family's lands in the film that pointed him toward a new career as a swashbuckler.

THE SHEIK, 1921

THE SON OF THE SHEIK, 1926

BEHIND THE SCENES

VALENTINO'S MARRIAGE TO FIRST WIFE JEAN ACKER MAY BE THE SHORTEST IN HOLLYWOOD HISTORY. (OFFICIALLY, IT LASTED FOUR YEARS, BUT IN REALITY IT WAS OVER WITHIN HOURS.) APPARENTLY, HE MARRIED HER BECAUSE OF HER CONNECTIONS IN HOLLYWOOD, NOT REALIZING SHE HAD BEEN INVOLVED IN A LESBIAN AFFAIR WITH ACTRESS ALLA NAZIMOVA. SHE LOCKED HIM OUT OF THEIR HOTEL ROOM SIX HOURS AFTER THE WEDDING. THEY NEVER EVEN LIVED TOGETHER.

VALENTINO MADE ONLY $350 A WEEK WHILE FILMING *THE FOUR HORSEMEN OF THE APOCALYPSE* (1921), LESS THAN SOME OF THE SUPPORTING PLAYERS WHO WERE UNDER CONTRACT AT METRO PICTURES. THE STUDIO ALSO MADE HIM BUY HIS OWN COSTUMES FOR THE PARIS SEQUENCE.

WITH THE SUCCESS OF *THE SHEIK* (1921), THE FILM'S TITLE BECAME A POPULAR SLANG TERM FOR AN ATTRACTIVE MAN.

THINKING HIS FIRST DIVORCE WAS FINAL, VALENTINO MARRIED DESIGNER NATACHA RAMBOVA IN 1923, ONLY TO BE HIT WITH BIGAMY CHARGES AND A $10,000 FINE.

WHEN VALENTINO RETURNED FROM A EUROPEAN VACATION WITH A BEARD HE PLANNED TO WEAR IN THE NEVER COMPLETED FILM, *THE HOODED FALCON* (1924), A NATIONAL BARBERS' ASSOCIATION THREATENED TO BOYCOTT THE FILM UNLESS HE SHAVED, WHICH HE DID IN A MASSIVE PR EVENT.

VALENTINO WAS SO DEEP IN DEBT WHEN HE DIED THAT HIS FAMILY COULDN'T AFFORD A BURIAL PLOT FOR HIM. WRITER JUNE MATHIS "LOANED" THEM A SPACE IN A MAUSOLEUM, WHERE HE REMAINS TODAY.

THROUGH THE YEARS, SEVERAL WOMEN HAVE CLAIMED TO BE THE LADY IN BLACK WHO PLACES ROSES AT VALENTINO'S GRAVE ON THE ANNIVERSARY OF HIS DEATH. IN 1947, DITRA FLAME MADE THE MOST RELIABLE CLAIM TO THAT IDENTITY. A DAUGHTER OF ONE OF VALENTINO'S FRIENDS, SHE HAD BEEN VISITED IN THE HOSPITAL BY VALENTINO, WHO BROUGHT HER A SINGLE RED ROSE AND PROMISED SHE WOULD GET BETTER.

No one rode taller in the saddle than "the Duke." His straight-talking drawl and ability to stare down the toughest opponent made him the embodiment of the men who tamed the West.

JOHN
WAYNE

John Wayne said it best himself: "Goddamn, I'm the stuff men are made of!" His films gave the impression he had conquered the Old West and won World War II single-handedly. Often defying authority to follow his own moral code, he was the epitome of frontier justice. Wayne got his first taste of pioneer life when his ailing father moved the family to a California ranch in search of a better climate. A good student, Wayne attended the University of Southern California on a football scholarship and got into the movies through a summer job arranged by team fan Tom Mix. While doing crew work, he befriended director John Ford, who recommended him for the leading role in *The Big Trail* (1930), and the studio renamed him John Wayne. When the film flopped, however, Wayne found himself consigned to Poverty Row studios, where he gradually carved a niche in low-budget westerns. Ford came to the rescue by casting him as the Ringo Kid in his "adult" western *Stagecoach* (1939), a major hit that made Wayne a star. Then Cecil B. DeMille put him in the historical epic *Reap the Wild Wind* (1942), exposing Wayne to an audience that didn't normally go to westerns. In 1948, director Howard Hawks gave him a chance to act as the tyrannical cattle baron in *Red River* (1948), and he surprised everyone with a critically acclaimed performance. Wayne continued with a series of demanding roles, most notably in *She Wore a Yellow Ribbon* (1949) and *The Searchers* (1956). By 1949, Wayne had entered the yearly list of top ten box office stars, where he would appear a record twenty-four times. He took a stab at directing with *The Alamo* (1960), but the expensive film almost bankrupted him. To bounce back, he increased his output, assembling a team in front of and behind the cameras (including actor son Patrick and producer son Michael) that made his films family affairs. Wayne took a chance on a character role—the one-eyed, aging lawman in *True Grit* (1969)—and walked off with the Oscar for Best Actor. He had already lost a lung to cancer when he made his final film appearance, as a dying gunman in *The Shootist* (1976). On his later films, he had to have oxygen on the set to help him breathe between takes. When he died in 1979, one Tokyo paper carried the headline, "Mr. America Is Dead," a fitting reflection of his place in film history.

Born
Marion Michael Morrison
May 26, 1907
Winterset, Iowa

Died
June 11, 1979
Los Angeles, California,
of lung and stomach cancer

Star Sign
Gemini

Height
6'4½"

Wives and Children
Socialite Josephine Saenz
(1933–1945, divorced)
sons, Michael and Patrick
daughters, Antonia Maria
and Melinda Ann

Singer-dancer
Esperanza "Chata" Bauer
(1946–1953, divorced)

Actress Pilar Pallete
(1954–1979, his death)
daughters, Aissa and Marissa
son, John Ethan

Essential
JOHNWAYNEFilms

STAGECOACH
(1939) United Artists
Wayne shot to stardom when John Ford cast him as a cowboy on the run who helped save the passengers of a stagecoach under Indian attack before once again escaping "the blessings of civilization."

SHE WORE A YELLOW RIBBON
(1949) RKO
In the second film of Ford's U.S. Cavalry trilogy, Wayne starred as an aging army captain leading one last, perilous campaign against the Indians before his retirement.

THE QUIET MAN
(1952) Republic
As a retired boxer who returned to his family home in Ireland, Wayne romanced his perfect leading lady, Maureen O'Hara, before joining Victor McLaglen for a rousing final fistfight.

THE SEARCHERS
(1956) Warner Bros.
Director John Ford turned this epic into a western revenge tragedy, with Wayne as a notorious Indian hunter on the trail of the Apaches who kidnapped his niece (Natalie Wood) and killed the rest of his brother's family.

TRUE GRIT
(1969) Paramount
Wayne finally won his Oscar playing a broken-down, lonely U.S. marshal who agreed to help a young girl (Kim Darby) track the outlaws who killed her father.

SHE WORE A YELLOW RIBBON, 1949

BEHINDTHE**SCENES**

JOHN WAYNE GOT HIS NICKNAME, "THE DUKE," AS A CHILD, WHEN HE OWNED A LARGE DOG NAMED DUKE. PEOPLE STARTED REFERRING TO THE DOG AS BIG DUKE AND WAYNE AS LITTLE DUKE.

WAYNE PLAYED MORE LEADING ROLES THAN ANY OTHER HOLLYWOOD ACTOR—142 IN 160 FILM CREDITS.

WAYNE'S MOST IMPRESSIVE ACTING JOB WAS SIMPLY PLAYING JOHN WAYNE. HE CREATED THE CHARACTER DURING HIS TIME IN LOW-BUDGET WESTERNS IN THE THIRTIES, MODELING HIS ROLLING WALK AND SLOW, DELIBERATE DRAWL ON LEGENDARY STUNTMAN YAKIMA CANUTT.

ALTHOUGH WAYNE SEEMED TO HAVE WON WORLD WAR II SINGLE-HANDEDLY ONSCREEN, HE NEVER SERVED IN THE MILITARY. AN EAR INJURY SUSTAINED DURING UNDERWATER PHOTOGRAPHY FOR *REAP THE WILD WIND* (1942) RENDERED HIM PHYSICALLY UNFIT FOR SERVICE.

WAYNE CONSIDERED THE PART OF ETHAN EDWARDS IN *THE SEARCHERS* (1956) THE BEST ROLE HE EVER HAD AND NAMED A SON FOR THE CHARACTER.

***THE CONQUEROR* (1956) WAS FILMED IN 1953 ON LOCATION IN UTAH, NOT FAR FROM A GOVERNMENT NUCLEAR-BOMB-TESTING SITE IN NEVADA. HOLLYWOOD HISTORIANS HAVE LONG SPECULATED THAT THE SURPRISING NUMBER OF CANCER DEATHS AMONG CAST AND CREW—INCLUDING WAYNE, DICK POWELL, SUSAN HAYWARD, AND AGNES MOOREHEAD—WERE THE RESULT OF FALLOUT.**

THE REPUBLICAN PARTY TRIED TO DRAFT WAYNE TO RUN FOR PRESIDENT IN 1968, BUT HE REFUSED, INSISTING VOTERS WOULDN'T TAKE HIM SERIOUSLY, BECAUSE HE WAS A MOVIE STAR.

ONE ROLE WAYNE CAMPAIGNED FOR VIGOROUSLY WAS GENERAL GEORGE S. PATTON IN *PATTON* (1970), A PART MANY OTHER STARS TURNED DOWN BEFORE IT WENT TO GEORGE C. SCOTT.

WHEN THE ROUGH CUT OF THE FINAL SHOOT-OUT IN *THE SHOOTIST* (1976) SHOWED HIM SHOOTING A MAN IN THE BACK, WAYNE INSISTED IT BE REEDITED, CLAIMING HE HAD NEVER DONE ANYTHING LIKE THAT IN ANY OF HIS FILMS BEFORE.

FILMOGRAPHIES

FRED ASTAIRE

Dancing Lady, 1933
Flying Down to Rio, 1933
The Gay Divorcee, 1934
Roberta, 1935
Top Hat, 1935
Follow the Fleet, 1936
Swing Time, 1936
Shall We Dance, 1937
A Damsel in Distress, 1937
Carefree, 1938
The Story of Vernon and Irene Castle, 1939
Broadway Melody of 1940, 1940
Second Chorus, 1940
You'll Never Get Rich, 1941
Holiday Inn, 1942
You Were Never Lovelier, 1942
The Sky's the Limit, 1943
Yolanda and the Thief, 1945
Blue Skies, 1946
Easter Parade, 1948
The Barkleys of Broadway, 1949
Three Little Words, 1950
Let's Dance, 1950
Royal Wedding, 1951
The Belle of New York, 1952
The Band Wagon, 1953
Daddy Long Legs, 1955
Funny Face, 1957
Silk Stockings, 1957
On the Beach, 1959
The Pleasure of His Company, 1961
The Notorious Landlady, 1962
Finian's Rainbow, 1968
Midas Run, 1969
The Towering Inferno, 1974
The Amazing Dobermans, 1976
The Purple Taxi, 1977
Ghost Story, 1981

JOHN BARRYMORE

An American Citizen, 1914
The Man from Mexico, 1914
Are You a Mason?, 1915
The Dictator, 1915
The Incorrigible Dukane, 1915
Nearly a King, 1916
The Lost Bridegroom, 1916
The Red Widow, 1916
Raffles, the Amateur Cracksman, 1917
On the Quiet, 1918
Here Comes the Bride, 1919
The Test of Honor, 1919
Dr. Jekyll and Mr. Hyde, 1920
The Lotus Eater, 1921
Sherlock Holmes, 1922
Beau Brummel, 1924
The Sea Beast, 1926
Don Juan, 1926
When a Man Loves, 1927
The Beloved Rogue, 1927
Tempest, 1928
Eternal Love, 1929

General Crack, 1930
The Man from Blankley's, 1930
Moby Dick, 1930
Svengali, 1931
The Mad Genius, 1931
Arsène Lupin, 1932
Grand Hotel, 1932
State's Attorney, 1932
A Bill of Divorcement, 1932
Rasputin and the Empress, 1933
Topaze, 1933
Reunion in Vienna, 1933
Dinner at Eight, 1933
Night Flight, 1933
Counsellor at Law, 1933
Long Lost Father, 1934
Twentieth Century, 1934
Romeo and Juliet, 1936
Maytime, 1937
Bulldog Drummond Comes Back, 1937
Night Club Scandal, 1937
True Confession, 1937
Bulldog Drummond's Revenge, 1938
Romance in the Dark, 1938
Bulldog Drummond's Peril, 1938
Marie Antoinette, 1938
Spawn of the North, 1938
Hold that Co-Ed, 1938
The Great Man Votes, 1939
Midnight, 1939
The Great Profile, 1940
The Invisible Woman, 1940
World Premiere, 1941
Playmates, 1941

HUMPHREY BOGART

Up the River, 1930
A Devil with Women, 1930
Body and Soul, 1931
Bad Sister, 1931
A Holy Terror, 1931
Love Affair, 1932
Big City Blues, 1932
Three on a Match, 1932
Midnight, 1934
The Petrified Forest, 1936
Bullets or Ballots, 1936
Two Against the World, 1936
China Clipper, 1936
Isle of Fury, 1936
Black Legion, 1937
The Great O'Malley, 1937
Marked Woman, 1937
Kid Galahad, 1937
San Quentin, 1937
Dead End, 1937
Stand-In, 1937
Swing Your Lady, 1938
Crime School, 1938
Racket Busters, 1938
Men Are Such Fools, 1938
The Amazing Dr. Clitterhouse, 1938

Angels with Dirty Faces, 1938
King of the Underworld, 1939
The Oklahoma Kid, 1939
Dark Victory, 1939
You Can't Get Away with Murder, 1939
The Roaring Twenties, 1939
The Return of Doctor X, 1939
Invisible Stripes, 1939
Virginia City, 1940
It All Came True, 1940
Brother Orchid, 1940
They Drive by Night, 1940
High Sierra, 1941
The Wagons Roll at Night, 1941
The Maltese Falcon, 1941
All Through the Night, 1942
The Big Shot, 1942
Across the Pacific, 1942
Casablanca, 1942
Action in the North Atlantic, 1943
Sahara, 1943
Passage to Marseille, 1944
To Have and Have Not, 1944
Conflict, 1945
The Big Sleep, 1946
Dead Reckoning, 1947
The Two Mrs. Carrolls, 1947
Dark Passage, 1947
The Treasure of the Sierra Madre, 1948
Key Largo, 1948
Knock on Any Door, 1949
Tokyo Joe, 1949
Chain Lightning, 1950
In a Lonely Place, 1950
The Enforcer, 1951
Sirocco, 1951
The African Queen, 1951
Deadline—U.S.A., 1952
Battle Circus, 1953
Beat the Devil, 1953
The Caine Mutiny, 1954
Sabrina, 1954
The Barefoot Contessa, 1954
We're No Angels, 1955
The Left Hand of God, 1955
The Desperate Hours, 1955
The Harder They Fall, 1956

CHARLES BOYER

L'Homme du Large, 1920
Chantelouve/Chante-Iouve, 1921
Le Grillon du Foyer, 1922
La Ronde Infernale/Infernal Circle, 1927
Le Capitaine Fracasse/Captain Fracasse, 1929
La Barcarolle d'Amour, 1929
Révolte dans la Prison, 1930
Le Procès de Mary Dugan, 1931
The Magnificent Lie, 1931
Tumultes, 1932
The Man from Yesterday, 1932
Red-Headed Woman, 1932
I.F. 1 Ne Répond Plus, 1932

L' Épervier/Les Amoureux, 1933
Moi et l'Impératrice/The Empress
    and I, 1933
The Only Girl/Heart Song, 1933
Caravane/Caravan, 1934
Liliom, 1934
La Bataille, 1934
Le Bonheur Happiness, 1934
Private Worlds, 1935
Break of Hearts, 1935
Shanghai, 1935
I Loved a Soldier, 1936
Mayerling, 1936
The Garden of Allah, 1936
History Is Made at Night, 1937
Conquest, 1937
Tovarich, 1937
Orage/Storm, 1938
Algiers, 1938
Le Corsaire, 1939
Love Affair, 1939
When Tomorrow Comes, 1939
All This, and Heaven Too, 1940
Back Street, 1941
Hold Back the Dawn, 1941
Appointment for Love, 1941
Tales of Manhattan, 1942
The Constant Nymph, 1943
Flesh and Fantasy, 1943
Gaslight, 1944
Together Again, 1944
Confidential Agent, 1945
Cluny Brown, 1946
A Woman's Vengeance, 1948
Arch of Triumph, 1948
The 13th Letter, 1951
The First Legion, 1951
The Happy Time, 1952
Thunder in the East, 1952
The Earrings of Madame de . . ., 1953
The Cobweb, 1955
Nana, 1955
La Fortuna di Essere/Donna What a
    Woman!, 1956
Around the World in Eighty Days, 1956
Paris, Palace Hôtel/Paris Hotel, 1956
Une Parisienne/La Parisienne, 1957
Maxime, 1958
The Buccaneer, 1958
Fanny, 1961
Les Démons de Minuit/Midnight Folly, 1961
Four Horsemen of the Apocalypse, 1962
Julia, Du Bist Zauberhaft/Adorable Julia,
    1962
Love Is a Ball, 1963
A Very Special Favor, 1965
How to Steal a Million, 1966
Is Paris Burning?, 1966
Casino Royale, 1967
Barefoot in the Park, 1967
The Day the Hot Line Got Hot, 1969

The April Fools, 1969
The Madwoman of Chaillot, 1969
Lost Horizon, 1973
L'Empire d'Alexandre/Stavisky . . ., 1974
A Matter of Time, 1976

MARLON BRANDO
The Men, 1950
A Streetcar Named Desire, 1951
Viva Zapata!, 1952
Julius Caesar, 1953
The Wild One, 1953
On the Waterfront, 1954
Désirée, 1954
Guys and Dolls, 1955
The Teahouse of the August Moon, 1956
Sayonara, 1957
The Young Lions, 1958
The Fugitive Kind, 1960
One-Eyed Jacks, 1961
Mutiny on the Bounty, 1962
The Ugly American, 1963
Bedtime Story, 1964
Morituri, 1965
The Chase, 1966
The Appaloosa, 1966
A Countess from Hong Kong, 1967
Reflections in a Golden Eye, 1967
Candy, 1968
The Night of the Following Day, 1969
Burn!, 1969
The Nightcomers, 1971
The Godfather, 1972
Last Tango in Paris, 1972
The Missouri Breaks, 1976
Superman, 1978
Apocalypse Now, 1979
The Formula, 1980
A Dry White Season, 1989
The Freshman, 1990
Christopher Columbus: The Discovery, 1992
Don Juan DeMarco, 1995
The Island of Dr. Moreau, 1996
The Brave, 1997
Free Money, 1998
The Score, 2001

JAMES CAGNEY
Sinners' Holiday, 1930
The Doorway to Hell, 1930
Other Men's Women, 1931
The Public Enemy, 1931
The Millionaire, 1931
Smart Money, 1931
Blonde Crazy, 1931
Taxi!, 1932
The Crowd Roars, 1932
Winner Take All, 1932
Hard to Handle, 1933
Picture Snatcher, 1933
The Mayor of Hell, 1933
Footlight Parade, 1933
Lady Killer, 1933
Jimmy the Gent, 1934

He Was Her Man, 1934
Here Comes the Navy, 1934
The St. Louis Kid, 1934
Devil Dogs of the Air, 1935
G-Men, 1935
The Irish in Us, 1935
A Midsummer Night's Dream, 1935
Frisco Kid, 1935
Ceiling Zero, 1936
Great Guy, 1936
Something to Sing About, 1937
Boy Meets Girl, 1938
Angels with Dirty Faces, 1938
The Oklahoma Kid, 1939
Each Dawn I Die, 1939
The Roaring Twenties, 1939
The Fighting 69th, 1940
Torrid Zone, 1940
City for Conquest, 1940
The Strawberry Blonde, 1941
The Bride Came C.O.D., 1941
Captains of the Clouds, 1942
Yankee Doodle Dandy, 1942
Johnny Come Lately, 1943
Blood on the Sun, 1945
13 Rue Madeleine, 1947
The Time of Your Life, 1948
White Heat, 1949
Kiss Tomorrow Goodbye, 1950
The West Point Story, 1950
Come Fill the Cup, 1951
What Price Glory?, 1952
A Lion Is in the Streets, 1953
Run for Cover, 1955
Love Me or Leave Me, 1955
The Seven Little Foys, 1955
Mister Roberts, 1955
Tribute to a Bad Man, 1956
These Wilder Years, 1956
Man of a Thousand Faces, 1957
Never Steal Anything Small, 1959
Shake Hands with the Devil, 1959
The Gallant Hours, 1960
One, Two, Three, 1961
Ragtime, 1981

LON CHANEY
Poor Jake's Demise, 1913
The Sea Urchin, 1913
The Blood Red Tape of Charity, 1913
Shon the Piper, 1913
The Trap, 1913
Almost an Actress, 1913
An Elephant on His Hands, 1913
Back to Life, 1913
Red Margaret, Moonshiner, 1913
Bloodhounds of the North, 1913
The Lie, 1914
The Honor of the Mounted, 1914
Remember Mary Magdalen, 1914
Discord and Harmony, 1914
The Menace to Carlotta, 1914

The Embezzler, 1914
The Lamb, the Woman, the Wolf, 1914
The End of the Feud, 1914
The Tragedy of Whispering Creek, 1914
The Unlawful Trade, 1914
The Forbidden Room, 1914
The Old Cobbler, 1914
The Hopes of Blind Alley, 1914
A Ranch Romance, 1914
Her Grave Mistake, 1914
By the Sun's Rays, 1914
The Oubliette, 1914
A Miner's Romance, 1914
Her Bounty, 1914
The Higher Law, 1914
Richelieu, 1914
The Pipes o' Pan, 1914
Virtue Is Its Own Reward, 1914
Her Life's Story, 1914
Lights and Shadows, 1914
The Lion, the Lamb, the Man, 1914
A Night of Thrills, 1914
Her Escape, 1914
The Sin of Olga Brandt, 1915
The Star of the Sea, 1915
The Smalltown Girl, 1915
The Measure of a Man, 1915
The Threads of Fate, 1915
When the Gods Played a Badger Game, 1915
Such Is Life, 1915
Where the Forest Ends, 1915
Outside the Gates, 1915
All for Peggy, 1915
The Desert Breed, 1915
Maid of the Mist, 1915
The Grind, 1915
The Girl of the Night, 1915
The Stool Pigeon, 1915
An Idyll of the Hills, 1915
The Stronger Mind, 1915
The Oyster Dredger, 1915
Steady Company, 1915
The Violin Maker, 1915
The Trust, 1915
Bound on the Wheel, 1915
Mountain Justice, 1915
Quits, 1915
The Chimney's Secret, 1915
The Pine's Revenge, 1915
The Fascination of the Fleur de Lis, 1915
Alas and Alack, 1915
A Mother's Atonement, 1915
Lon of Lone Mountain, 1915
The Millionaire Paupers, 1915
Under a Shadow, 1915
Father and the Boys, 1915
Stronger than Death, 1915
Dolly's Scoop, 1916
The Grip of Jealousy, 1916
Tangled Hearts, 1916
The Gilded Spider, 1916
Bobbie of the Ballet, 1916
The Grasp of Greed, 1916
The Mark of Cain, 1916
If My Country Should Call, 1916

Felix on the Job, 1916
The Place Beyond the Winds, 1916
Accusing Evidence, 1916
The Price of Silence, 1916
The Piper's Price, 1917
Hell Morgan's Girl, 1917
The Mask of Love, 1917
The Girl in the Checkered Coat, 1917
The Flashlight, 1917
A Doll's House, 1917
Fires of Rebellion, 1917
The Rescue, 1917
Pay Me!, 1917
Triumph, 1917
The Empty Gun, 1917
Anything Once, 1917
The Scarlet Car, 1917
The Grand Passion, 1918
Broadway Love, 1918
The Kaiser, the Beast of Berlin, 1918
Fast Company, 1918
A Broadway Scandal, 1918
Riddle Gawne, 1918
That Devil, Bateese, 1918
The Talk of the Town, 1918
Danger, Go Slow, 1918
The False Faces, 1919
The Wicked Darling, 1919
A Man's Country, 1919
The Miracle Man, 1919
Paid in Advance, 1919
When Bearcat Went Dry, 1919
Victory, 1919
Daredevil Jack, 1920
Treasure Island, 1920
The Gift Supreme, 1920
The Penalty, 1920
Nomads of the North, 1920
Outside the Law, 1920
For Those We Love, 1921
The Ace of Hearts, 1921
Bits of Life, 1921
Voices of the City, 1921
The Trap, 1922
Flesh and Blood, 1922
The Light in the Dark, 1922
Oliver Twist, 1922
Shadows, 1922
Quincy Adams Sawyer, 1922
A Blind Bargain, 1922
All the Brothers Were Valiant, 1923
While Paris Sleeps, 1923
The Shock, 1923
The Hunchback of Notre Dame, 1923
The Next Corner, 1924
He Who Gets Slapped, 1924
The Monster, 1925
The Unholy Three, 1925
The Phantom of the Opera, 1925
The Tower of Lies, 1925
The Blackbird, 1926

The Road to Mandalay, 1926
Tell It to the Marines, 1926
Mr. Wu, 1927
The Unknown, 1927
Mockery, 1927
London After Midnight, 1927
The Big City, 1928
Laugh, Clown, Laugh, 1928
While the City Sleeps, 1928
West of Zanzibar, 1928
Where East is East, 1929
Thunder, 1929
The Unholy Three, 1930

CHARLES CHAPLIN
Making a Living, 1914
Kid Auto Races at Venice, 1914
Mabel's Strange Predicament, 1914
Between Showers, 1914
A Film Johnnie, 1914
Tango Tangles, 1914
His Favorite Pastime, 1914
Cruel, Cruel Love, 1914
The Star Boarder, 1914
Mabel at the Wheel, 1914
Twenty Minutes of Love, 1914
Caught in a Cabaret, 1914
Caught in the Rain, 1914
A Busy Day, 1914
The Fatal Mallet, 1914
Her Friend the Bandit, 1914
The Knockout, 1914
Mabel's Busy Day, 1914
Mabel's Married Life, 1914
Laughing Gas, 1914
The Property Man, 1914
The Face on the Bar Room Floor, 1914
Recreation, 1914
The Masquerader, 1914
His New Profession, 1914
The Rounders, 1914
The New Janitor, 1914
Those Love Pangs, 1914
Dough and Dynamite, 1914
Gentlemen of Nerve, 1914
His Musical Career, 1914
His Trysting Place, 1914
Tillie's Punctured Romance, 1914
Getting Acquainted, 1914
His Prehistoric Past, 1914
His New Job, 1915
A Night Out, 1915
The Champion, 1915
In the Park, 1915
A Jitney Elopement, 1915
The Tramp, 1915
By the Sea, 1915
Work, 1915
A Woman, 1915
The Bank, 1915
Shanghaied, 1915
A Night in the Show, 1915
Police, 1916
Burlesque on Carmen, 1916
The Floorwalker, 1916

The Fireman, 1916
The Vagabond, 1916
One A.M., 1916
The Count, 1916
The Pawnshop, 1916
Behind the Screen, 1916
The Rink, 1916
Easy Street, 1917
The Cure, 1917
The Immigrant, 1917
The Adventurer, 1917
A Dog's Life, 1918
Triple Trouble, 1918
Shoulder Arms, 1918
Sunnyside, 1919
A Day's Pleasure, 1919
The Kid, 1921
The Idle Class, 1921
Pay Day, 1922
The Pilgrim, 1923
Souls for Sale, 1923
The Gold Rush, 1925
The Circus, 1928
City Lights, 1931
Modern Times, 1936
The Great Dictator, 1940
Monsieur Verdoux, 1947
Limelight, 1952
A King in New York, 1957
A Countess from Hong Kong, 1967

MONTGOMERY CLIFT

The Search, 1948
Red River, 1948
The Heiress, 1949
The Big Lift, 1950
A Place in the Sun, 1951
I Confess, 1953
Terminal Station/Indiscretion of an
   American Wife, 1953
From Here to Eternity, 1953
Raintree County, 1957
Lonelyhearts, 1958
The Young Lions, 1958
Suddenly, Last Summer, 1959
Wild River, 1960
The Misfits, 1961
Judgment at Nuremberg, 1961
Freud, 1962
The Defector, 1966

RONALD COLMAN

The Toilers, 1919
Snow in the Desert, 1919
Anna the Adventuress, 1920
A Son of David, 1920
The Black Spider, 1920
Handcuffs or Kisses, 1921
The White Sister, 1923
Twenty Dollars a Week, 1924
Tarnish, 1924
Her Night of Romance, 1924
Romola, 1925

A Thief in Paradise, 1925
The Sporting Venus, 1925
His Supreme Moment, 1925
Her Sister from Paris, 1925
The Dark Angel, 1925
Stella Dallas, 1925
Lady Windermere's Fan, 1925
Kiki, 1926
Beau Geste, 1926
The Winning of Barbara Worth, 1926
The Night of Love, 1927
The Magic Flame, 1927
Two Lovers, 1928
The Rescue, 1929
Bulldog Drummond, 1929
Condemned, 1929
Raffles, 1930
The Devil to Pay!, 1930
The Unholy Garden, 1931
Arrowsmith, 1931
Cynara, 1932
The Masquerader, 1933
Bulldog Drummond Strikes Back, 1934
Clive of India, 1935
The Man Who Broke the Bank at Monte
   Carlo, 1935
A Tale of Two Cities, 1935
Under Two Flags, 1936
Lost Horizon, 1937
The Prisoner of Zenda, 1937
If I Were King, 1938
The Light That Failed, 1939
Lucky Partners, 1940
My Life with Caroline, 1941
The Talk of the Town, 1942
Random Harvest, 1942
Kismet, 1944
The Late George Apley, 1947
A Double Life, 1947
Champagne for Caesar, 1950
Around the World in Eighty Days, 1956
The Story of Mankind, 1957

GARY COOPER

The Winning of Barbara Worth, 1926
It, 1927
Arizona Bound, 1927
Children of Divorce, 1927
The Last Outlaw, 1927
Wings, 1927
Nevada, 1927
Half a Bride, 1928
Beau Sabreur, 1928
Doomsday, 1928
The Legion of the Condemned, 1928
Lilac Time, 1928
The First Kiss, 1928
The Shopworn Angel, 1928
Wolf Song, 1929
Betrayal, 1929
The Virginian, 1929
Seven Days Leave, 1930
Only the Brave, 1930
The Texan, 1930
A Man from Wyoming, 1930

The Spoilers, 1930
Morocco, 1930
Fighting Caravans, 1931
City Streets, 1931
I Take This Woman, 1931
His Woman, 1931
Devil and the Deep, 1932
If I Had a Million, 1932
A Farewell to Arms, 1932
Today We Live, 1933
One Sunday Afternoon, 1933
Alice in Wonderland, 1933
Design for Living, 1933
Operator 13, 1934
Now and Forever, 1934
The Lives of a Bengal Lancer, 1935
The Wedding Night, 1935
Peter Ibbetson, 1935
Desire, 1936
Mr. Deeds Goes to Town, 1936
The General Died at Dawn, 1936
The Plainsman, 1936
Souls at Sea, 1937
Bluebeard's Eighth Wife, 1938
The Adventures of Marco Polo, 1938
The Cowboy and the Lady, 1938
Beau Geste, 1939
The Real Glory, 1939
The Westerner, 1940
North West Mounted Police, 1940
Meet John Doe, 1941
Sergeant York, 1941
Ball of Fire, 1941
The Pride of the Yankees, 1942
For Whom the Bell Tolls, 1943
The Story of Dr. Wassell, 1944
Casanova Brown, 1944
Along Came Jones, 1945
Saratoga Trunk, 1945
Cloak and Dagger, 1946
Unconquered, 1947
Good Sam, 1947
The Fountainhead, 1949
Task Force, 1949
Bright Leaf, 1950
Dallas, 1950
You're in the Navy Now, 1951
It's a Big Country, 1951
Distant Drums, 1951
High Noon, 1952
Springfield Rifle, 1952
Return to Paradise, 1953
Blowing Wild, 1953
Garden of Evil, 1954
Vera Cruz, 1954
The Court-Martial of Billy Mitchell, 1955
Friendly Persuasion, 1956
Love in the Afternoon, 1957
Ten North Frederick, 1958
Man of the West, 1958
The Hanging Tree, 1959
They Came to Cordura, 1959
The Wreck of the Mary Deare, 1959
The Naked Edge, 1961

BING CROSBY

Reaching for the Moon, 1930
Confessions of a Co-Ed, 1931
The Big Broadcast, 1932
College Humor, 1933
Too Much Harmony, 1933
Going Hollywood, 1933
We're Not Dressing, 1934
She Loves Me Not, 1934
Here Is My Heart, 1934
Mississippi, 1935
Two for Tonight, 1935
Anything Goes, 1936
Rhythm on the Range, 1936
Pennies from Heaven, 1936
Waikiki Wedding, 1937
Double or Nothing, 1937
Dr. Rhythm, 1938
Sing You Sinners, 1938
Paris Honeymoon, 1939
East Side Heaven, 1939
The Star Maker, 1939
Road to Singapore, 1940
Rhythm on the River, 1940
If I Had My Way, 1940
Road to Zanzibar, 1941
Birth of the Blues, 1941
Holiday Inn, 1942
Road to Morocco, 1942
Dixie, 1943
Going My Way, 1942
Here Come the Waves, 1944
The Bells of St. Mary's, 1945
Road to Utopia, 1946
Blue Skies, 1946
Welcome Stranger, 1947
Road to Rio, 1947
The Emperor Waltz, 1948
A Connecticut Yankee in King Arthur's
    Court, 1949
Top o' the Morning, 1949
Riding High, 1950
Mr. Music, 1950
Here Comes the Groom, 1951
Just for You, 1952
Road to Bali, 1952
Little Boy Lost, 1953
White Christmas, 1954
The Country Girl, 1954
Anything Goes, 1956
High Society, 1956
Man on Fire, 1957
Say One for Me, 1959
High Time, 1960
The Road to Hong Kong, 1962
Robin and the 7 Hoods, 1964
Stagecoach, 1966

JAMES DEAN

East of Eden, 1955
Rebel without a Cause, 1955
Giant, 1956

KIRK DOUGLAS

The Strange Love of Martha Ivers, 1946
Out of the Past, 1947
Mourning Becomes Electra, 1947
I Walk Alone, 1948
The Walls of Jericho, 1948
My Dear Secretary, 1948
A Letter to Three Wives, 1949
Champion, 1949
Young Man with a Horn, 1950
The Glass Menagerie, 1950
Along the Great Divide, 1951
Ace in the Hole, 1951
Detective Story, 1951
The Big Trees, 1952
The Big Sky, 1952
The Bad and the Beautiful, 1952
The Story of Three Loves, 1953
The Juggler, 1953
Act of Love, 1953
20,000 Leagues Under the Sea, 1954
The Racers, 1955
Ulysses, 1955
Man Without a Star, 1955
The Indian Fighter, 1955
Lust for Life, 1956
Top Secret Affair, 1957
Gunfight at the O.K. Corral, 1957
Paths of Glory, 1957
The Vikings, 1958
Last Train from Gun Hill, 1959
The Devil's Disciple, 1959
Strangers When We Meet, 1960
Spartacus, 1960
Town Without Pity, 1961
The Last Sunset, 1961
Lonely Are the Brave, 1962
Two Weeks in Another Town, 1962
The Hook, 1963
The List of Adrian Messenger, 1963
For Love or Money, 1963
Seven Days in May, 1964
The Heroes of Telemark, 1965
In Harm's Way, 1965
Cast a Giant Shadow, 1966
Is Paris Burning?, 1966
The Way West, 1967
The War Wagon, 1967
A Lovely Way to Die, 1968
The Brotherhood, 1968
The Arrangement, 1969
There Was a Crooked Man . . ., 1970
Catch Me a Spy, 1971
The Light at the Edge of the World, 1971
A Gunfight, 1971
The Master Touch, 1972
Scalawag, 1973
Jacqueline Susann's Once Is Not Enough,
    1975
Posse, 1975
Holocaust 2000, 1977
The Fury, 1978
Home Movies, 1979
The Villain, 1979
Saturn 3, 1980

The Final Countdown, 1980
The Man from Snowy River, 1982
Eddie Macon's Run, 1983
Tough Guys, 1986
Oscar, 1991
Veraz, 1991
Greedy, 1994
Diamonds, 1999
It Runs in the Family, 2003
Illusion, 2004

DOUGLAS FAIRBANKS

The Lamb, 1915
The Martyrs of the Alamo, 1915
Double Trouble, 1915
His Picture in the Papers, 1916
The Habit of Happiness, 1916
The Good Bad Man, 1916
Reggie Mixes In, 1916
Flirting with Fate, 1916
The Half Breed, 1916
Manhattan Madness, 1916
American Aristocracy, 1916
The Matrimaniac, 1916
The Americano, 1916
In Again, Out Again, 1917
Wild and Woolly, 1917
Down to Earth, 1917
The Man from Painted Post, 1917
Reaching for the Moon, 1917
A Modern Musketeer, 1917
Headin' South, 1918
Mr. Fix-It, 1918
Say! Young Fellow, 1918
Bound in Morocco, 1918
He Comes Up Smiling, 1918
Arizona, 1918
The Knickerbocker Buckaroo, 1919
His Majesty, the American, 1919
When the Clouds Roll By, 1919
The Mollycoddle, 1920
The Mark of Zorro, 1920
The Nut, 1921
The Three Musketeers, 1921
The Thief of Baghdad, 1924
Don Q Son of Zorro, 1925
The Black Pirate, 1926
The Gaucho, 1927
The Iron Mask, 1929
The Taming of the Shrew, 1929
Reaching for the Moon, 1930
Mr. Robinson Crusoe, 1932
The Private Life of Don Juan, 1934

ERROL FLYNN

In the Wake of the Bounty, 1933
Murder at Monte Carlo, 1934
The Case of the Curious Bride, 1935
Don't Bet on Blondes, 1935
Captain Blood, 1935
The Charge of the Light Brigade, 1936
Green Light, 1937
The Prince and the Pauper, 1937
Another Dawn, 1937
The Perfect Specimen, 1937
The Adventures of Robin Hood, 1938
Four's a Crowd, 1938
The Sisters, 1938
The Dawn Patrol, 1938
Dodge City, 1939
The Private Lives of Elizabeth and Essex, 1939
Virginia City, 1940
The Sea Hawk, 1940
Santa Fe Trail, 1940
Footsteps in the Dark, 1941
Dive Bomber, 1941
They Died with Their Boots On, 1941
Desperate Journey, 1942
Gentleman Jim, 1942
Edge of Darkness, 1943
Northern Pursuit, 1943
Uncertain Glory, 1944
Objective, Burma!, 1945
San Antonio, 1945
Never Say Goodbye, 1946
Cry Wolf, 1947
Escape Me Never, 1947
Silver River, 1948
Adventures of Don Juan, 1948
That Forsyte Woman, 1949
Montana, 1950
Rocky Mountain, 1950
Kim, 1950
Hello God, 1951
Adventures of Captain Fabian, 1951
Mara Maru, 1952
Against All Flags, 1952
The Master of Ballantrae, 1953
Crossed Swords, 1954
Lilacs in the Spring, 1955
King's Rhapsody, 1955
The Dark Avenger, 1955
Istanbul, 1957
The Big Boodle, 1957
The Sun Also Rises, 1957
Too Much, Too Soon, 1958
The Roots of Heaven, 1958
Cuban Rebel Girls, 1959

HENRY FONDA

The Farmer Takes a Wife, 1935
Way Down East, 1935
I Dream Too Much, 1935
The Trail of the Lonesome Pine, 1936
The Moon's Our Home, 1936
Spendthrift, 1936
Wings of the Morning, 1937
You Only Live Once, 1937
Slim, 1937
That Certain Woman, 1937
I Met My Love Again, 1938
Jezebel, 1938
Blockade, 1938
Spawn of the North, 1938
The Mad Miss Manton, 1938
Jesse James, 1939
Let Us Live! 1939
The Story of Alexander Graham Bell, 1939
Young Mr. Lincoln, 1939
Drums Along the Mohawk, 1939
The Grapes of Wrath, 1940
Lillian Russell, 1940
The Return of Frank James, 1940
Chad Hanna, 1940
The Lady Eve, 1941
Wild Geese Calling, 1941
You Belong to Me, 1941
Rings on Her Fingers, 1942
The Male Animal, 1942
The Magnificent Dope, 1942
Tales of Manhattan, 1942
The Big Street, 1942
Immortal Sergeant, 1943
The Ox-Bow Incident, 1943
My Darling Clementine, 1946
The Long Night, 1947
The Fugitive, 1947
Daisy Kenyon, 1947
On Our Merry Way, 1948
Fort Apache, 1948
Mister Roberts, 1955
War and Peace, 1956
The Wrong Man, 1956
12 Angry Men, 1957
The Tin Star, 1957
Stage Struck, 1958
Warlock, 1959
The Man Who Understood Women, 1959
Advise and Consent, 1962
The Longest Day, 1962
How the West Was Won, 1962
Spencer's Mountain, 1963
The Best Man, 1964
Fail-Safe, 1964
Sex and the Single Girl, 1964
The Rounders, 1965
In Harm's Way, 1965
The Dirty Game, 1965
Battle of the Bulge, 1965
A Big Hand for the Little Lady, 1966
Welcome to Hard Times, 1967
Firecreek, 1968
Madigan, 1968
Yours, Mine, and Ours, 1968
The Boston Strangler, 1968
Once upon a Time in the West, 1968
Too Late the Hero, 1970
The Cheyenne Social Club, 1970
There Was a Crooked Man . . ., 1970
Sometimes a Great Notion, 1971
The Serpent, 1973
Ash Wednesday, 1973
My Name Is Nobody, 1973
The Last Days of Mussolini, 1974
Midway, 1976
The Last of the Cowboys, 1977
Tentacles, 1977
Rollercoaster, 1977
The Biggest Battle, 1978
The Swarm, 1978
Meteor, 1979
City on Fire, 1979
Wanda Nevada, 1979
On Golden Pond, 1981

CLARK GABLE

White Man, 1924
North Star, 1925
The Painted Desert, 1931
The Easiest Way, 1931
Dance, Fools, Dance, 1931
The Finger Points, 1931
The Secret Six, 1931
Laughing Sinners, 1931
A Free Soul, 1931
Night Nurse, 1931
Sporting Blood, 1931
Susan Lenox (Her Fall and Rise), 1931
Possessed, 1931
Hell Divers, 1931
Polly of the Circus, 1932
Red Dust, 1932
No Man of Her Own, 1932
Strange Interlude, 1932
The White Sister, 1933
Hold Your Man, 1933
Night Flight, 1933
Dancing Lady, 1933
It Happened One Night, 1934
Men in White, 1934
Manhattan Melodrama, 1934
Chained, 1934
Forsaking All Others, 1934
After Office Hours, 1935
China Seas, 1935
The Call of the Wild, 1935
Mutiny on the Bounty, 1935
Wife vs. Secretary, 1936
San Francisco, 1936
Cain and Mabel, 1936
Love on the Run, 1936
Parnell, 1937
Saratoga, 1937
Test Pilot, 1938
Too Hot to Handle, 1938
Idiot's Delight, 1939
Gone with the Wind, 1939
Strange Cargo, 1940
Boom Town, 1940
Comrade X, 1940
They Met in Bombay, 1941
Honky Tonk, 1941
Somewhere I'll Find You, 1942
Adventure, 1945
The Hucksters, 1947

Homecoming, 1948
Command Decision, 1948
Any Number Can Play, 1949
Key to the City, 1950
To Please a Lady, 1950
Across the Wide Missouri, 1951
Lone Star, 1952
Never Let Me Go, 1953
Mogambo, 1953
Betrayed, 1954
Soldier of Fortune, 1955
The Tall Men, 1955
The King and Four Queens, 1956
Band of Angels, 1957
Run Silent, Run Deep, 1958
Teacher's Pet, 1958
But Not for Me, 1959
It Started in Naples, 1960
The Misfits, 1961

JOHN GARFIELD

Four Daughters, 1938
They Made Me a Criminal, 1939
Blackwell's Island, 1939
Juarez, 1939
Daughters Courageous, 1939
Dust Be My Destiny, 1939
Four Wives, 1939
Castle on the Hudson, 1940
Saturday's Children, 1940
Flowing Gold, 1940
East of the River, 1940
The Sea Wolf, 1941
Out of the Fog, 1941
Dangerously They Live, 1942
Tortilla Flat, 1942
Air Force, 1943
The Fallen Sparrow, 1943
Destination Tokyo, 1943
Between Two Worlds, 1944
Pride of the Marines, 1945
The Postman Always Rings Twice, 1946
Nobody Lives Forever, 1946
Humoresque, 1946
Body and Soul, 1947
Gentleman's Agreement, 1947
Force of Evil, 1948
We Were Strangers, 1949
Under My Skin, 1950
The Breaking Point, 1950
He Ran All the Way, 1951

JOHN GILBERT

The Phantom, 1916
The Apostle of Vengeance, 1916
Shell 43, 1916
The Sin Ye Do, 1916
The Bride of Hate, 1917
Princess of the Dark, 1917
The Dark Road, 1917
Happiness, 1917
The Millionaire Vagrant, 1917
The Hater of Men, 1917
The Mother Instinct, 1917
Golden Rule Kate, 1917

The Devil Dodger, 1917
Up or Down?, 1917
Nancy Comes Home, 1918
Shackled, 1918
More Trouble, 1918
Wedlock, 1918
The Mask, 1918
Three X Gordon, 1918
The Dawn of Understanding, 1918
The White Heather, 1919
The Busher, 1919
The Man Beneath, 1919
A Little Brother of the Rich, 1919
The Red Viper, 1919
For a Woman's Honor, 1919
Widow by Proxy, 1919
Heart o' the Hills, 1919
Should a Woman Tell?, 1919
The White Circle, 1920
Deep Waters, 1920
The Servant in the House, 1921
Shame, 1921
Ladies Must Live, 1921
Gleam O'Dawn, 1922
Arabian Love, 1922
The Yellow Stain, 1922
Honor First, 1922
Monte Cristo, 1922
Calvert's Valley, 1922
The Love Gambler, 1922
A California Romance, 1922
While Paris Sleeps, 1923
Truxton King, 1923
Madness of Youth, 1923
St. Elmo, 1923
The Exiles, 1923
Cameo Kirby, 1923
Just Off Broadway, 1924
The Wolf Man, 1924
A Man's Mate, 1924
The Lone Chance, 1924
Romance Ranch, 1924
His Hour, 1924
He Who Gets Slapped, 1924
The Snob, 1924
The Wife of the Centaur, 1924
The Merry Widow, 1925
The Big Parade, 1925
La Boheme, 1926
Bardelys the Magnificent, 1926
Flesh and the Devil, 1926
The Show, 1927
Twelve Miles Out, 1927
Man, Woman and Sin, 1927
Love, 1927
Four Walls, 1928
The Masks of the Devil, 1928
A Woman of Affairs, 1928
The Cossacks, 1928
Desert Nights, 1929
His Glorious Night, 1929

Redemption, 1930
Way for a Sailor, 1930
Gentleman's Fate, 1931
The Phantom of Paris, 1931
West of Broadway, 1931
Downstairs, 1932
Fast Workers, 1933
Queen Christina, 1933
The Captain Hates the Sea, 1934

CARY GRANT

This Is the Night, 1932
Sinners in the Sun, 1932
Merrily We Go to Hell, 1932
Devil and the Deep, 1932
Blonde Venus, 1932
Hot Saturday, 1932
Madame Butterfly, 1932
She Done Him Wrong, 1933
The Woman Accused, 1933
The Eagle and the Hawk, 1933
Gambling Ship, 1933
I'm No Angel, 1933
Alice in Wonderland, 1933
Thirty Day Princess, 1934
Born to Be Bad, 1934
Kiss and Make Up, 1934
Ladies Should Listen, 1934
Enter Madame, 1935
Wings in the Dark, 1935
The Last Outpost, 1935
Sylvia Scarlett, 1935
The Amazing Quest of Ernest Bliss, 1936
Big Brown Eyes, 1936
Suzy, 1936
Wedding Present, 1936
When You're in Love, 1937
Topper, 1937
The Toast of New York, 1937
The Awful Truth, 1937
Bringing Up Baby, 1938
Holiday, 1938
Gunga Din, 1939
Only Angels Have Wings, 1939
In Name Only, 1939
His Girl Friday, 1940
My Favorite Wife, 1940
The Howards of Virginia, 1940
The Philadelphia Story, 1940
Penny Serenade, 1941
Suspicion, 1941
The Talk of the Town, 1942
Once Upon a Honeymoon, 1942
Mr. Lucky, 1943
Destination Tokyo, 1943
Once Upon a Time, 1944
None But the Lonely Heart, 1944
Arsenic and Old Lace, 1944
Night and Day, 1946
Notorious, 1946
The Bachelor and the Bobby-Soxer, 1947
The Bishop's Wife, 1947
Mr. Blandings Builds His Dream House, 1948
Every Girl Should Be Married, 1948
I Was a Male War Bride, 1949

Crisis, 1950
People Will Talk, 1951
Room for One More, 1952
Monkey Business, 1952
Dream Wife, 1953
To Catch a Thief, 1955
An Affair to Remember, 1957
The Pride and the Passion, 1957
Kiss Them for Me, 1957
Indiscreet, 1958
Houseboat, 1958
North by Northwest, 1959
Operation Petticoat, 1959
The Grass Is Greener, 1960
That Touch of Mink, 1962
Charade, 1963
Father Goose, 1964
Walk Don't Run, 1966

WILLIAM HOLDEN

Golden Boy, 1939
Invisible Stripes, 1939
Our Town, 1940
Those Were the Days!, 1940
Arizona, 1940
I Wanted Wings, 1941
Texas, 1941
The Fleet's In, 1942
The Remarkable Andrew, 1942
Meet the Stewarts, 1942
Young and Willing, 1943
Blaze of Noon, 1947
Dear Ruth, 1947
The Man from Colorado, 1948
Rachel and the Stranger, 1948
Apartment for Peggy, 1948
The Dark Past, 1948
Streets of Laredo, 1949
Miss Grant Takes Richmond, 1949
Dear Wife, 1949
Father Is a Bachelor, 1950
Sunset Blvd., 1950
Union Station, 1950
Born Yesterday, 1950
Force of Arms, 1951
Submarine Command, 1951
Boots Malone, 1952
The Turning Point, 1952
Stalag 17, 1953
The Moon Is Blue, 1953
Escape from Fort Bravo, 1953
Forever Female, 1953
Executive Suite, 1954
Sabrina, 1954
The Country Girl, 1954
The Bridges at Toko-Ri, 1955
Love is a Many-Splendored Thing, 1955
Picnic, 1955
The Proud and Profane, 1956
Toward the Unknown, 1956
The Bridge on the River Kwai, 1957

The Key, 1958
The Horse Soldiers, 1959
The World of Suzie Wong, 1960
Satan Never Sleeps, 1962
The Counterfeit Traitor, 1962
The Lion, 1962
Paris—When It Sizzles, 1964
The 7th Dawn, 1964
Alvarez Kelly, 1966
Casino Royale, 1967
The Devil's Brigade, 1968
The Wild Bunch, 1969
The Christmas Tree, 1969
Wild Rovers, 1971
The Revengers, 1972
Breezy, 1973
Open Season, 1974
The Towering Inferno, 1974
Network, 1976
Fedora, 1978
Damien: Omen II, 1978
Ashanti, 1979
When Time Ran Out, 1980
The Earthling, 1980
S.O.B., 1981

BOB HOPE

The Big Broadcast of 1938, 1938
College Swing, 1938
Give Me a Sailor, 1938
Thanks for the Memory, 1938
Never Say Die, 1939
Some Like It Hot, 1939
The Cat and the Canary, 1939
Road to Singapore, 1940
The Ghost Breakers, 1940
Road to Zanzibar, 1941
Caught in the Draft, 1941
Nothing but the Truth, 1941
Louisiana Purchase, 1941
My Favorite Blonde, 1942
Road to Morocco, 1942
They Got Me Covered, 1943
Let's Face It, 1943
The Princess and the Pirate, 1944
Road to Utopia, 1946
Monsieur Beaucaire, 1946
My Favorite Brunette, 1947
Where There's Life, 1947
Road to Rio, 1947
The Paleface, 1948
Sorrowful Jones, 1949
The Great Lover, 1949
Fancy Pants, 1950
The Lemon Drop Kid, 1951
My Favorite Spy, 1951
Son of Paleface, 1952
Road to Bali, 1952
Off Limits, 1953
Here Comes the Girls, 1953
Casanova's Big Night, 1954
The Seven Little Foys, 1955
That Certain Feeling, 1956
The Iron Petticoat, 1956
Beau James, 1957

Paris Holiday, 1958
Alias Jesse James, 1959
The Facts of Life, 1960
Bachelor in Paradise, 1961
The Road to Hong Kong, 1962
Critic's Choice, 1963
Call Me Bwana, 1963
A Global Affair, 1964
I'll Take Sweden, 1965
Boy, Did I Get a Wrong Number!, 1966
Eight on the Lam, 1967
The Private Navy of Sgt. O'Farrell, 1968
How to Commit Marriage, 1969
Cancel My Reservation, 1972

ROCK HUDSON

I Was a Shoplifter, 1950
Peggy, 1950
Winchester '73, 1950
The Desert Hawk, 1950
Shakedown, 1950
Tomahawk, 1951
Air Cadet, 1951
The Fat Man, 1951
Bright Victory, 1951
Iron Man, 1951
Bend of the River, 1952
Here Come the Nelsons, 1952
Scarlet Angel, 1952
Has Anybody Seen My Gal?, 1952
Horizons West, 1952
The Lawless Breed, 1953
Seminole, 1953
Sea Devils, 1953
The Golden Blade, 1953
Gun Fury, 1953
Back to God's Country, 1953
Taza, Son of Cochise, 1954
Magnificent Obsession, 1954
Bengal Brigade, 1954
Captain Lightfoot, 1955
One Desire, 1955
All That Heaven Allows, 1955
Never Say Goodbye, 1956
Giant, 1956
Written on the Wind, 1956
Battle Hymn, 1957
Something of Value, 1957
A Farewell to Arms, 1957
The Tarnished Angels, 1958
Twilight for the Gods, 1958
The Earth Is Mine, 1959
Pillow Talk, 1959
The Last Sunset, 1961
Come September, 1961
Lover Come Back, 1961
The Spiral Road, 1962
A Gathering of Eagles, 1963
Man's Favorite Sport?, 1964
Send Me No Flowers, 1964
Strange Bedfellows, 1965

The Great Gatsby, 1949
Chicago Deadline, 1949
Captain Carey, U.S.A., 1950
Branded, 1950
Appointment with Danger, 1951
Red Mountain, 1951
The Iron Mistress, 1952
Thunder in the East, 1952
Botany Bay, 1953
Desert Legion, 1953
Shane, 1953
The Red Beret, 1953
Hell Below Zero, 1954
Saskatchewan, 1954
The Black Knight, 1954
Drum Beat, 1954
Hell on Frisco Bay, 1955
The McConnell Story, 1955
Santiago, 1956
The Big Land, 1957
Boy on a Dolphin, 1957
The Deep Six, 1958
The Proud Rebel, 1958
The Badlanders, 1958
The Man in the Net, 1959
Guns of the Timberland, 1960
All the Young Men, 1960
One Foot in Hell, 1960
Duel of the Champions, 1961
13 West Street, 1962
The Carpetbaggers, 1964

BURT LANCASTER

The Killers, 1946
Brute Force, 1947
Desert Fury, 1947
I Walk Alone, 1949
All My Sons, 1948
Sorry, Wrong Number, 1948
Kiss the Blood off My Hands, 1948
Criss Cross, 1949
Rope of Sand, 1949
The Flame and the Arrow, 1950
Mister 880, 1950
Vengeance Valley, 1951
Jim Thorpe—All-American, 1951
Ten Tall Men, 1951
The Crimson Pirate, 1952
Come Back, Little Sheba, 1952
South Sea Woman, 1953
From Here to Eternity, 1953
His Majesty O'Keefe, 1954
Apache, 1954
Vera Cruz, 1954
The Kentuckian, 1955
The Rose Tattoo, 1955
Trapeze, 1956
The Rainmaker, 1956
Gunfight at the O.K. Corral, 1957
Sweet Smell of Success, 1957
Run Silent, Run Deep, 1958
Separate Tables, 1958
The Devil's Disciple, 1959
The Unforgiven, 1960
Elmer Gantry, 1960

The Young Savages, 1961
Judgment at Nuremberg, 1961
Birdman of Alcatraz, 1962
A Child Is Waiting, 1963
The Leopard, 1963
Seven Days in May, 1964
The Train, 1964
The Hallelujah Trail, 1965
The Professionals, 1966
The Scalphunters, 1968
The Swimmer, 1968
Castle Keep, 1969
The Gypsy Moths, 1969
Airport, 1970
Lawman, 1971
Valdez Is Coming, 1971
Ulzana's Raid, 1972
Scorpio, 1973
Executive Action, 1973
The Midnight Man, 1974
Conversation Piece, 1974
Buffalo Bill and the Indians, or Sitting Bull's
    History Lesson, 1976
1900, 1976
The Cassandra Crossing, 1976
Twilight's Last Gleaming, 1977
The Island of Dr. Moreau, 1977
Go Tell the Spartans, 1978
Zulu Dawn, 1979
Atlantic City, 1980
Cattle Annie and Little Britches, 1981
La Pelle, 1981
Local Hero, 1983
The Osterman Weekend, 1983
Little Treasure, 1985
Tough Guys, 1986
Rocket Gibraltar, 1988
The Jeweller's Shop, 1989
Field of Dreams, 1989

JACK LEMMON

It Should Happen to You, 1954
Phffft!, 1954
Three for the Show, 1955
Mister Roberts, 1955
My Sister Eileen, 1955
You Can't Run Away from It, 1956
Fire Down Below, 1957
Operation Mad Ball, 1957
Cowboy, 1958
Bell, Book and Candle, 1958
Some Like It Hot, 1959
It Happened to Jane, 1959
The Apartment, 1960
The Wackiest Ship in the Army, 1960
The Notorious Landlady, 1962
Days of Wine and Roses, 1962
Irma la Douce, 1963
Under the Yum Yum Tree, 1963
Good Neighbor Sam, 1964
How to Murder Your Wife, 1965

The Great Race, 1965
The Fortune Cookie, 1966
Luv, 1967
The Odd Couple, 1968
The April Fools, 1969
The Out-of-Towners, 1970
The War Between Men and Women, 1972
Avanti!, 1972
Save the Tiger, 1973
The Front Page, 1974
The Prisoner of Second Avenue, 1975
Alex and the Gypsy, 1976
Airport '77, 1977
The China Syndrome, 1979
Tribute, 1980
Buddy Buddy, 1981
Missing, 1982
Mass Appeal, 1984
Macaroni, 1985
That's Life!, 1986
Dad, 1989
JFK, 1991
Glengarry Glen Ross, 1992
Short Cuts, 1993
Grumpy Old Men, 1993
The Grass Harp, 1995
Grumpier Old Men, 1995
Getting Away with Murder, 1996
My Fellow Americans, 1996
Hamlet, 1996
Out to Sea, 1997
The Odd Couple II, 1998

HAROLD LLOYD

Pete, the Pedal Polisher, 1915
Close-Cropped Clippings, 1915
Beyond His Fondest Hopes, 1915
Willie Runs the Park, 1915
Just Nuts, 1915
Their Social Splash, 1915
Miss Fatty's Seaside Lovers, 1915
From Italy's Shores, 1915
The Greater Courage, 1915
The Hungry Actors, 1915
Spit-Ball Sadie, 1915
Terribly Stuck Up, 1915
A Mixup for Mazie, 1915
Some Baby, 1915
Fresh from the Farm, 1915
Giving Them the Fits, 1915
Bughouse Bellhops, 1915
Tinkering with Trouble, 1915
Great While It Lasted, 1915
Ragtime Snap Shots, 1915
A Foozle at the Tee Party, 1915
Ruses, Rhymes, and Roughnecks, 1915
Peculiar Patients' Pranks, 1915
Lonesome Luke, Social Gangster, 1915
Lonesome Luke Leans to the Literary, 1916
Luke Lugs Luggage, 1916
Lonesome Luke Lolls in Luxury, 1916
Luke, the Candy Cut-up, 1916
Luke Foils the Villain, 1916
Lonesome Luke, Circus King, 1916
Luke's Double, 1916

Them Was the Happy Days!, 1916
Luke and the Bomb Throwers, 1916
Luke's Late Lunchers, 1916
Luke Laughs Last, 1916
Luke's Fatal Flivver, 1916
Luke's Society Mixup, 1916
Luke's Washful Waiting, 1916
Luke Rides Roughshod, 1916
Luke, Crystal Gazer, 1916
Luke's Lost Lamb, 1916
Luke Does the Midway, 1916
Luke Joins the Navy, 1916
Luke and the Mermaids, 1916
Luke's Speedy Club Life, 1916
Luke and the Bang-Tails, 1916
Luke, the Chauffeur, 1916
Luke's Preparedness Preparations, 1916
Luke, the Gladiator, 1916
Luke, Patient Provider, 1916
Luke's Newsie Knockout, 1916
Luke's Movie Muddle, 1916
Luke, Rank Impersonator, 1916
Luke's Fireworks Fizzle, 1916
Luke Locates the Loot, 1916
Luke's Shattered Sleep, 1916
Lonesome Luke's Lovely Rifle, 1917
Luke's Lost Liberty, 1917
Luke's Busy Day, 1917
Drama's Dreadful Deal, 1917
Luke's Trolley Troubles, 1917
Lonesome Luke, Lawyer, 1917
Luke Wins Ye Ladye Faire, 1917
Lonesome Luke's Lively Life, 1917
Lonesome Luke on Tin Can Alley, 1917
Lonesome Luke's Honeymoon, 1917
Lonesome Luke, Plumber, 1917
Stop! Luke! Listen!, 1917
Lonesome Luke, Messenger, 1917
Lonesome Luke, Mechanic, 1917
Luke's Wild Women, 1917
Over the Fence, 1917
Lonesome Luke Loses Patients, 1917
Pinched, 1917
By the Sad Sea Waves, 1917
Birds of a Feather, 1917
Bliss, 1917
From London to Laramie, 1917
Rainbow Island, 1917
Love, Laughs, and Lather, 1917
The Flirt, 1917
Clubs Are Trump, 1917
All Aboard, 1917
We Never Sleep, 1917
Move On, 1917
Bashful, 1917
Step Lively, 1817
The Tip, 1918
The Big Idea, 1918
The Lamb, 1918
Hit Him Again, 1918
Beat It, 1918
A Gasoline Wedding, 1918
Look Pleasant, Please, 1918
Here Come the Girls, 1918
Let's Go, 1918

On the Jump, 1918
Follow the Crowd, 1918
Pipe the Whiskers, 1918
It's a Wild Life, 1918
Hey There!, 1918
Kicked Out, 1918
The Non-Stop Kid, 1918
Two-Gun Gussie, 1918
Fireman, Save My Child, 1918
The City Slicker, 1918
Sic 'Em, Towser, 1918
Somewhere in Turkey, 1918
Are Crooks Dishonest?, 1918
An Ozark Romance, 1918
Kicking the Germ Out of Germany, 1918
That's Him, 1918
Bride and Gloom, 1918
Two Scrambled, 1918
Swing Your Partners, 1918
Bees in His Bonnet, 1918
Why Pick on Me?, 1918
Nothing but Trouble, 1918
Hear 'Em Rave, 1918
Take a Chance, 1918
She Loves Me Not, 1918
Wanted—$5,000, 1919
Back to the Woods, 1919
Going! Going! Gone!, 1919
Ask Father, 1919
On the Fire, 1919
I'm on My Way, 1919
Look out Below!, 1919
The Dutiful Dub, 1919
Next Aisle Over, 1919
A Sammy in Siberia, 1919
Just Dropped In, 1919
Young Mr. Jazz, 1919
Crack Your Heels, 1919
Ring up the Curtain, 1919
Si, Senor, 1919
Before Breakfast, 1919
The Marathon, 1919
Pistols for Breakfast, 1919
Swat the Crook, 1919
Off the Trolley, 1919
Spring Fever, 1919
Billy Blazes, Esq., 1919
Just Neighbors, 1919
At the Old Stage Door, 1919
Never Touched Me, 1919
A Jazzed Honeymoon, 1919
Count Your Change, 1919
Chop Suey & Co., 1919
Be My Wife, 1919
Heap Big Chief, 1919
Don't Shove, 1919
The Rajah, 1919
He Leads, Others Follow, 1919
Soft Money, 1919
Count the Votes, 1919
Pay Your Dues, 1919

Bumping into Broadway, 1919
His Only Father, 1919
Captain Kidd's Kids, 1919
From Hand to Mouth, 1919
His Royal Slyness, 1920
Haunted Spooks, 1920
An Eastern Westerner, 1920
High and Dizzy, 1920
Get out and Get Under, 1920
Number, Please?, 1920
Now or Never, 1921
Among Those Present, 1921
I Do, 1921
Never Weaken, 1921
A Sailor-Made Man, 1921
Grandma's Boy, 1922
Dr. Jack, 1922
Safety Last!, 1923
Why Worry?, 1923
Girl Shy, 1924
Hot Water, 1924
The Freshman, 1925
For Heaven's Sake, 1926
The Kid Brother, 1927
Speedy, 1928
Welcome Danger, 1929
Feet First, 1930
Movie Crazy, 1932
The Cat's-Paw, 1934
The Milky Way, 1936
Professor Beware, 1938
The Sin of Harold Diddlebock, 1947

FREDRIC MARCH
The Dummy, 1929
The Wild Party, 1929
The Studio Murder Mystery, 1929
Paris Bound, 1929
Jealousy, 1929
Footlights and Fools, 1929
The Marriage Playground, 1929
Sarah and Son/Wiegenlied, 1930
Ladies Love Brutes, 1930
True to the Navy, 1930
Manslaughter, 1930
Laughter, 1930
The Royal Family of Broadway, 1930
Honor Among Lovers, 1931
The Night Angel, 1931
My Sin, 1931
Dr. Jekyll and Mr. Hyde, 1932
Strangers in Love, 1932
Merrily We Go to Hell, 1932
Smilin' Through, 1932
The Sign of the Cross, 1932
Tonight Is Ours, 1933
The Eagle and the Hawk, 1933
Design for Living, 1933
All of Me, 1934
Death Takes a Holiday, 1934
Good Dame, 1934
The Affairs of Cellini, 1934
The Barretts of Wimpole Street, 1934
We Live Again, 1934
Les Misérables, 1935

Anna Karenina, 1935
The Dark Angel, 1935
The Road to Glory, 1936
Mary of Scotland, 1936
Anthony Adverse, 1936
A Star Is Born, 1937
Nothing Sacred, 1937
The Buccaneer, 1938
There Goes My Heart, 1938
Trade Winds, 1938
Susan and God, 1940
Victory, 1940
So Ends Our Night, 1941
One Foot in Heaven, 1941
Bedtime Story, 1941
I Married a Witch, 1942
The Adventures of Mark Twain, 1944
Tomorrow, the World!, 1944
The Best Years of Our Lives, 1946
Another Part of the Forest, 1948
An Act of Murder, 1948
Christopher Columbus, 1949
It's a Big Country, 1951
Death of a Salesman, 1951
Man on a Tightrope, 1953
Executive Suite, 1954
The Bridges at Toko-Ri, 1955
The Desperate Hours, 1955
Alexander the Great, 1956
The Man in the Gray Flannel Suit, 1956
Middle of the Night, 1959
Inherit the Wind, 1960
The Young Doctors, 1961
The Condemned of Altona, 1962
Seven Days in May, 1964
Hombre, 1967
. . . tick . . . tick . . . tick . . ., 1970
The Iceman Cometh, 1973

JOEL MCCREA

The Jazz Age, 1929
Dynamite, 1929
The Silver Horde, 1930
Lightnin', 1930
Once a Sinner, 1931
Kept Husbands, 1931
Born to Love, 1931
The Common Law, 1931
Girls About Town, 1931
Business and Pleasure, 1932
The Lost Squadron, 1932
Bird of Paradise, 1932
The Most Dangerous Game, 1932
The Sport Parade, 1932
Rockabye, 1932
The Silver Cord, 1933
Bed of Roses, 1933
One Man's Journey, 1933
Chance at Heaven, 1933
Gambling Lady, 1934
Half a Sinner, 1934
The Richest Girl in the World, 1934
Private Worlds, 1935

Our Little Girl, 1935
Woman Wanted, 1935
Barbary Coast, 1935
Splendor, 1935
These Three, 1936
Two in a Crowd, 1936
Adventure in Manhattan, 1936
Come and Get It, 1936
Banjo on My Knee, 1936
Internes Can't Take Money, 1937
Woman Chases Man, 1937
Dead End, 1937
Wells Fargo, 1937
Three Blind Mice, 1938
Youth Takes a Fling, 1938
Union Pacific, 1939
They Shall Have Music, 1939
Espionage Agent, 1939
He Married His Wife, 1940
Primrose Path, 1940
Foreign Correspondent, 1940
Reaching for the Sun, 1941
Sullivan's Travels, 1941
The Great Man's Lady, 1942
The Palm Beach Story, 1942
The More the Merrier, 1943
Buffalo Bill, 1944
The Great Moment, 1944
The Unseen, 1945
The Virginian, 1946
Ramrod, 1947
Four Faces West, 1948
South of St. Louis, 1949
Colorado Territory, 1949
The Outriders, 1950
Stars in My Crown, 1950
Saddle Tramp, 1950
Frenchie, 1950
Cattle Drive, 1951
The San Francisco Story, 1952
Rough Shoot, 1953
Lone Hand, 1953
Border River, 1954
Black Horse Canyon, 1954
Stranger on Horseback, 1955
Wichita, 1955
The First Texan, 1956
The Oklahoman, 1957
Trooper Hook, 1957
Gunsight Ridge, 1957
The Tall Stranger, 1957
Cattle Empire, 1958
Fort Massacre, 1958
The Gunfight at Dodge City, 1959
Ride the High Country, 1962
Cry Blood, Apache, 1970
Mustang Country, 1976

STEVE MCQUEEN

Somebody up There Likes Me, 1956
Never Love a Stranger, 1958
The Blob, 1958
The Great St. Louis Bank Robbery, 1959
Never So Few, 1959
The Magnificent Seven, 1960

The Honeymoon Machine, 1961
Hell Is for Heroes, 1962
The War Lover, 1962
The Great Escape, 1963
Soldier in the Rain, 1963
Love with the Proper Stranger, 1963
Baby, the Rain Must Fall, 1965
The Cincinnati Kid, 1965
Nevada Smith, 1966
The Sand Pebbles, 1966
The Thomas Crown Affair, 1968
Bullitt, 1968
The Reivers, 1969
Le Mans, 1971
Junior Bonner, 1972
The Getaway, 1972
Papillon, 1973
The Towering Inferno, 1974
An Enemy of the People, 1978
Tom Horn, 1980
The Hunter, 1980

ROBERT MITCHUM

Hoppy Serves a Writ, 1943
Border Patrol, 1943
Follow the Band, 1943
Colt Comrades, 1943
We've Never Been Licked, 1943
Lone Star Trail, 1943
Beyond the Last Frontier, 1943
Bar 20, 1943
Doughboys in Ireland, 1943
False Colors, 1943
Minesweeper, 1943
Riders of the Deadline, 1943
Gung Ho!, 1943
Johnny Doesn't Live Here Any More, 1944
When Strangers Marry, 1944
Girl Rush, 1944
Thirty Seconds over Tokyo, 1944
Nevada, 1944
Story of G.I. Joe, 1944
West of the Pecos, 1945
Till the End of Time, 1946
Undercurrent, 1946
The Locket, 1946
Pursued, 1947
Crossfire, 1947
Desire Me, 1947
Out of the Past, 1947
Rachel and the Stranger, 1948
Blood on the Moon, 1948
The Red Pony, 1949
The Big Steal, 1949
Holiday Affair, 1949
Where Danger Lives, 1950
My Forbidden Past, 1951
His Kind of Woman, 1951
The Racket, 1951
Macao, 1952
One Minute to Zero, 1952
The Lusty Men, 1952
Angel Face, 1952

White Witch Doctor, 1953
Second Chance, 1953
She Couldn't Say No, 1954
River of No Return, 1954
Track of the Cat, 1954
Not as a Stranger, 1955
The Night of the Hunter, 1955
Man with the Gun, 1955
Foreign Intrigue, 1956
Bandido, 1956
Heaven Knows, Mr. Allison, 1957
Fire Down Below, 1957
The Enemy Below, 1957
Thunder Road, 1958
The Hunters, 1958
The Angry Hills, 1959
The Wonderful Country, 1959
Home from the Hill, 1960
A Terrible Beauty, 1960
The Sundowners, 1960
The Grass Is Greener, 1960
The Last Time I Saw Archie, 1961
Cape Fear, 1962
The Longest Day, 1962
Two for the Seesaw, 1962
Rampage, 1963
Man in the Middle, 1964
What a Way to Go!, 1964
Mister Moses, 1965
El Dorado, 1966
The Way West, 1967
Villa Rides, 1968
Anzio, 1968
5 Card Stud, 1968
Secret Ceremony, 1968
Young Billy Young, 1969
The Good Guys and the Bad Guys, 1969
Ryan's Daughter, 1970
Going Home, 1971
The Wrath of God, 1972
The Friends of Eddie Coyle, 1973
The Yakuza, 1975
Farewell, My Lovely, 1975
Midway, 1976
The Last Tycoon, 1976
The Amsterdam Kill, 1977
Matilda, 1978
The Big Sleep, 1978
Breakthrough, 1979
Agency, 1980
Nightkill, 1980
That Championship Season, 1983
The Ambassador, 1984
Maria's Lovers, 1984
Mr. North, 1988
Scrooged, 1988
Midnight Ride, 1990
Présumé Dangereux, 1990
Cape Fear, 1991
The Seven Deadly Sins, 1992
Woman of Desire, 1993
Backfire!, 1995
Dead Man, 1995
Pakten, 1995
James Dean: Race with Destiny, 1997

PAUL MUNI

The Valiant, 1929
Seven Faces, 1929
Scarface: The Shame of the Nation, 1932
I Am a Fugitive from a Chain Gang, 1932
The World Changes, 1933
Hi, Nellie!, 1934
Bordertown, 1935
Black Fury, 1935
Dr. Socrates, 1935
The Story of Louis Pasteur, 1936
The Good Earth, 1937
The Woman I Love, 1937
The Life of Emile Zola, 1937
Juarez, 1939
We Are Not Alone, 1939
Hudson's Bay, 1941
Commandos Strike at Dawn, 1942
A Song to Remember, 1945
Counter-Attack, 1945
Angel on My Shoulder, 1946
Imbarco a mezzanote/Stranger on the
    Prowl, 1951
The Last Angry Man, 1959

PAUL NEWMAN

The Silver Chalice, 1954
Somebody Up There Likes Me, 1956
The Rack, 1956
The Helen Morgan Story, 1957
Until They Sail, 1957
The Long, Hot Summer, 1958
The Left Handed Gun, 1958
Cat on a Hot Tin Roof, 1958
Rally 'Round the Flag, Boys!, 1958
The Young Philadelphians, 1959
Exodus, 1960
From the Terrace, 1960
The Hustler, 1961
Paris Blues, 1961
Sweet Bird of Youth, 1962
Hemingway's Adventures of a Young Man,
    1962
Hud, 1963
A New Kind of Love, 1963
The Prize, 1963
What a Way to Go!, 1964
The Outrage, 1964
Lady L, 1965
Harper, 1966
Torn Curtain, 1966
Hombre, 1967
Cool Hand Luke, 1967
The Secret War of Harry Frigg, 1968
Winning, 1969
Butch Cassidy and the Sundance Kid, 1969
WUSA, 1970
Sometimes a Great Notion, 1971
Pocket Money, 1972
The Life and Times of Judge Roy Bean, 1972
The MacKintosh Man, 1973
The Sting, 1973
The Towering Inferno, 1974
The Drowning Pool, 1975

Buffalo Bill and the Indians, or Sitting Bull's
    History Lesson, 1976
Slap Shot, 1977
Quintet, 1979
When Time Ran Out . . ., 1980
Fort Apache, the Bronx, 1981
Absence of Malice, 1981
The Verdict, 1982
Harry and Son, 1984
The Color of Money, 1986
Fat Man and Little Boy, 1989
Blaze, 1989
Mr. & Mrs. Bridge, 1990
The Hudsucker Proxy, 1994
Nobody's Fool, 1994
Twilight, 1998
Message in a Bottle, 1999
Where the Money Is, 2000
Road to Perdition, 2002

LAURENCE OLIVIER

The Temporary Widow, 1930
Potiphar's Wife, 1931
Friends and Lovers, 1931
The Yellow Ticket, 1931
Westward Passage, 1932
No Funny Business, 1933
Perfect Understanding, 1933
Moscow Nights, 1935
As You Like It, 1936
Fire over England, 1937
The Divorce of Lady X, 1938
Q Planes, 1939
Wuthering Heights, 1939
21 Days, 1940
Rebecca, 1940
Pride and Prejudice, 1940
That Hamilton Woman, 1941
49th Parallel, 1941
The Demi-Paradise, 1943
Henry V, 1944
Hamlet, 1948
The Magic Box, 1951
Carrie, 1952
The Beggar's Opera, 1953
Richard III, 1955
The Prince and the Showgirl, 1957
The Devil's Disciple, 1959
The Entertainer, 1960
Spartacus, 1960
Term of Trial, 1962
Uncle Vanya, 1963
Bunny Lake Is Missing, 1965
Othello, 1965
Khartoum, 1966
The Shoes of the Fisherman, 1968
Oh! What a Lovely War, 1969
The Dance of Death, 1969
Battle of Britain, 1969
Three Sisters, 1970
Nicholas and Alexandra, 1971
Lady Caroline Lamb, 1972
Sleuth, 1972
The Rehearsal, 1974
Marathon Man, 1976

The Seven-Per-Cent Solution, 1976
A Bridge too Far, 1977
The Betsy, 1978
The Boys from Brazil, 1978
A Little Romance, 1979
Dracula, 1979
The Jazz Singer, 1980
Inchon, 1981
Clash of the Titans, 1981
The Jigsaw Man, 1983
The Bounty, 1984
Wild Geese II, 1985
War Requiem, 1989

PETER O'TOOLE

The Savage Innocents, 1959
Kidnapped, 1960
The Day They Robbed the Bank of England, 1960
Lawrence of Arabia, 1962
Becket, 1964
Lord Jim, 1965
What's New, Pussycat?, 1965
How to Steal a Million, 1966
The Bible, 1966
The Night of the Generals, 1967
The Lion in Winter, 1968
Great Catherine, 1968
Goodbye, Mr. Chips, 1969
Country Dance, 1969
Murphy's War, 1971
Under Milk Wood, 1971
The Ruling Class, 1972
Man of La Mancha, 1972
Rosebud, 1975
Man Friday, 1975
Foxtrot, 1976
Power Play, 1978
Zulu Dawn, 1979
Caligula, 1979
The Stunt Man, 1980
My Favorite Year, 1982
Supergirl, 1984
Creator, 1985
Club Paradise, 1986
The Last Emperor, 1987
High Spirits, 1988
On a Moonlit Night, 1989
The Rainbow Thief, 1990
Wings of Fame, 1990
King Ralph, 1991
Rebecca's Daughters, 1992
Isabelle Eberhardt, 1992
The Seventh Coin, 1993
FairyTale: A True Story, 1997
Phantoms, 1998
The Manor, 1999
Molokai: The Story of Father Damien, 1999
Global Heresy, 2002
The Final Curtain, 2002
Bright Young Things, 2003
Romeo and Me, 2004
Troy, 2004
One Night with the King, 2005
Lassie, 2005

GREGORY PECK

Days of Glory, 1944
The Keys of the Kingdom, 1944
The Valley of Decision, 1945
Spellbound, 1945
The Yearling, 1946
Duel in the Sun, 1946
The Macomber Affair, 1947
Gentleman's Agreement, 1947
The Paradine Case, 1947
Yellow Sky, 1949
The Great Sinner, 1949
Twelve O'Clock High, 1949
The Gunfighter, 1950
Captain Horatio Hornblower, 1951
Only the Valiant, 1951
David and Bathsheba, 1951
The Snows of Kilimanjaro, 1952
The World in His Arms, 1952
Man with a Million, 1953
Roman Holiday, 1953
Night People, 1954
The Purple Plain, 1954
The Man in the Gray Flannel Suit, 1956
Moby Dick, 1956
Designing Woman, 1957
The Bravados, 1958
The Big Country, 1958
Pork Chop Hill, 1959
Beloved Infidel, 1959
On the Beach, 1959
The Guns of Navarone, 1961
Cape Fear, 1962
How the West Was Won, 1962
To Kill a Mockingbird, 1962
Captain Newman, M.D., 1963
Behold a Pale Horse, 1964
Mirage, 1965
Arabesque, 1966
The Stalking Moon, 1969
Mackenna's Gold, 1969
The Chairman, 1969
Marooned, 1969
I Walk the Line, 1970
Shoot Out, 1971
Billy Two Hats, 1974
The Omen, 1976
MacArthur, 1977
The Boys from Brazil, 1978
The Sea Wolves: The Last Charge of the Calcutta Light Horse, 1980
Amazing Grace and Chuck, 1987
Old Gringo, 1989
Other People's Money, 1991
Cape Fear, 1991

SIDNEY POITIER

No Way Out, 1950
Cry, the Beloved Country, 1951
Red Ball Express, 1952
Go, Man, Go!, 1954
Blackboard Jungle, 1955
Good-bye, My Lady, 1956
Edge of the City, 1957
Something of Value, 1957
Band of Angels, 1957
Virgin Island, 1958
The Mark of the Hawk, 1958
The Defiant Ones, 1958
Porgy and Bess, 1959
All the Young Men, 1960
A Raisin in the Sun, 1961
Paris Blues, 1961
Pressure Point, 1962
Lilies of the Field, 1963
The Long Ships, 1964
The Bedford Incident, 1965
The Greatest Story Ever Told, 1965
A Patch of Blue, 1965
The Slender Thread, 1965
Duel at Diablo, 1966
To Sir, with Love, 1967
In the Heat of the Night, 1967
Guess Who's Coming to Dinner, 1967
For Love of Ivy, 1968
The Lost Man, 1969
They Call Me MISTER Tibbs!, 1970
Brother John, 1971
The Organization, 1971
Buck and the Preacher, 1972
A Warm December, 1973
Uptown Saturday Night, 1974
Let's Do It Again, 1975
The Wilby Conspiracy, 1975
A Piece of the Action, 1977
Shoot to Kill, 1988
Little Nikita, 1988
Sneakers, 1992
The Jackal, 1997

WILLIAM POWELL

Sherlock Holmes, 1922
When Knighthood Was in Flower, 1922
Outcast, 1922
The Bright Shawl, 1923
Under the Red Robe, 1923
Dangerous Money, 1924
Romola, 1924
Too Many Kisses, 1925
Faint Perfume, 1925
My Lady's Lips, 1925
The Beautiful City, 1925
White Mice, 1926
Sea Horses, 1926
Desert Gold, 1926
The Runaway, 1926
Aloma of the South Seas, 1926
Beau Geste, 1926
Tin Gods, 1926
The Great Gatsby, 1926
New York, 1927

Love's Greatest Mistake, 1927
Señorita, 1927
Special Delivery, 1927
Time to Love, 1927
Paid to Love, 1927
Nevada, 1927
She's a Sheik, 1927
Beau Sabreur, 1928
The Last Command, 1928
Feel My Pulse, 1928
Partners in Crime, 1928
The Dragnet, 1928
The Vanishing Pioneer, 1928
Forgotten Faces, 1928
Interference, 1928
The Canary Murder Case, 1929
The Four Feathers, 1929
The Greene Murder Case, 1929
Charming Sinners, 1929
Pointed Heels, 1929
Behind the Make-Up, 1930
Street of Chance, 1930
The Benson Murder Case, 1930
Shadow of the Law, 1930
For the Defense, 1930
Man of the World, 1931
Ladies' Man, 1931
The Road to Singapore, 1931
High Pressure, 1932
Jewel Robbery, 1932
One Way Passage, 1932
Lawyer Man, 1933
Private Detective 62, 1933
Double Harness, 1933
The Kennel Murder Case, 1933
Fashions of 1934, 1934
Manhattan Melodrama, 1934
The Thin Man, 1934
The Key, 1934
Evelyn Prentice, 1934
Star of Midnight, 1935
Reckless, 1935
Escapade, 1935
Rendezvous, 1935
The Great Ziegfeld, 1936
The Ex-Mrs. Bradford, 1936
My Man Godfrey, 1936
Libeled Lady, 1936
After the Thin Man, 1936
The Last of Mrs. Cheyney, 1937
The Emperor's Candlesticks, 1937
Double Wedding, 1937
The Baroness and the Butler, 1938
Another Thin Man, 1939
I Love You Again, 1940
Love Crazy, 1941
Shadow of the Thin Man, 1941
Crossroads, 1942
The Heavenly Body, 1944
The Thin Man Goes Home, 1945
Zigfield Follies, 1946
The Hoodlum Saint, 1946
Life with Father, 1947

Song of the Thin Man, 1947
The Senator Was Indiscreet, 1947
Mr. Peabody and the Mermaid, 1948
Take One False Step, 1949
Dancing in the Dark, 1949
It's a Big Country, 1951
The Treasure of Lost Canyon, 1952
The Girl Who Had Everything, 1953
How to Marry a Millionaire, 1953
Mister Roberts, 1955

ANTHONY QUINN

Parole, 1936
The Plainsman, 1936
Swing High, Swing Low, 1937
The Last Train from Madrid, 1937
Partners in Crime, 1937
Waikiki Wedding, 1937
Daughter of Shanghai, 1937
The Buccaneer, 1938
Dangerous to Know, 1938
Tip-Off Girls, 1938
Hunted Men, 1938
Bulldog Drummond in Africa, 1938
King of Alcatraz, 1938
Island of Lost Men, 1939
King of Chinatown, 1939
Union Pacific, 1939
Television Spy, 1939
Emergency Squad, 1940
Road to Singapore, 1940
Parole Fixer, 1940
The Ghost Breakers, 1940
City for Conquest, 1940
The Texas Rangers Ride Again, 1940
Knockout, 1941
Thieves Fall Out, 1941
Blood and Sand, 1941
Bullets for O'Hara, 1941
They Died with Their Boots On, 1941
The Perfect Snob, 1941
Larceny, Inc., 1942
Road to Morocco, 1942
The Black Swan, 1942
The Ox-Bow Incident, 1943
Guadalcanal Diary, 1943
Buffalo Bill, 1944
Ladies of Washington, 1944
Roger Touhy, Gangster, 1944
Irish Eyes Are Smiling, 1944
China Sky, 1945
Where Do We Go from Here?, 1945
Back to Bataan, 1945
California, 1946
Sinbad the Sailor, 1947
The Imperfect Lady, 1947
Black Gold, 1947
Tycoon, 1947
The Brave Bulls, 1951
Mask of the Avenger, 1951
Viva Zapata!, 1952
The Brigand, 1952
The World in His Arms, 1952
Against All Flags, 1952
Donne Proibite/Angels of Darkness, 1953

Cavalleria Rusticana/Fatal Desire, 1953
City Beneath the Sea, 1953
Seminole, 1953
Ride, Vaquero!, 1953
East of Sumatra, 1953
Blowing Wild, 1953
The Long Wait, 1954
La Strada, 1954
Attila, 1954
Ulysses, 1955
The Magnificent Matador, 1955
The Naked Street, 1955
Seven Cities of Gold, 1955
Lust for Life, 1956
Man from Del Rio, 1956
The Hunchback of Notre Dame, 1956
The Wild Party, 1956
The River's Edge, 1957
The Ride Back, 1957
Wild Is the Wind, 1957
Hot Spell, 1958
The Black Orchid, 1958
The Savage Innocents, 1959
Warlock, 1959
Last Train from Gun Hill, 1959
Heller in Pink Tights, 1960
Portrait in Black, 1960
The Guns of Navarone, 1961
Barabbas, 1962
Requiem for a Heavyweight, 1962
Lawrence of Arabia, 1962
Behold a Pale Horse, 1964
The Visit, 1964
Zorba the Greek, 1964
A High Wind in Jamaica, 1965
La Fabuleuse Aventure de Marco Polo/
    Marco the Magnificent, 1965
Lost Command, 1966
The Rover, 1967
*La Vingt-Cinquième Heure/*The 25th Hour,
    1967
The Happening, 1967
*La Bataille de San Sebastian/*Guns for San
    Sebastian, 1968
The Shoes of the Fisherman, 1968
The Magus, 1968
The Secret of Santa Vittoria, 1969
A Dream of Kings, 1969
Walk in the Spring Rain, 1970
R.P.M., 1970
Flap, 1970
*Los Amigos/*Deaf Smith and Johnny Ears,
    1972
Across 110th Street, 1972
The Don Is Dead, 1973
The Marseille Contract, 1974
Target of an Assassin, 1976
The Message, 1976
The Con Artists, 1976
The Inheritance, 1976
The Greek Tycoon, 1978
Caravans, 1978

The Children of Sanchez, 1978
The Passage, 1979
The Salamander, 1981
Lion of the Desert, 1981
High Risk, 1981
Regina Roma/Regina, 1982
Valentina, 1982
Stradivari, 1989
A Man of Passion, 1989
Revenge, 1990
Ghosts Can't Do It, 1990
A Star for Two, 1991
Only the Lonely, 1991
Jungle Fever, 1991
Mobsters, 1991
Last Action Hero, 1993
Somebody to Love, 1994
A Walk in the Clouds, 1995
Il Sindaco/The Mayor, 1996
Seven Servants, 1996
Oriundi, 1999
Terra de Canons, 1999
Avenging Angelo, 2002

EDWARD G. ROBINSON

Arms and the Woman, 1916
The Bright Shawl, 1923
The Hole in the Wall, 1929
Night Ride, 1930
A Lady to Love, 1930
Outside the Law, 1930
East Is West, 1930
The Widow from Chicago, 1930
Little Caesar, 1931
Smart Money, 1931
Five Star Final, 1931
The Hatchet Man, 1932
Two Seconds, 1932
Tiger Shark, 1932
Silver Dollar, 1932
The Little Giant, 1933
I Loved a Woman, 1933
Dark Hazard, 1933
The Man with Two Faces, 1934
The Whole Town's Talking, 1935
Barbary Coast, 1935
Bullets or Ballots, 1936
Thunder in the City, 1937
Kid Galahad, 1937
The Last Gangster, 1937
A Slight Case of Murder, 1938
The Amazing Dr. Clitterhouse, 1938
I Am the Law, 1938
Confessions of a Nazi Spy, 1939
Blackmail, 1939
Dr. Ehrlich's Magic Bullet, 1940
Brother Orchid, 1940
A Dispatch from Reuters, 1940
The Sea Wolf, 1941
Manpower, 1941
Unholy Partners, 1941
Larceny, Inc., 1942
Tales of Manhattan, 1942
Destroyer, 1943
Flesh and Fantasy, 1943

Tampico, 1944
Mr. Winkle Goes to War, 1944
Double Indemnity, 1944
The Woman in the Window, 1945
Our Vines Have Tender Grapes, 1945
Scarlet Street, 1945
Journey Together, 1946
The Stranger, 1946
The Red House, 1947
All My Sons, 1948
Key Largo, 1948
Night Has a Thousand Eyes, 1948
House of Strangers, 1949
My Daughter Joy, 1950
Actors and Sin, 1952
Vice Squad, 1953
Big Leaguer, 1953
The Glass Web, 1953
Black Tuesday, 1954
Hell on Frisco Bay, 1956
The Violent Men, 1955
Tight Spot, 1955
A Bullet for Joey, 1955
Illegal, 1955
Nightmare, 1956
The Ten Commandments, 1956
A Hole in the Head, 1959
Seven Thieves, 1960
My Geisha, 1962
Two Weeks in Another Town, 1962
Sammy Going South, 1963
The Prize, 1963
Good Neighbor Sam, 1964
Cheyenne Autumn, 1964
The Outrage, 1964
The Cincinnati Kid, 1965
Grand Slam, 1967
Peking Blonde, 1967
Operazione San Pietro, 1967
The Biggest Bundle of Them All, 1968
Never a Dull Moment, 1968
It's Your Move, 1969
Mackenna's Gold, 1969
Song of Norway, 1970
Neither by Day nor by Night, 1972
Soylent Green, 1973

MICKEY ROONEY

Mickey's Circus, 1927
Mickey's Pals, 1927
Mickey's Eleven, 1927
Mickey's Battle, 1927
Mickey's Minstrels, 1928
Mickey's Parade, 1928
Mickey in School, 1928
Mickey's Nine, 1928
Mickey's Little Eva, 1928
Mickey's Wild West, 1928
Mickey in Love, 1928
Mickey's Triumph, 1928
Mickey's Babies, 1928
Mickey's Movies, 1928

Mickey's Rivals, 1928
Mickey the Detective, 1928
Mickey's Athletes, 1928
Mickey's Big Game Hunt, 1928
Mickey's Great Idea, 1929
Mickey's Explorers, 1929
Mickey's Menagerie, 1929
Mickey's Last Chance, 1929
Mickey's Brown Derby, 1929
Mickey's Northwest Mounted, 1929
Mickey's Initiation, 1929
Mickey's Midnight Follies, 1929
Mickey's Surprise, 1929
Mickey's Mix-Up, 1929
Mickey's Big Moment, 1929
Mickey's Strategy, 1929
Mickey Wins the Day, 1930
Mickey's Champs, 1930
Mickey's Master Mind, 1930
Mickey's Luck, 1930
Mickey's Whirlwinds, 1930
Mickey's Warriors, 1930
Mickey the Romeo, 1930
Mickey's Merry Men, 1930
Mickey's Winners, 1930
Mickey's Musketeers, 1930
Mickey's Bargain, 1930
Mickey's Sideline, 1931
Mickey's Stampede, 1931
Mickey's Crusaders, 1931
Mickey's Rebellion, 1931
Mickey's Diplomacy, 1931
Mickey's Wildcats, 1931
Mickey's Thrill Hunters, 1931
Mickey's Helping Hand, 1931
Mickey's Busy Day, 1931
Mickey's Travels, 1932
Mickey's Holiday, 1932
Mickey's Big Business, 1932
Mickey's Golden Rule, 1932
Mickey's Charity, 1932
Sin's Pay Day, 1932
High Speed, 1932
Fast Companions, 1932
My Pal, the King, 1932
Mickey's Ape Man, 1933
Mickey's Race, 1933
Mickey's Big Broadcast, 1933
Mickey's Touchdown, 1933
Mickey's Tent Show, 1933
Mickey's Disguises, 1933
Mickey's Covered Wagon, 1933
The Big Cage, 1933
The Big Chance, 1933
Broadway to Hollywood, 1933
The Chief, 1933
Beloved, 1934
Mickey's Medicine Man, 1934
Mickey's Rescue, 1934
The Lost Jungle, 1934
I Like It That Way, 1934
Manhattan Melodrama, 1934
Love Birds, 1934
Hide-Out, 1934
Blind Date, 1934

Death on the Diamond, 1934
The County Chairman, 1935
The Healer, 1935
A Midsummer Night's Dream, 1935
Ah, Wilderness!, 1935
Mickey's Derby Day, 1936
Riffraff, 1936
Little Lord Fauntleroy, 1936
Down the Stretch, 1936
The Devil Is a Sissy, 1936
A Family Affair, 1937
Captains Courageous, 1937
Slave Ship, 1937
Live, Love and Learn, 1937
Thoroughbreds Don't Cry, 1937
You're Only Young Once, 1937
Love Is a Headache, 1938
Judge Hardy's Children, 1938
Hold That Kiss, 1938
Lord Jeff, 1938
Love Finds Andy Hardy, 1938
Boys Town, 1938
Stablemates, 1938
Out West with the Hardys, 1938
The Adventures of Huckleberry Finn, 1939
The Hardys Ride High, 1939
Andy Hardy Gets Spring Fever, 1939
Babes in Arms, 1939
Judge Hardy and Son, 1939
Young Tom Edison, 1940
Andy Hardy Meets Debutante, 1940
Strike up the Band, 1940
Andy Hardy's Private Secretary, 1941
Men of Boys Town, 1941
Life Begins for Andy Hardy, 1941
Babes on Broadway, 1941
The Courtship of Andy Hardy, 1942
A Yank at Eton, 1942
Andy Hardy's Double Life, 1942
The Human Comedy, 1943
Girl Crazy, 1943
Andy Hardy's Blonde Trouble, 1944
National Velvet, 1944
Love Laughs at Andy Hardy, 1947
Killer McCoy, 1947
Summer Holiday, 1948
Words and Music, 1948
The Big Wheel, 1949
Quicksand, 1950
The Fireball, 1950
He's a Cockeyed Wonder, 1950
My Outlaw Brother, 1951
The Strip, 1951
Sound Off, 1952
Off Limits, 1953
All Ashore, 1953
A Slight Case of Larceny, 1953
Drive a Crooked Road, 1954
The Atomic Kid, 1954
The Bridges at Toko-Ri, 1955
The Twinkle in God's Eye, 1955
The Bold and the Brave, 1956
Francis in the Haunted House, 1956
Magnificent Roughnecks, 1956
Operation Mad Ball, 1957

Baby Face Nelson, 1957
A Nice Little Bank that Should Be Robbed, 1958
Andy Hardy Comes Home, 1958
The Big Operator, 1959
The Last Mile, 1959
Platinum High School, 1960
The Private Lives of Adam and Eve, 1960
King of the Roaring 20's—The Story of Arnold Rothstein, 1961
Breakfast at Tiffany's, 1961
Everything's Ducky, 1961
Requiem for a Heavyweight, 1962
It's a Mad Mad Mad Mad World, 1963
The Secret Invasion, 1964
Twenty-Four Hours to Kill, 1965
How to Stuff a Wild Bikini, 1965
L'Arcidiavolo, 1966
Ambush Bay, 1966
Skidoo, 1968
The Extraordinary Seaman, 1969
The Comic, 1969
80 Steps to Jonah, 1969
Cockeyed Cowboys of Calico County, 1970
The Manipulator, 1971
Pulp, 1972
Richard, 1972
The Godmothers, 1973
Thunder County, 1974
Rachel's Man, 1974
Ace of Hearts, 1975
From Hong Kong with Love, 1975
Find the Lady, 1976
The Domino Principle, 1977
Pete's Dragon, 1977
The Magic of Lassie, 1978
The Black Stallion, 1979
Arabian Adventure, 1979
The Emperor of Peru, 1982
Lightning, the White Stallion, 1986
Erik the Viking, 1989
My Heroes Have Always Been Cowboys, 1991
La Vida Láctea/The Milky Life, 1992
Silent Night, Deadly Night 5. The Toy Maker, 1992
Maximum Force, 1992
The Legend of Wolf Mountain, 1993
Revenge of the Red Baron, 1994
The Outlaws: Legend of O.B. Taggart, 1994
Making Waves, 1994
Killing Midnight, 1997
Boys Will Be Boys, 1997
Animals and the Tollkeeper, 1998
Michael Kael Contre la World News Company/Michael Kael vs. the World News Company, 1998
Sinbad: The Battle of the Dark Nights, 1998
Babe: Pig in the City, 1998
The First of May, 1999
Topa Topa Bluffs, 2002
Paradise, 2003
Strike the Tent, 2005

FRANK SINATRA

Higher and Higher, 1943
Step Lively, 1944
Anchors Aweigh, 1945
It Happened in Brooklyn, 1947
The Miracle of the Bells, 1948
The Kissing Bandit, 1948
Take Me Out to the Ball Game, 1949
On the Town, 1949
Double Dynamite, 1951
Meet Danny Wilson, 1952
From Here to Eternity, 1953
Suddenly, 1954
Young at Heart, 1954
Not as a Stranger, 1955
Guys and Dolls, 1955
The Tender Trap, 1955
The Man with the Golden Arm, 1955
High Society, 1956
Johnny Concho, 1956
Around the World in Eighty Days, 1956
The Pride and the Passion, 1957
The Joker Is Wild, 1957
Pal Joey, 1957
Kings Go Forth, 1958
Some Came Running, 1958
A Hole in the Head, 1959
Never So Few, 1959
Can-Can, 1960
Ocean's Eleven, 1960
The Devil at 4 O'Clock, 1961
Sergeants 3, 1962
The Manchurian Candidate, 1962
Come Blow Your Horn, 1963
4 for Texas, 1963
Robin and the 7 Hoods, 1964
None but the Brave, 1965
Von Ryan's Express, 1965
Marriage on the Rocks, 1965
Cast a Giant Shadow, 1966
Assault on a Queen, 1966
The Naked Runner, 1967
Tony Rome, 1967
The Detective, 1968
Lady in Cement, 1968
Dirty Dingus Magee, 1970
The First Deadly Sin, 1980

JAMES STEWART

Murder Man, 1935
Rose-Marie, 1936
Next Time We Love, 1936
Wife vs. Secretary, 1936
Small Town Girl, 1936
Speed, 1936
The Gorgeous Hussy, 1936
Born to Dance, 1936
After the Thin Man, 1936
Seventh Heaven, 1937
The Last Gangster, 1937
Navy Blue and Gold, 1937
Of Human Hearts, 1938
Vivacious Lady, 1938
The Shopworn Angel, 1938
You Can't Take it With You, 1938

Made for Each Other, 1939
The Ice Follies of 1939, 1939
It's a Wonderful World, 1939
Mr. Smith Goes to Washington, 1939
Destry Rides Again, 1939
The Shop Around the Corner, 1940
The Mortal Storm, 1940
No Time for Comedy, 1940
The Philadelphia Story, 1940
Come Live with Me, 1941
Pot o' Gold, 1941
Ziegfeld Girl, 1941
It's a Wonderful Life, 1946
Magic Town, 1947
Call Northside 777, 1948
On Our Merry Way, 1948
Rope, 1948
You Gotta Stay Happy, 1948
The Stratton Story, 1949
Malaya, 1949
Winchester '73, 1950
Broken Arrow, 1950
Harvey, 1950
The Jackpot, 1950
No Highway in the Sky, 1951
The Greatest Show on Earth, 1952
Bend of the River, 1952
Carbine Williams, 1952
The Naked Spur, 1953
Thunder Bay, 1953
The Glenn Miller Story, 1953
Rear Window, 1954
The Far Country, 1954
Strategic Air Command, 1955
The Man from Laramie, 1955
The Man Who Knew Too Much, 1956
The Spirit of St. Louis, 1957
Night Passage, 1957
Vertigo, 1958
Bell, Book and Candle, 1958
Anatomy of a Murder, 1959
The FBI Story, 1959
The Mountain Road, 1960
Two Rode Together, 1961
The Man Who Shot Liberty Valance, 1962
Mr. Hobbs Takes a Vacation, 1962
How the West Was Won, 1962
Take Her, She's Mine, 1963
Cheyenne Autumn, 1964
Dear Brigitte, 1965
Shenandoah, 1965
The Flight of the Phoenix, 1965
The Rare Breed, 1966
Firecreek, 1968
Bandolero!, 1969
The Cheyenne Social Club, 1970
Fools' Parade, 1971
The Shootist, 1976
Airport '77, 1977
The Big Sleep, 1978
The Magic of Lassie, 1978
The Green Horizon, 1981

ROBERT TAYLOR

Handy Andy, 1934
There's Always Tomorrow, 1934
A Wicked Woman, 1934
Society Doctor, 1935
Times Square Lady, 1935
West Point of the Air, 1935
Murder in the Fleet, 1935
Broadway Melody of 1936, 1935
Magnificent Obsession, 1935
Small Town Girl, 1936
Private Number, 1936
His Brother's Wife, 1936
The Gorgeous Hussy, 1936
Camille, 1936
Personal Property, 1937
This is My Affair, 1937
Broadway Melody of 1938, 1937
A Yank at Oxford, 1938
Three Comrades, 1938
The Crowd Roars, 1938
Stand Up and Fight, 1939
Lucky Night, 1939
Lady of the Tropics, 1939
Remember?, 1939
Waterloo Bridge, 1940
Escape, 1940
Flight Command, 1940
Billy the Kid, 1941
When Ladies Meet, 1941
Johnny Eager, 1942
Her Cardboard Lover, 1942
Stand by for Action, 1942
Bataan, 1943
Song of Russia, 1944
Undercurrent, 1946
High Wall, 1947
The Bribe, 1949
Conspirator, 1949
Ambush, 1950
Devil's Doorway, 1950
Westward Women, 1951
Quo Vadis?, 1951
Ivanhoe, 1952
Above and Beyond, 1952
Knights of the Round Table, 1953
Ride, Vaquero!, 1953
All the Brothers Were Valiant, 1953
Valley of the Kings, 1954
Rogue Cop, 1954
Many Rivers to Cross, 1955
The Adventures of Quentin Durward, 1955
The Last Hunt, 1956
D-Day the Sixth of June, 1956
The Power and the Prize, 1956
Tip on a Dead Jockey, 1957
Saddle the Wind, 1958
The Law and Jake Wade, 1958
Party Girl, 1958
The Hangman, 1959
The House of the Seven Hawks, 1959
Killers of Kilimanjaro, 1960
Miracle of the White Stallions, 1963
Cattle King, 1963
A House Is Not a Home, 1964

The Night Walker, 1964
Johnny Tiger, 1966
Savage Pampas, 1966
La Sfinge d'Oro/The Glass Sphinx, 1967
Return of the Gunfighter, 1967
The Day the Hot Line Got Hot, 1968
Where Angels Go, Trouble Follows, 1968

SPENCER TRACY

Up the River, 1930
Quick Millions, 1931
Six Cylinder Love, 1931
Goldie, 1931
She Wanted a Millionaire, 1932
Sky Devils, 1932
Disorderly Conduct, 1932
Young America, 1932
Society Girl, 1932
The Painted Woman, 1932
Me and My Gal, 1932
20,000 Years in Sing Sing, 1932
Face in the Sky, 1933
Shanghai Madness, 1933
The Power and the Glory, 1933
Man's Castle, 1933
The Mad Game, 1933
The Show-Off, 1934
Looking for Trouble, 1934
Bottoms Up, 1934
Now I'll Tell, 1934
Marie Galante, 1934
It's a Small World, 1935
The Murder Man, 1935
Dante's Inferno, 1935
Whipsaw, 1935
Riffraff, 1936
Fury, 1936
San Francisco, 1936
Libeled Lady, 1936
They Gave Him a Gun, 1937
Captains Courageous, 1937
Big City, 1937
Mannequin, 1937
Test Pilot, 1938
Boys Town, 1938
Stanley and Livingstone, 1939
I Take this Woman, 1940
Northwest Passage, 1940
Edison, the Man, 1940
Boom Town, 1940
Men of Boys Town, 1941
Dr. Jekyll and Mr. Hyde, 1941
Woman of the Year, 1942
Tortilla Flat, 1942
Keeper of the Flame, 1942
A Guy Named Joe, 1943
The Seventh Cross, 1944
Thirty Seconds over Tokyo, 1944
Without Love, 1945
The Sea of Grass, 1947
Cass Timberlane, 1947
State of the Union, 1948
Edward, My Son, 1949
Adam's Rib, 1949

Malaya, 1949
Father of the Bride, 1950
Father's Little Dividend, 1951
The People Against O'Hara, 1951
Pat and Mike, 1952
Plymouth Adventure, 1952
The Actress, 1953
Broken Lance, 1954
Bad Day at Black Rock, 1955
The Mountain, 1956
Desk Set, 1957
The Old Man and the Sea, 1958
The Last Hurrah, 1958
Inherit the Wind, 1960
The Devil at 4 O'Clock, 1961
Judgment at Nuremberg, 1961
It's a Mad Mad Mad Mad World, 1963
Guess Who's Coming to Dinner, 1967

RUDOLPH VALENTINO

A Society Sensation, 1918
All Night, 1918
The Married Virgin, 1918
The Delicious Little Devil, 1919
The Big Little Person, 1919
A Rogue's Romance, 1919
Nobody Home, 1919
Eyes of Youth, 1919
An Adventuress, 1920
Passion's Playground, 1920
Once to Every Woman, 1920
The Wonderful Chance, 1920
Stolen Moments, 1920
The Four Horsemen of the Apocalypse, 1921
Uncharted Seas, 1921
The Conquering Power, 1921
Camille, 1921
The Sheik, 1921
Moran of the Lady Letty, 1922
Beyond the Rocks, 1922
Blood and Sand, 1922
The Young Rajah, 1922
Monsieur Beaucaire, 1924
A Sainted Devil, 1924
The Eagle, 1925
Cobra, 1925
The Son of the Sheik, 1926

JOHN WAYNE

Bardelys the Magnificent, 1926
Words and Music, 1929
The Big Trail, 1930
Girls Demand Excitement, 1931
Three Girls Lost, 1931
Arizona, 1931
Range Feud, 1931
The Deceiver, 1931
Maker of Men, 1931
Texas Cyclone, 1932
Two-Fisted Law, 1932
Lady and Gent, 1932
The Shadow of the Eagle, 1932
Ride Him, Cowboy, 1932
The Big Stampede, 1932
Haunted Gold, 1932

The Hurricane Express, 1932
The Telegraph Trail, 1933
Somewhere in Sonora, 1933
His Private Secretary, 1933
The Life of Jimmy Dolan, 1933
Baby Face, 1933
The Man From Monterey, 1933
The Three Musketeers, 1933
Riders of Destiny, 1933
Sagebrush Trail, 1933
The Lucky Texan, 1934
West of the Divide, 1934
Blue Steel, 1934
The Man from Utah, 1934
Randy Rides Alone, 1934
The Star Packer, 1934
The Trail Beyond, 1934
The Lawless Frontier, 1934
'Neath the Arizona Skies, 1934
Texas Terror, 1935
Rainbow Valley, 1935
The Desert Trail, 1935
The Dawn Rider, 1935
Paradise Canyon, 1935
Westward Ho, 1935
The New Frontier, 1935
Lawless Range, 1935
The Oregon Trail, 1936
The Lawless Nineties, 1936
King of the Pecos, 1936
The Lonely Trail, 1936
Winds of the Wasteland, 1936
Sea Spoilers, 1936
Conflict, 1936
California Straight Ahead!, 1937
I Cover the War, 1937
Idol of the Crowds, 1937
Adventure's End, 1937
Born to the West, 1937
Pals of the Saddle, 1938
Overland Stage Raiders, 1938
Santa Fe Stampede, 1938
Red River Range, 1938
Stagecoach, 1939
The Night Riders, 1939
Three Texas Steers, 1939
Wyoming Outlaw, 1939
New Frontier, 1939
Allegheny Uprising, 1939
Dark Command, 1940
Three Faces West, 1940
The Long Voyage Home, 1940
Seven Sinners, 1940
A Man Betrayed, 1941
Lady from Louisiana, 1941
The Shepherd of the Hills, 1941
Lady for a Night, 1942
Reap the Wild Wind, 1942
The Spoilers, 1942
In Old California, 1942
Flying Tigers, 1942
Pittsburgh, 1942
Reunion in France, 1942
A Lady Takes a Chance, 1943
In Old Oklahoma, 1943

The Fighting Seabees, 1944
Tall in the Saddle, 1944
Flame of Barbary Coast, 1945
Back to Bataan, 1945
They Were Expendable, 1945
Dakota, 1945
Without Reservations, 1946
Angel and the Badman, 1947
Tycoon, 1947
Fort Apache, 1948
Red River, 1948
3 Godfathers, 1948
Wake of the Red Witch, 1948
The Fighting Kentuckian, 1949
She Wore a Yellow Ribbon, 1949
Sands of Iwo Jima, 1949
Rio Grande, 1950
Operation Pacific, 1951
Flying Leathernecks, 1951
The Quiet Man, 1952
Big Jim McLain, 1952
Trouble Along the Way, 1953
Island in the Sky, 1953
Hondo, 1953
The High and the Mighty, 1954
The Sea Chase, 1955
Blood Alley, 1955
The Conqueror, 1956
The Searchers, 1956
The Wings of Eagles, 1957
Jet Pilot, 1957
Legend of the Lost, 1957
The Barbarian and the Geisha, 1958
Rio Bravo, 1959
The Horse Soldiers, 1959
The Alamo, 1960
North to Alaska, 1960
The Comancheros, 1961
The Man Who Shot Liberty Valance, 1962
Hatari!, 1962
The Longest Day, 1962
How the West Was Won, 1962
McLintock!, 1963
Donovan's Reef, 1963
Circus World, 1964
The Greatest Story Ever Told, 1965
In Harm's Way, 1965
The Sons of Katie Elder, 1965
Cast a Giant Shadow, 1966
El Dorado, 1966
The War Wagon, 1967
The Green Berets, 1968
Hellfighters, 1968
True Grit, 1969
The Undefeated, 1969
Chisum, 1970
Rio Lobo, 1970
Big Jake, 1971
The Cowboys, 1972
The Train Robbers, 1973
Cahill U.S. Marshal, 1973
McQ, 1974
Brannigan, 1975
Rooster Cogburn, 1975
The Shootist, 1976

RY GRANT IN *MY FAVORITE WIFE*, 1940

JAMES STEWART, CIRCA 1930s

ABOUT THE AUTHORS

TEXT

Frank Miller is the head of the theater program at Georgia State University, where he also lectures. He is the author of *Casablanca: As Time Goes By* and *Censored Hollywood: Sin, Sex & Violence on the Screen*, and he edited the companion volume to this book, *Leading Ladies: The 50 Most Unforgettable Actresses of the Studio Era*.

RESEARCHERS

Aubry Anne D'Arminio is a master's student in film studies at Emory University. Her work has appeared in the *Journal of Popular Film and Television, Leading Ladies: The 50 Most Unforgettable Actresses of the Studio Era*, and online at the All Movie Guide.

Alexa L. Foreman is a senior researcher/producer at Turner Classic Movies. She is the author of *Women in Motion*, coauthor of *In the Picture: Production Stills from the TCM Archives*, and a contributor to *The St. James Women Filmmakers Encyclopedia* and *International Dictionary of Films and Filmmakers*.

WILLIAM POWELL, 1935

BUSTER KEATON, 1932

HUMPHREY BOGART IN *CASABLANCA*, 1942